THE POLITICAL ECONOMY OF GERMANY UNDER CHANCELLORS KOHL AND SCHRÖDER

Monographs in German History

THE POLITICAL ECONOMY OF GERMANY UNDER CHANCELLORS KOHL AND SCHRÖDER

Decline of the German Model?

Jeremy Leaman

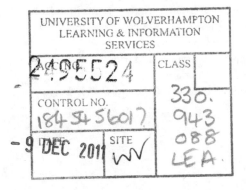

Berghahn Books
New York • Oxford

First published in 2009 by
Berghahn Books
www.berghahnbooks.com

Library of Congress Cataloging-in-Publication Data
Leaman, Jeremy, 1947-
 The political economy of Germany under Chancellors Kohl and Schroder :
decline of the German model? / by Jeremy Leaman.
    p. cm. -- (Monographs in German history ; 29)
 Includes bibliographical references and index.
 ISBN 978-1-84545-601-6 (alk. paper)
 1. Germany--Economic policy--1990- 2. Germany--Economic policy--1945-1990.
I. Title.

 HC286.8.L42 2009
 330.943'088--dc22

                                                                    2009013506

British Library Cataloguing in Publication Data
A catalogue record for this book is available from the British Library

Printed on acid-free paper.

ISBN 978-1-84545-601-6 (hardback)

CONTENTS

For K.

LIST OF TABLES AND FIGURES

List of Tables

List of Figures

INTRODUCTION

Writing about the German economy, the social arrangements that underpin it and the political management of its structures and processes invariably involves a paradox. On the one hand, this core political economy of greater Europe has maintained its leading status as a highly productive trading nation, exporting more goods in 2007 ($1.36 trillion) than either China ($1.22 trillion) or the United States ($1.12 trillion), which have, respectively, populations sixteen times and three-and-a-half times that of Germany. Without Germany's massive balance of trade surplus, the European Union's and the eurozone's external balances would look much less favourable. Secondly, its engineering products, most notably its investment goods and its motor vehicles, carry a badge of quality which makes them less price-sensitive than those of their rivals, both because of their established reliability and because of the quality of after-sales service provided to their customers. Thirdly, it produces more industrial patents per head of population than practically any other European country, except Sweden. It continues to attract relatively high levels of foreign direct investment (2006 stock levels, approximately $763.9 billion) despite the comparatively high marginal wage costs (social insurance etc.) paid by enterprises in Germany.

As a catalogue of virtues, this kind of record would satisfy most superficial judges of economic fitness and successful political management. The paradox, the other side of the coin of success, is – inevitably – the set of indicators that question the sustainability of that success. Germany's rate of economic growth – its average annual increase of real gross domestic product (GDP) – has been comparatively disappointing in recent decades. Since 1993 there have been two business cycles; the first from the recession year in 1993 to the pre-recession year of 2002 showed an annual average rate of growth of just 1.24 per cent; in the, as yet unfinished, cycle from the recession year of 2003 to 2007, it is probable that it will result in a similarly low average. Growth in 2006 (3.1 per cent) and 2007 (2.6 per cent) indicated a cyclical recovery, but such recoveries have historically always occurred; in Germany's case they have been fewer and farther between in recent years. Notwithstanding the huge shock of German–German unification in 1990, growth in this core industrial economy has been weaker than any other EU-15 country since 1993; the GDP growth weakness has translated into weaker employment growth and more particularly into less favourable unemployment. In 1993 the standard rate of unemployment in

Germany – at 7.6 per cent – was lower than the Organisation for Economic Co-operation and Development (OECD) average of 7.8 per cent (OECD 2007: Statistical Annex Table 14) but by 2005 had risen to 10.6 per cent while the OECD average had fallen to 6.7 per cent; the 2006–07 recovery has helped to reduce unemployment, but in all likelihood Germany will end this current cycle, as in all others since 1975, with higher unemployment than at the end of the previous cycle. A rule of thumb among economists contends that economies currently require an average rate of GDP growth of around 2 per cent to prevent unemployment rising inexorably from cycle to cycle. The medium-term signs for the German labour market are not favourable, therefore. Structural unemployment was well embedded even before unification and, reinforced by the tribulations of East Germany's transition to market economics, is set to remain firmly entrenched in the united country's political economy. This is in part a result of a relative decline in the proportion of GDP that is reinvested in the national economy, the investment ratio, which has fallen from a typically high average of over 20 per cent before 2000 to 18.4 per cent in 2007 (after two years of strong growth in investments); the average investment ratio for the new cycle since 2001 is thus set to decline further, compared to previous cycles. Without a significant reversal of investment activity in the domestic economy, Germany's overall trend of GDP and employment growth is therefore likely to be disappointing.

The paradox of evident strengths side-by-side with evident weaknesses should not be so surprising, even if one sets aside the problems associated with unification. The political economy of the Federal Republic had identifiable structural problems in the 1970s and 1980s (Leaman 1988) which have in part only been reinforced by unification; part of the purpose of this book is to examine the threads of continuity and the longer-term determinants of the country's paradoxical status and to assess whether Europe's industrial Colossus has more obvious 'feet of clay' today than in the 1980s (ibid. 263ff).

****

A fundamental point of departure for this analysis is the assumption that Germany's 'economic order', like that of all other social formations, has changed markedly over the last century and will continue to change – probably more rapidly – in the twenty-first century. This truism needs to be stated for one simple reason: it challenges the theoretical and practical political assumptions based on the notion of an ideal-typical market order that underpins neoclassical economics and the political orthodoxy of neoliberalism, which is currently *en vogue* in Germany and elsewhere. Market fundamentalism, for which 'neoliberalism' is the most commonly used label, has theological characteristics in its postulation of a purity of market mechanisms which have supposedly been distorted or disabled by state interference but which could be restored through a programme of reversal ('roll-back') towards the pure *status quo ante*. Polanyi describes this school of thought as 'liberal utopianism'. The 'roll-back' is akin to Jeremiah's plea to the corrupted citizens of Jerusalem to 'return to the Lord' and was reinforced by the apparent triumph of market capitalism over state socialism after 1989 and by the (admittedly absurd) notion of the 'end of history' (Fukuyama) and the seeming convergence of a purified West with a fundamentally restructured 'East'.

The details of the paradigm shift from Keynesianism/Marxism 'back to' market fundamentalism will be dealt with in subsequent chapters. It is sufficient to say, in the introduction, that this study of Germany's political economy rejects entirely the notion of the ideal-typical model of economic and social organisation which can be restored to health and permanently fixed. Every teleological state of perfection, be it the sanctified Prussian state in Hegelian conservatism, communism as 'final stage' of social development in Marxian thought or the paradise of market freedoms for neoliberals, defies the overwhelming evidence of flux, of change, of irreversible history and the uncertainty of future human development. The *desirability* of distributional fairness, social justice and sustainable human welfare will never make these *inevitable*. The constitutional, legislative and normative anchors which societies develop individually as nation states or even collectively as international bodies are also not bound to prevent change, favourable or unfavourable. In the history of economic and social 'orders', the discontinuities arguably far outweigh the continuities. This is more than evident in the case of the development of the German political economy in the last 150 years. Periods of relative stability (e.g., 1949 to 1989) were preceded and followed by periods of extreme change. There were dramatic discontinuities at the level of the state-form presiding over economic development, from the autocratic particularism of the mid-nineteenth century, through the federal autocracy of the 'Second Empire' 1870–1918, the federal democracy of the Weimar Republic 1918–1933, the centralised autocracy of German fascism 1933–1945 and – after the interregnum of Allied occupation – the extreme federalism of the Federal Republic of Germany (FRG) and the state socialist autocracy of the German Democratic Republic (GDR). While this extreme discontinuity of state-form concealed significant continuities in the structures of ownership and their respective economic and political elites – the 'cartel of rye and iron' (Kitchen 1978) – it also reflected significant shifts in the contextual conditions of economic and political activity. The sectoral shifts in production and employment – firstly from agriculture to industry and then, after the Second World War, from industry to the service sector, produced major demographic changes, above all in the process of urbanisation, which in their turn presented major challenges to the political management of change in a political economy dominated by the land-owning aristocracy until at least 1916. The subsequent evolution of Germany's particular forms of political management has been variously described by economic and social historians in terms of a 'special path' (*Sonderweg*) (Blackbourn and Ely 1984), a 'German path' (Abelshauser 2005: 127) etc. This was in large part to explain the world historical catastrophe of Germany's genocidal imperialism, but also to account for the particular features of what Abelshauser describes as 'the German production regime' (ibid. 77ff). Such accounts are invaluable for tracing the origins of the traditions which have evolved in Germany over the last century, in particular when contrasting this development with that of other political economies.

The military-aristocratic mercantilism of Bismarckian and Wilhelmine Germany can be seen to predefine the particular pathway towards industrial modernisation pursued by subsequent generations of economic and political leaders. The toleration/promotion of universal banks and cartels by the Prussian–German state was informed by and in turn nurtured the 'aversion to risk' generally accepted to characterise the investment, production and distribution regimes in Germany in the critical first half of the twentieth century. The strong preference for bipartite corporatist regimes (state plus trade associations) up to 1945 and for tripartite corporatism (state, trade associations and trade unions) in the Federal Republic after 1949 equally reflects a culture which more readily sought to prevent or avoid the unnecessary costs of conflict and/or competition.

This much would justify the student of comparative economics in using the concept 'organised capitalism' to characterise (in admittedly very general terms) the way in which Germany's political economy was managed and regulated, and in placing it in the 'conservative' (Esping-Andersen 1990) or 'Rhenish' (Albert 1992) segment of the spectrum of governance in the family of capitalist states. It is far less convincing to describe Germany's variant form of capitalism as 'non-liberal' (Streeck and Yamamura 2001) in contrast to the 'liberal' capitalism represented by the United States and Britain (ibid. 5). Firstly, as Streeck himself concedes, 'liberal' or 'standard' capitalism 'is no more than an ideal type' (ibid.), i.e., a heuristic abstraction, never actually realised, even in Anglo-Saxon economies. It is in fact a pretty crude abstraction which, with the polarity to nonliberal, implicitly applies the theological yardsticks of Hayek, Mises and the Chicago School to the measurement of 'liberality'. This adds confusion rather than clarity to the analysis of both liberalism and the German political economy. It thus arguably plays into the hands of the high priests of market fundamentalism, by implying that German (and Japanese) elites have constructed an organisational framework for the operation of capitalism which excludes 'liberty'. However, the most basic analysis of the concept 'liberalism' reveals a veritable bran-tub of confusing choice and the unhelpful knowledge that, as a semantic blanket, it covers a political spectrum from Beveridge to Pinochet. The rhetorical malleability of 'liberty' reflects both the political potential of its use/abuse (Harvey 2005: 39ff) and the frequent intellectual 'poverty' of liberalism (Wolff 1969).

It does not require a great deal of reflection to ask of the proponents of 'liberalism' what particular liberties are primary and how they are constituted and protected. Whose freedom is involved, from what bondage and to what end? This kind of enquiry would reveal that 'liberalism' is deployed to justify a host of 'liberties', some of which can clearly be seen to be antithetical: e.g., the freedom to exploit other human beings (as owner of land, commercial property, means of production, scarce resources) clearly collides with the freedom from exploitation. The list of such potential contradictions is endless. They can at the very least be deployed to suggest that certain provisions of 'organised' or 'embedded' capitalism, e.g., in health and safety legislation, consumer rights, contract law, licensing laws etc., are designed to maximise the potential of certain (market) freedoms by curbing harmful, negative 'liberties'. 'Nonliberal' as a category of analysis and as a vehicle for understanding the evolution of Germany's political economy is at best a provocative heuristic fiction, at worst a misleading and crude simplification.

If we therefore examine the main constituent elements of Germany's variant of organised capitalism, it is possible to identify a considerable number of features which limit, regulate or constrain the operations of 'the' market or particular markets, but also other features which favour and promote those operations in ways which market fundamentalists would generally applaud. Conversely, an examination of the recent practice of 'liberal' states, e.g., the United States and the United Kingdom, reveals features of statist intervention, mercantilism and rule setting which the Chicago School would eschew – 'Reagonomics' in the 1980s is a perfect example of this (see Palley 2005: 24).

The economic order established in the Federal Republic after 1945 was very much the product of historically embedded structures and beliefs as well as the experience of defeat and political failure. The extreme federalism imposed on the architects of the temporary constitution, the Basic Law, by the Western occupying powers created a relatively weak central government and extensive devolution of powers to regional and local government. Central (federal) government was further weakened by the establishment of a central bank – the Bank deutscher Länder, later the Bundesbank – which was independent of government control. This fragmentation of executive power meant that there was effectively 'no place for Keynesianism' (Abelshauser 1983). Furthermore, the architects of West Germany's 'social market economy' – within the governing Christian Democratic parties after 1949 – were strongly influenced by the 'ordoliberal' school of economists based in Freiburg under the leadership of the German economist Walter Eucken (Leaman 1988: 50ff); the Christian Democratic Union's (CDU's) Düsseldorf Principles from 1949 reflect this influence quite fundamentally with an explicit disavowal of the need for state interventionism. Through the establishment of a competitive market order with the help of monopoly control, 'the state is … freed from the worry of central direction. There remains the task of making and protecting the law, of encouraging competition and organising monetary affairs' (cited in Leaman 1988: 54). While the reality of CDU government policy during the period of postwar reconstruction clearly did contain elements of intervention and shrewd mercantilism, there was never anything remotely resembling the programmatic application of state intervention as evident in most other European economies in the 1950s and 1960s. The brief experiment with Keynesian 'global steering' under Karl Schiller from 1967 to 1972 was ill-starred and ultimately self-defeating, as it coincided with the upheavals of Bretton Woods and the building boom prior to the Munich Olympics and, in any case, involved delays to fiscal stimuli – compounded by a fragmented policy architecture – which produced a massive pro-cyclical surge and high inflation on the eve of the first oil crisis. From the early 1970s onward, German economic management was increasingly dominated by monetary policy and the preferences of the independent Bundesbank (Marsh 1993; Leaman 2001). As David Harvey has rightly observed, the insulation of 'key institutions, such as the central bank, from democratic pressures', is a strong preference of neoliberals (Harvey 2005: 66). German (and more recently EU) monetary policy has thus arguably been more compatible with neoliberal fundamentalism than in the case of the United States where the Federal Reserve Board is statutorily obliged to consider the effects of its policies on the growth cycle. The Bundesbank and the European Central Bank are required to focus primarily on price stability and the money supply.

The statism reflected in Germany's 'organised capitalism' is thus not to be found in the pursuit of the orthodox antithesis of neoliberalism – Keynesianism – but in the modes of state regulation and private sector self-regulation which emerged in the exceptional context of defeat and occupation. These features include the system of mandatory social insurance, which had four pillars (health, unemployment, old age and accident) until 1995 when a fifth (long-term care) was added. With the exception of accident insurance, which is the exclusive responsibility of employers, the funding of the other four schemes is shared by employees and employers; the federal state has subsidised the pensions system from the very beginning, averaging almost a quarter of total pensions payments in the early 1960s, but after unification has been obliged to raise its contribution to more than a third (some €80 billion per annum), in part to reduce pressure on employers' 'non-wage' costs. Nevertheless, employers' contributions to the social insurance funds can be regarded as employee income (qua wage mass) set aside for the insuree's benefit, payable – in the case of pensions and unemployment benefit – as a proportion of final or latest salaries. Germany's individualised social insurance system, established by the shrewd tactician Bismarck in the 1880s, differs markedly from the more obviously statist systems of social security funded by general government revenue, as in the United Kingdom or Denmark.

A second feature of state 'organisation' of market forces can be found in the body of legislation governing employment relations. While wage-setting is rooted in the principle of free collective bargaining (*Tarifautonomie*) by centralised trade associations and trade unions, industrial disputes deriving from the comparatively rare failure of such bargaining are subject to very strict statutory procedures, involving state sponsored arbitration, cooling-off periods, mandatory secret ballots and an independent branch of labour jurisdiction (*Arbeitsgerichtsbarkeit*). Germany has extended employment law to include a highly developed system of workers' participation, generally dubbed 'codetermination' (*Mitbestimmung*), which in its most extensive form (in heavy industrial companies with more than 1,000 employees and other industrial and commercial enterprises with more than 2,000) confers on the company workforce the right to representation on the supervisory boards of joint stock companies. This elaborate and (superficially at least) expensive statutory system of codetermination, developed between 1951 and 1976, has been in the firing line of neoliberal critics of German 'statism' as a hindrance to market-driven decision-making processes (Institut der deutschen Wirtschaft 2008; Münchau 2008); supporters of German codetermination (Friedrich Ebert Stiftung 2005: 19) assert the institution's contribution to the promotion of economic competition and the prevention of damaging disputes. Interestingly, a 'Codetermination Commission', co-sponsored by the Bertelsmann Foundation and the union-funded Hans-Böckler Foundation in the 1990s, attested to the institution's positive achievements, while criticising only aspects of its practice in individual cases (discussed by Abelshauser 2005: 138). Codetermination is nevertheless a clear example of a conscious regulating corporatism and of a juridification of social relations designed to manage the vicissitudes of market forces. The institutionalised 'social partnership' of employers and employees is evident in their joint oversight of social insurance schemes, in their parity status in Labour Court panels, in the deeply embedded system of apprenticeship training and in sectoral schemes of participation, e.g., in the health service and in higher education.

One of the strongest structural contrasts between the political economy of Germany and that of Anglo-Saxon countries has been the emphasis on long-term stakeholder relationships within the corporate sector and between industrial and commercial corporations on the one hand and Germany's universal banks (both private and state-owned) on the other.

The security and predictability afforded by Germany's bank industry relations has historically underpinned the operations of both the large corporations and, through local state banks, the renowned *Mittelstand* of innovative small and medium-sized enterprises. The banks' privileged knowledge of corporate activities may raise all sorts of worries about insider advantages and distortions of competition, but there is strong evidence that the 'patience of the banks' has enhanced the long-term international competitiveness of German companies (Hutton 1995: 263f). Bank parcel holdings in Germany's 'nonbanks' are a vivid illustration of a general 'enmeshing' of private businesses and of the strongly cooperative behaviour within the corporate sector in general. In terms of maintaining Germany's technological and trading competitiveness, it functions very effectively alongside the horizontal and vertical concentration that German companies share with their counterparts in other major OECD countries.

The original conception of the politically ordered 'social market' gave absolute centrality to 'monopoly control' (Christlich Demokratische Union 1949: 440) and preventing the abuse of market power. However, while the Federal Cartel Office in Berlin, together with the EU's Competition Directorate (DG IV), has been relatively effective in prosecuting cartels, it has been powerless to prevent the inexorable process of concentration in the major branches of German industry and commerce. Statism or market ordering has been imperceptible in the process of national and international agglomeration of capital. On a scale of 'liberality' one would have to describe the political context for mergers in Germany – and elsewhere in the world – as benign.

****

The above thumbnail sketch of Germany's political economy is intended to provide a point of departure for the study of the progress that political economy has undergone over the last quarter of a century and the changes that have affected that progress through the so-called paradigm shift in the 1980s and the turmoil of German unification. When describing the 'German model' and the threats to its survival, this study certainly does not proceed from any strong advocacy or defence of its merits as a blueprint for other societies to copy. The high levels of capital concentration, the oligarchic features of corporate cooperation and the weak democratic credentials of the state's economic policy architecture (independent central bank, fragmented fiscal authorities) do not recommend themselves for any new democracy based on openness and social justice. That said, there are other features of Germany's economic and political culture which are not simply worth defending, but which offer the promise of a civilised escape from the current global trajectory of increasing disparity and the conflictual resolution of the problems of resource distribution that threaten to engulf human society: Germany's tradition of skill, of consensual politics, of social solidarity and reflective long-termism could, if allowed, be deployed to navigate its citizens away from the calamities which an obsessive adoption of neoliberalism has arguably hastened.

Jeremy Leaman,
Loughborough 2008

Chapter 1

1982: CRISIS AND TRANSITION

The removal of Helmut Schmidt as Federal Chancellor in October 1982 by means of the first successful 'constructive' vote of no confidence in the history of the German Bundestag is seen to a greater or lesser degree as a turning point in the development of economic policy in Europe's strongest national economy. There is, of course, always a danger of overstating the significance of the regime change (Borchardt 1990: 32), the replacement of the 'social–liberal' coalition (Social Democratic Party of Germany [SPD] and Free Democratic Party [FDP]) with a centre-right coalition (Christian Democratic Union/Christian Social Union [CDU/ CSU] and FDP) under Helmut Kohl, particularly given the usual political/electoral rhetoric of the *Wende* (the 'turn-around' or 'great change') deployed by Kohl's party machine. One is instinctively reluctant to give credence to the electoral propaganda of Germany's Conservative Party, better known for its slogan 'no experiments' that had been rolled out repeatedly during the Party's seventeen-year stint under Adenauer and Erhard up to 1966. There are also both marked elements of continuity between the Schmidt and Kohl regimes and of policy change prefigured by legislative measures taken under Schmidt's chancellorship with the particular encouragement of the FDP. And yes, the epistemology of discontinuity is riddled with syllogisms and overworked notions of 'eras' – the Adenauer, Erhard, Brandt, Schmidt, Kohl, and Schröder eras which conceal fundamental, structural constants qua social power hierarchies and corresponding policy imperatives. Nevertheless, this chapter will seek to demonstrate that there was indeed a significant *Wende* in the political and economic culture of the Federal Republic involving a paradigm shift in policy ambitions.

Paradigm Shift: Indicators 1982–89

As implied above, the neat periodisation of developments in a political economy like that of Germany suits many actors in the process as well as statisticians and historians. It allows the construction of narratives of merit, of blame, of pride in responsibility and relief in the perceived responsibility of others. It allows the truncation of causality and the convenience of selection: the trends of macroeconomic indicators, for example, can be linked or isolated according to the interests or ideological preferences of the narrator. So it is with the dramatic regime change of October 1982 with the added piquancy of the whiff of 'betrayal'; SPD and trade union banners in late 1982 and early 1983 stressed the FDP's *Verrat* and even invoked the memory of Bismarck's demise with demands that the 'pilot [Schmidt–Bismarck] should stay on board', alluding to the famous cartoon of 1890 where Bismarck's resignation is depicted as the 'pilot disembarking' and Schmidt's nautical background and reputation as fixer are implied.

Periodisation allows the convenient self-demarcation of predecessor/ successor from the errors of the future or the past respectively. However, in the case of the 1982 *Wende*, the periodisation into Schmidt and Kohl eras belies the significant features of continuity between one regime and the other. It is therefore important to assess the evidence of continuity before identifying the key changes in Germany's political economy since the early 1980s. It is helpful to separate the features of continuity into two generic categories.

Structural Economic Constants

a) The German macroeconomy was – either side of the watershed of 1982 – distinctively organised, with high levels of capital concentration, particularly in the key sectors of heavy industry, mechanical and electrical engineering, automotive and chemicals.

b) The governance of Germany's corporate sector was (and remains) highly centralised with a characteristic network of reciprocal holdings, involving both banks and 'non-banks' (productive and trading enterprises) where universal banks in both the private and the public sector wield – as long-term stakeholders – significant influence over the strategic decision making (research, development, investment, marketing, employment) of the major corporations; centralisation was/is also evident in the organisational density of the individual branches of the economy, in particular in the centralised system of collective bargaining, where national trade associations negotiate branchwide wage agreements with a corresponding national trade union.

c) The political economy was and remains heavily integrated in, and thus highly dependent on, the global trading economy, with a characteristic pattern of high value-added exports (predominantly capital goods, motor vehicles and consumer durables) and lower value-added imports.

d) Germany's renowned depth of skills training and high levels of qualified blue- and white-collar workers was – before and beyond 1982 – administered within a tripartite system of employment regulation, where employers, trade unionists and state agencies operated a predominantly cooperative regime of consultation, 'co-determination' and co-supervision (e.g., of the statutory social insurance funds), as well as consensual conflict resolution in the network of Labour Courts.

e) Germany's economic culture, in contrast to Anglo-Saxon systems, has been historically more 'risk-averse' in the sense of manifesting a preference for security, reliability and long-termism at both the micro- and the macroeconomic level. This arguably reflects both Germany's latecomer status as a unified industrialised power, in which state mercantilism and private cartels sought predictability in a hostile commercial environment, and the real experience of social and political turmoil which overwhelmed the country between 1914 and 1949, of two wars, two hyperinflations, slump, death and bereavement on an unimaginable scale, three changes of state form and the overwhelming shame of genocide. The result was a conservative investment culture in which capital was mobilised far less via equity markets – as in the United States and the United Kingdom – and predominantly via the banks and insurance companies as house banks *and* long-term stakeholders. A consistent 7 per cent of German households own shares, compared to over a quarter in the United Kingdom and (currently) 49 per cent in the United States. Equity returns – qua dividends and asset prices – were in turn traditionally less generous, with a higher propensity to retain profits for reinvestment. Despite a comprehensive system of social insurance, the household savings ratio was and is high and constant (1982: 12.7 per cent; 1991: 13.7 per cent; 2004: 10.5 per cent) compared to the United States (1982: 8.9 per cent; 1991: 5.4 per cent; 2004: 1.8 per cent) or Japan (16.7 per cent; 14.1 per cent; 2.4 per cent respectively).

Structural Political Constants

a) The pronounced devolution of powers in Germany's federal system remained in place after 1982, and with it the inbuilt weakness of central government powers, by which the paradigm shift must be measured. With key competencies in the hands of the eleven (now sixteen) regional governments and their associated district and local councils – notably education, policing, regional transport, tax collection, environment and spatial planning – the scope for 'shifting' the axis of the economic paradigm was limited at best. Subsidiarity continued to be reflected firstly in the higher volume of resources deployed at regional and local level; in 1980, the federated states and local councils accounted for 69 per cent of the total expenditure of state territorial authorities. Secondly, they employed many more civil servants than the Federation (Bund); out of a total of 3,041,700 full-time *Beamte* in 1980 only 553,400 worked for the Bund (18 per cent), 1,567,900 for the Länder (52 per cent) and a further 920,000 for local authorities (30 per cent). These ratios had changed insignificantly by 1990 (Bund: 17.9 per cent; Länder : 49.6 per cent; local authorities: 32.5 per cent) (Figures: *Statistisches Jahrbuch der Bundesrepublik*). The power of the lower-tier authorities was compounded by statutory entitlements to agreed shares of income taxes and value added tax (VAT) and by revenue from specific regional and local taxes.

b) Within Germany's extreme federalism, the Upper House (Bundesrat), representing the governments of the regional states, has the statutory power to initiate legislation, but notably to influence or indeed block some 70 per cent of all national legislation. Throughout most of the period of social–liberal rule under Brandt and Schmidt, the Bundesrat was controlled by the opposition parties (CDU/CSU), influencing legislation either directly in debate and revision or indirectly through the anticipation of revision on the part of the federal government. (Bräuninger and König 2000). In particular, the Bundesrat was 'extraordinarily' active in the initiation of legislation in the ninth legislative period, i.e.,1980–82 (ibid. 14).

c) The power of the federal government was likewise constrained by the ceding of sovereignty to the European Communities and by the increasing influence of European Commission (EC) directives on domestic (federal and regional) legislation (Bulmer and Radaelli 2004). In this context, Sturm and Pehle raise the question of 'The Bundestag as a "junior Partner" of European institutions' (Sturm and Pehle 2001: 57), referring in particular to the number of EC/European Union (EU) directives incorporated in Federal Law; in the eighth legislative period (Schmidt's second cabinet) they amounted to 1,706; in the tenth legislative period (Kohl II) it rose slightly to 1,828.

d) Arguably the most significant structural political constraint on federal executive power and thus on the latter's ability to define the dominant paradigms of macroeconomic policy was and remained the influence of the autonomous Bundesbank; this influence had grown after the collapse of Bretton Woods, the floating of all convertible currencies and the erosion of exchange controls (Leaman 2001: 155ff; Kennedy 1991). The European Monetary System (EMS), with its core feature of the Exchange Rate Mechanism (ERM), was in part designed to moderate the dominance of 'the bank that rules Europe' (Marsh 1993); the design – conceived by Valéry Giscard D'Estaing and Helmut Schmidt – failed; the EMS/ERM were effectively managed by the strongest central bank in the strongest trading economy with the strongest currency in Europe. The EMS period (1979–99) indeed arguably represents the pinnacle of the Bundesbank's power and influence; more than any elected government in Europe, this unelected, unanswerable institution defined the rules by which the turbulent waters of the post-Bretton Woods era were to be navigated, rules by which all the other (democratically answerable) monetary and fiscal authorities in Europe had to abide. While this volume will argue strongly in support of the notion of a paradigm shift in German economic policy since 1982, there is a persuasive case for the foundations of that shift having been laid early in the 1970s by the Bundesbank's version of monetarism.

Arguments in Support of the Paradigm Shift Hypothesis

Despite the strong elements of continuity in both structural economic and structural political terms, 1982 can still be seen as a very significant marker in the history of Germany's political economy, not because of any immediate radicalism as manifested by Kohl's ostensible policy models, Thatcher and Reagan, but rather because it ushered in a period in which there was a gradual but inexorable shift in the quality of economic policy decisions, the ideological paradigm within which they were consistently framed and the global context within which national, regional and global institutions operated.

The main reasons for highlighting the above features of continuity were to relativise the importance of regime change at the federal level but also to underscore the relative weakness of the SPD-led governments of the 1970s in a global economic and institutional environment which did not favour the coordinated nation-state interventionism normally associated with social democratic preferences. More particularly, the policy mix and reform measures of the social–liberal coalition are seen to prefigure the programme adopted by the Kohl governments of the 1980s by a number of commentators. Butterwegge sees the Law on Improving the Budget Structure of December 1975 as a clear 'caesura' (Butterwegge 2005: 117), in that with the Bill:

> the period of expansion in social policy which had lasted several decades came to an end and a phase of stagnation or regression began. The dismantling of the Social Democratic 'Model Germany', successfully invoked in the federal election campaign in 1976 against Helmut Kohl as chancellor candidate, did not just begin with the latter in 1982; rather it was 're-adjusted' already under Federal Chancellor Helmut Schmidt, restructured step-by-step and attuned to the goal of 'securing the location' [*Standortsicherung*] by means of the transformation of the welfare state.

Against the background of the exogenous shock of the oil crises, the furious debate within Germany's economic, political and academic elites about the supposed causes of 'the' crisis (Leaman 1988: 240ff) and the increasing fragility of the SPD–FDP coalition, it is not difficult to interpret the changes to pension and employment law in 1978 and the major expenditure cutbacks in the 'Operation '82', agreed in October 1981, and in particular in the Second Law on Improving the Budget Structure as confirmation of Schmidt's preparedness to accept policies 'which towards the end of his period in office hardly bore any resemblance to social democracy, and in practical terms prepared the ground for the [Christian-Democratic] Union to take over power' (Butterwegge 2005: 118f). It is no coincidence, perhaps, that the intensification of austerity policies at the expense of the subjects of social policy began when Lambsdorff took over as Federal Economics Minister in October 1977 from his party colleague, Hans Friderichs.

'Preparing the Ground': The SPD and the Path to Neoliberalism

Apart from the need to consider the views of an increasingly strident coalition partner, the prefiguring of the neoliberal revolution on the part of Helmut Schmidt and the SPD can above all be identified in the seemingly contradictory views within the Party towards the country's macroeconomic policy architecture. In his 1983 review of 'social democratic parties in Europe' Anton Pelinka (1983: 3) identifies the extension and strengthening of democratic controls in society as the central and enduring principles of social democracy; this 'consummation of political democracy' (ibid.) is furthermore centrally linked to the perception of the flawed nature of markets in advanced capitalism in the eyes of all social democrats – a perception shared with Keynesians, Marxists and ordoliberals – and the corresponding need for the political management of economic activity to avoid cyclical and structural crises and to remedy the distributive ills of capitalist society. There have been significant differences between different social democratic movements at any given point in time, and modifications in the goals, strategies and policies of individual parties over time, but the core belief in the democratically legitimated political management of national economic affairs has remained a constant. Thus, while views concerning the collective ownership of productive assets have altered markedly over time, European social democracy remained consistently associated with Keynesianism in the half century following the 1930s depression, i.e., with the politics of the anti-cyclical management of aggregate demand and the welfarist redistribution of social wealth to provide both public goods (qua physical and social infrastructure) and to prevent the kind of multiple deprivation evident in the history of capitalism hitherto. Scharpf (1987: 23) talks correctly of the 'intellectual hegemony' of Keynesianism in the period up to the 1970s. It was this hegemony that persuaded Germany's political and academic elites in the 1960s to modify the 'intervention phobia' of the Adenauer era (Ambrosius 1984: 108), firstly by establishing the Council of Economic Experts

(*Sachverständigenrat*) in 1963, which was designed to monitor macroeconomic policy and provide scientific guidance and in its early years had strong Keynesian leanings; secondly, with the establishment of a grand coalition between Christian Democrats and Social Democrats in 1966, Keynesians within both parties were given key positions under Kiesinger's chancellorship: Franz-Josef Strauss (CSU) as federal Finance Minister and Karl Schiller (SPD) as federal Economics Minister. Thus, in the latter days of the Keynesian consensus, even Germany's ordoliberal 'social market' was modified by the Stability and Growth Law of 1967, Keynesian in tooth and claw, which provided for extensive levels of policy coordination between the central and regional executive authorities, for state demand management and for tripartite consultations involving business associations, trade unions and the state (See Leaman 1988: 197ff).

The brief Keynesian experiment under Schiller and Strauss and, from 1969 to 1972 under Schiller, barely had time to bed in to the – in any case unpromising – humus of a fragmented German economic culture, when the end of fixed exchange rates and cheap oil thrust the whole of the Organisation for Economic Co-operation and Development (OECD) into the political turmoil of stagflation. Schiller's resignation as double Minister of Finance and Economics on 7 July 1972, while interpreted at the time as a reflection of his maverick personality (see Leaman 1988: 194), quite clearly marked a decisive shift away from a confident technocratic approach to macroeconomic policy to one that reflected the fundamental weakness of national social democratic regimes in the context of unstable trading and monetary conditions worldwide. As Keynes himself implied in the revealing Preface to the 1936 German edition of the *General Theory*, the most favourable conditions for the implementation of his policy prescriptions were provided by a highly centralised, territorially discreet political economy such as existed at the time in Germany! In 1972/73, Germany's extreme federal polity was faced with exchange rate mayhem, with sterling and dollar crises and (imminently) with an energy crisis.

A key factor in Schiller's departure was the decision of the Brandt cabinet to support the exchange rate strategy proposed by Karl Klasen, the then president of the Bundesbank, against that proposed by Karl Schiller. The difference of opinion revolved around the way in which the Federal Republic could neutralise the inflow of vagabond capital which was escaping from dollar and sterling assets and seeking refuge in DM securities. The fact that Klasen expressed a preference for strict exchange controls, effectively licensing foreign purchases of DM securities, against Schiller's less dirigiste preference for higher minimum deposits on foreign loans (Leaman 1988: 194f), is irrelevant. More significant was the alignment of the federal cabinet with the institution that was now effectively managing the external value of the DM within an exchange rate system that no longer had the security of the dollar standard, namely the

Bundesbank; this alignment was all the more crucial in the run-up to the federal elections in November 1972, which the social–liberal coalition won with an increased majority. The appearance of unanimity between Federal Bank and federal government was tactically more important than the retention of the dominant figure of Schiller in the Brandt cabinet.

There are two ironies in the economic policy events of 1972 which underscore the haplessness of the SPD in a crucial period of transition. Firstly, the consolidation of parliamentary power coincided with the effective ceding of macroeconomic control to the Bundesbank and the consolidation of monetarism as dominant orthodoxy, pursued with increasing ruthlessness through the remainder of the crisis-laden years of social–liberal rule. Secondly, Schiller's orthodox countercyclical credentials had produced a confrontation within Brandt's cabinet, where he opposed an increase in the PSBR on the grounds that it would contribute to the further overheating of a buoyant economy and suggested budget cuts instead, cuts which would have hit Helmut Schmidt's Defence Ministry. After Schiller's resignation, he was in fact replaced by Helmut Schmidt as double Minister for Finance and Economics. When in 1973 the reshuffled cabinet was confronted with further budgetary shortfalls, it elected initially to implement measures designed to stabilise both budget and inflationary tendencies, except that the indicators of a cyclical downturn were already evident, in particular with a rise in bankruptcies, a fall in capacity utilisation and the stagnation of private investment (Leaman 1988: 202). The reduction of state investments in 1973 was, above all, pro-cyclical – i.e., compounding the downturn – where Schiller's 1972 proposals would have been anti-cyclical. Faced with the stagflationary dilemma of promoting growth *or* price stability, both the federal cabinet and the Bundesbank identified inflation as the primary evil in 1973. There was, albeit, an attempt by the federal government later in 1973 to reverse the austerity measures and, after Schmidt's accession to the chancellorship in May 1974, a special fiscal programme for stimulating the economy was approved along with increased federal borrowing. In the context of an intensification of the Bundesbank's deflationary squeeze, however – which among other things raised the cost of federal and other state borrowing – the fiscal measures were too little, too late; at the height of the recession in 1975, state investment fell again by 3 per cent after a 7 per cent rise in 1974.

The transition to the new orthodoxy of monetarism was easiest in Germany, firstly as it represented the strongest trading economy in Europe, secondly because the DM as strongest European reserve currency was presided over by an independent central bank, which was statutorily committed to 'safeguard the value of the currency' (§3 Bundesbank Law 1958) and to ignore the demands of other political authorities if these 'prejudice ... the fulfilment of its duty' (§12). The Bundesbank's independence allowed it to apply the principles of the quantity theory of money as it saw fit, employing central bank refinancing rates (and minimum reserve ratios) to influence the national money stock and match the growth in the money stock to the growth of the national economy (or its productive potential). The Bundesbank traditionally operated under the assumption that price stability existed when annual price inflation was 2 per cent or less; thus monetary policy was considered successful if the money stock grew by 5 per cent, real gross domestic product (GDP) (or productive potential) by 3 per cent and prices by 2 per cent. The fact that this kind of monetarist target was missed more often than it was achieved (Marsh 1993) impressed observers less than Germany's above-average growth rate, its below-average rate of inflation and its almost permanent trade surplus. The causal linking of the success of the Federal Republic's low inflation trading economy with the operations of the autonomous Bundesbank was clearly shared by Social Democratic parliamentarians who, in a 1995 survey (Leaman 1995: 38) expressed strong approval (90.3 per cent) of EMU being 'administered by an independent European Central Bank', in contrast to British Labour Members of Parliament and Members of European Parliament, only 29.1 per cent of whom were of a similar opinion.

SPD support for an independent central bank was of long standing, predating the Bad Godesberg 'modernisation' by at least three years. In the Bundestag debates on the Bundesbank Law in 1956, Walter Seuffert (SPD) was unequivocal: 'Ladies and Gentlemen, it is ... the view of the Social Democratic opposition that the bank of issue must be independent at all costs, independent of every political influence, independent of the government, independent, I would like to say, of every government' (cited in: Leaman 1995: 26). The Bundesbank Law was passed with the full support of the SPD opposition at its final reading in July 1957. Since then, despite clear conflicts with SPD-led administrations and strong criticism of the bank by leading social democrats like Herbert Ehrenberg (1991) and even Helmut Schmidt (1994: 90), there has been no serious attempt to alter the bank's statutory autonomy.

In the immediate postwar years, the SPD had in fact insisted on the subordination of monetary policy to democratic controls in a framework of industrial and financial planning (Leaman 1995: 27). This kind of dirigisme, consistent with Left Keynesianism, was nevertheless sacrificed on the altar of conformity to the 'social market economy' in the Godesberg Programme of 1959. When, seven years later, Schiller instituted his Keynesian experiment to counteract the cyclical crisis of 1966/67, the policy coordination mechanisms of the Stability and Growth Act (1967) did not modify the separation of powers between fiscal and monetary authorities, even though, as Fritz Scharpf observed (1987: 119) this was 'contrary to Keynesian logic'. The Bundesbank tolerated Schiller's and Strauss' fiscal stimulation programme between 1967 and 1969. However, when the Keynesian experiment got seemingly out of hand with pro-cyclical overheating from 1970 to 1972 (Leaman 1988: 187), the bank reverted to its single-minded stability policies.

It would be misleading to suggest that the SPD accepted the state's fragmented policy architecture unquestioningly; the long-term party strategy document 'Orientation Framework '85' (published in 1975) has more of a resignatory tone in relation to the 'diffusion of state responsibilities' and the 'narrow constraints' on policy (SPD 1975: 26, 19). The Orientation Framework does propose that the Bundesbank be 'committed legally to all the goals of the Stability and Growth Law' (ibid. 35) but it confirms the Bank's autonomy and talks only very vaguely about monitoring its 'compliance with legal regulations'. In the context of the stagflationary crisis of 1975 in which one *Spiegel* headline asked 'Will tight money bring down the SPD?' (*Der Spiegel*: 17 February 1975), the reticence of Schmidt's party to elaborate a clearer plan for improving strategic policy coordination reflected the very constraints it bemoaned and its need to consider its liberal coalition partner and the opposition majority in the *Bundesrat* and the Bundesbank's power to 'topple governments' (Marsh 1993: 169ff). It is significant that the Orientation Framework only mentions the Bundesbank twice in its 127 pages. A decade later, after the Party's return to opposition in the Bundestag, the 1986 Irrsee 'Programme of Principles' makes only one fleeting and anodyne mention of the central bank, where it expresses the need to organise the 'constant dialogue between the two sides of industry, interest groups, the Bundesbank and the various levels of state responsibility' (SPD 1986: 54). It is perhaps surprising that, in the wake of Schmidt's demise, the SPD's defeat and the twin advance of monetarism and neoliberalism, the Party tabuises the Bundesbank as one of two key institutions (along with the US Federal Reserve Board) in the new global political economy. On the other hand, the imperative of political survival in the post-Bretton Woods era was central to the strategic manoeuvring within all European social democratic movements facing, as they did, a collective crisis (Scharpf 1987).

In the context of examining the provenance of the paradigm shift, it is most relevant to underline that the SPD contributed directly and indirectly to that shift through its ambivalence towards the separation of powers between monetary and fiscal policy and its failure to develop policy alternatives. It should nevertheless be stressed that one core element of neoliberal strategy – the redistribution of national income from labour to capital as a key incentive for wealth and job creation – was neither prefigured in the policy programmes or evident in the results of social–liberal rule between 1969 and 1982. It is noteworthy indeed that the wages ratio – wages and salaries as a proportion of national income – rose during the Brandt and Schmidt chancellorships (Table 1.1). Setting aside the crisis-related austerity measures at the end of Schmidt's term of office, the thrust of the social–liberal coalition's reform programme had been to enhance the social security of all citizens at risk of unemployment and sickness, to enhance an already generous statutory pension system, to widen educational participation and to extend workers' participation and other employment rights.

Table 1.1 Gross Wages Ratio in West Germany 1960–1980

	1960	1970	1979	1980
Gross Wages Ratio* (unadjusted)	60.1	68.0	71.5	73.5
Gross Wages Ratio (structurally adjusted)**	65	68	68.5	70

* Wages and Salaries as a proportion of National Income in percent
** GWR adjusted to account for increase of waged and salaried employees as a proportion of total workforce
Source: Hartmut Görgens (1990)

Most notable among the reform measures of the 1970s were:
- Pension reform in 1972 with the introduction of a flexible retirement age (full pension entitlement at sixty-three with thirty-five years of contributions) and generous settlements for pensioners with twenty-five years and above (at least 75 per cent of the normal full entitlement).
- Increases in Unemployment Benefit (*Arbeitslosengeld*) – from 62.5 per cent to 68 per cent of net income – and of Unemployment Assistance (*Arbeitslosenhilfe*) – from 52.5 per cent to 58 per cent - from 1 January 1975.
- The controversial extension of Parity Codetermination – equal worker representation on company supervisory boards – from heavy industrial corporations to all corporations with more than 2,000 employees became law in 1976, albeit with critical concessions to the business-friendly FDP.
- The Federal Law for the Promotion of Training (*Bundesausbildungs-förderungsgesetz* or *BaföG*) of 1971 – involving, in particular, grants to poorer university applicants as well as interest-free loans – survived the pressures for budgetary consolidation until Kohl's accession to power in October 1982.

Thus, while the exigencies of power – federalism, an autonomous Federal Bank, an opposition majority in the *Bundesrat* and a coalition government – reduced the room for manoeuvre in macroeconomic management, the SPD arguably was able to maintain the redistributive dimension of its politics, both in terms of a more equitable distribution of national income and access by wider sections of the population to key sources of power and influence – knowledge and information – and to the institutions of economic power. Whether measured by a relatively favourable Gini-Coefficient or by the strengthening of corporatist structures (in Labour Law, the supervision of social insurance funds, skills training, works councils, supervisory board representation) or by the dramatic expansion of higher education in the 1970s, the SPD's claim to promote a measure of redistribution and social justice cannot be dismissed. It is the persistence of a redistribution imperative from richer to poorer up until 1982 that represents the fundamental discontinuity in Germany's political economy; it is the key indicator of the subsequent paradigm shift. With Kohl's *Wende* comes namely the popularisation of the view that greater inequality is a precondition for economic recovery and lower unemployment.

The *Wende* as Normative Revolution

What happened in Germany in the winter of 1982/83 was thus less the deployment of a dramatically different set of policy tools and more of a change of normative emphasis within an already emerging new orthodoxy, in which monetarism held centre stage and supply-sidism was supplanting direct management of demand through state investment. The new consensus involving the centre-right federal coalition, the Bundesrat, the Bundesbank, the Council of Economic Experts and leading academic research institutes centred around the (dys)functional relationship between the businesses as 'creators of wealth' and employment, the employees of those businesses and the nonworking population, above all around the optimal incentivisation of these three groups. Neoliberal critics of West Germany's pre-1982 status quo focus on the demotivation of entrepreneurs through the pressures of labour cost and regulatory costs as well as the demotivation of employees through state social policy. Thus Otto von Lambsdorff, while still Economics Minister, was able to write:

> It is with concern that I observe a development over several years where a large number of social policy decisions – sensible when looked at in isolation – add up to a total system which no longer produces a sensible picture. ...There are today numerous cases in which the role of the wage income is rendered relatively less significant by the level of state transfer payments, yes even cases of otherwise identically structured households where the one with the lower income from work ends up with a higher disposable income. (Lambsdorff 1980: 84–5)

Two years before the *Wende*, Lambsdorff advocates tax relief for entrepreneurs and households (ibid. 86), deregulation (ibid. 87) and privatisation (ibid. 88f) as preferable strategies to state redistribution. Lambsdorff's views (expressed when still a member of the Schmidt administration!) were replicated widely within the political and economic elites of the Federal Republic during the severe stagflationary crisis. Kurt Biedenkopf, CDU spokesman on economic affairs, and economist Meinhard Miegel, produced a market-radical critique of welfare

Keynesianism under Schmidt in their 1979 book *Die Programmierte Krise* (*The Preprogrammed Crisis*) which cites the negative effect of narrow wage differentials on employment (Biedenkopf and Miegel 1979: 104); of state social policy on employer costs (109f); and of public debt on capital markets and private investment (66f). The Council of Economic Experts in its annual report for 1978/79 invoked the theory of 'crowding out' within capital markets in its critique of government deficit-financed demand management: by additional borrowing on tight capital markets, state authorities simply end up with a situation in which 'the additional private expenditure which fiscal policy stimulates through state demand is largely lost again at another point as a result of a reluctance to spend [on the part of enterprises]' (SVR 1978/79: 186). Based on this classic supply-side diagnosis of West Germany's politicoeconomic deficiencies, the prescribed cures are predictable:

- The state must reduce its interference in factor markets, reduce its expenditure on branch subsidies, on social transfer payments, the civil service and on public goods.
- The state must forego a portion of its revenue, reduce the state ratio and leave a larger proportion of gross national income in the hands of private companies and private households.
- The state must abandon its guarantee of full employment (Biedenkopf and Miegel 1979: 114ff) and allow the emergence of wider income differentials.
- The state must, through the reform of taxation and social levies and through deregulation improve the profitability of enterprises (ibid. 109) and the individual accumulation of wealth (111).
- Through the 'privatisation of public services' (Lambsdorff 1980: 88) the state can reduce its responsibilities, its costs and, through the greater efficiency of private enterprise, reduce the cost of services to the general public.

The simple diagnosis and prescription outlined above clearly seized the intellectual imagination of wide sections of the political, academic and corporate elite in West Germany. By conquering Europe's most powerful economy, *neoliberal supply-sidism* slowly consolidated its grip on the rest of Western Europe as the momentous first stage in the march towards global liberalisation.

The paradigm shift from Keynesian welfarism to neoliberalism was, like most economic paradigm shifts in the past, the product of crisis (Borchardt 1990: 32). Just as Prussian mercantilism was driven forward by, among other things, population growth and the Napoleonic wars; Wilhelmine imperialism by the crisis of (aristocratic) agriculture and the dynamism of (bourgeois) industry and banking (Jäger 1988); just as Keynesianism was the product of the Great Depression and the Second World War, so neoliberalism can in large measure be seen as the product of the crises which brought the 'Golden Age' of postwar reconstruction and growth to an end at the beginning of the 1970s (Hobsbawm 1994: 403ff). The transition to the new orthodoxy of neoliberalism was facilitated both by the militancy of the academic, political and popular critique of welfare Keynesianism within Germany's economic and political elite and by the lack of effective resistance on the part of the old orthodoxy that found itself suddenly and surprisingly with very few friends; academic and political proponents of welfare Keynesianism were suddenly very thin on the ground and – in the face of the real flaws revealed by stagflation – very defensive and susceptible to revisionism or wholesale revocation of its key tenets.

Just as the theory and practice of welfare Keynesianism in the postwar period contained 'a normative objective, namely the primacy of full employment' (AAW 1984: 250), so the downgrading or even abandonment of full employment as primary policy goal represents a shift in the normative focus of state policy. Whereas Keynes saw full employment as an important yardstick of macroeconomic equilibrium, as a key test of politicoeconomic success, supply-side theory sees every level of employment/unemployment as 'natural' in terms of a moving equilibrium in which the supply of and demand for labour resolve market changes around the price of labour (Tobin 1999: 38f). Friedman's notion of a 'natural' rate of unemployment implies not just that the representatives of labour are primarily responsible for the supply of jobs and the level of unemployment through their bargaining but that the political attempt to influence the demand for labour and, by fiscal and other means, to achieve a Beveridge definition of full employment (excess of vacancies over total number of registered unemployed) is counterproductive. A further implication of the 'natural unemployment' hypothesis is that a higher level of unemployment can be used as a means of achieving wage moderation and reducing employers' costs; reducing or removing the constraints of full employment on employer costs releases, in the logic of capital-friendly supply-sidism, the virtuous circle of increased profit, a higher preparedness to invest, a higher propensity to take on additional workers, higher turnover, higher profit etc. (The speciousness of this logic will be discussed later.) The popularisation of the concept of natural unemployment or 'minimum wage unemployment' is the strongest indicator of the erosion of the so-called 'Keynesian accommodation' which, since the catastrophes of the Great Depression and the Second World War, had involved the acceptance by capital interests of both increased state fiscal redistribution qua 'social wage' and the influence of labour organisations on macro- and microeconomic affairs (Scharpf 1987: 23; Bowles and Gintis 1994: 55ff). While Germany was not the natural home of Keynesianism, the 'organised capitalism' of the 'social market economy' did involve a dense and complex architecture of corporatism, as outlined above and replicating the 'compromise between capital and labour' (AAW 1984: 249), which had its strongest expression in the 'social partnership' of Germany's employers and workers. This partnership was facilitated by two decades of unparalleled growth and unprecedented social peace; the end of the 'golden age' of growth ushered in a period of unease and increased labour unrest; the wildcat strikes of 1969 took employers, trade unions and state authorities by surprise but reflected a spontaneous rejection of a voluntary wage policy which benefited company profits more than household income (Leaman 1988: 180–81) and spelled the effective end of the tripartite consultative forum dubbed 'Concerted Action' long before its official demise in 1977 and the political *Wende* of 1982.

The rhetoric of the neoliberal revolution stressed the importance of 'freedom' and 'choice' for both enterprises and households; far less frequent was the articulation of the logic of new and necessary inequalities. George Gilder, the guru of supply-sidism, comes close to demanding greater inequality when he attacks the destructiveness of 'the egalitarian programme' and its tendency 'to promote greed over giving' (Gilder 1981: 99, 38–39). However, the Heidelberg economist, Hermann May (cited in Butterwegge 2005: 77) has more recently explicitly stated that, 'economic inequality must not be regarded as a regrettable failure of the market, but must be identified rather as a highly gratifying, indeed necessary consequence of individual economic action'. One can applaud May at the very least for the honest exposition of a banal truth, namely that market capitalism operates on the basis of functional inequalities. The fact of inequality in economic rewards and in the related distribution of national income and wealth is justified predominantly in terms of the meritocratic principle of reward for better achievement. The logic of supply-sidism is to enhance the meritocratic principle: improving the profitability of a company (Biedenkopf and Miegel 1979) involves increasing the margin between turnover and cost, retaining a higher proportion of revenue as profit before and after tax, i.e., shifting the distribution of benefit from economic activity to the entrepreneur and away from concrete factors of production (materials, preproducts, services, labour) and the tax-raising arm of the state. The direct cost of labour is influenced by a number of factors, notably the degree to which increases in compensation per employee are adjusted to account for consumer price inflation and increases in labour productivity (turnover per employee). The logic of supply-sidism is to avoid the full compensation and to reduce the ratio of labour (and other) costs to turnover. The net effect of this strategy should be a shift in the *functional distribution of income* from labour to capital as the first essential step in regenerating a growth dynamic that benefits all and generates employment. The functional distribution of income is expressed commonly in the wages ratio and the profits ratio. The wages ratio denotes the share of wages and salaries as a proportion of national income, the profits ratio the corresponding share of income from business profit and accumulated wealth. The two ratios are not exact indicators of *personal income distribution* or the situation of individual households, as the latter also derive disposable income from accumulated wealth qua savings and other securities. Nevertheless, they can be used to indicate distributional trends. As noted previously (Table 1.1), the wages ratio rose in the 1970s, with a corresponding decline in the profits ratio, suggesting a reduction in levels of income inequality between wage earners and the self-employed under the social–liberal coalition. However, as Figure 1.1 shows, the improvement was reversed, starting in the early 1980s.

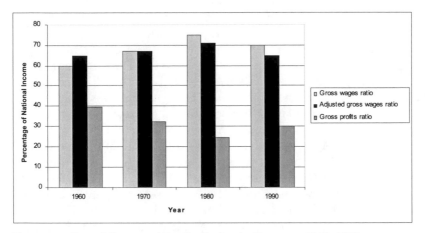

Figure 1.1 Gross Wages and Profits Ratios in Germany 1960–1990
Source: Claus Schäfer (2004)

The unadjusted gross wages ratio rose from 60.1 per cent of national income in 1960 to a peak of 75.2 per cent in 1980 but dropped back to 69.8 per cent by 1990; the gross profits ratio dropped correspondingly from an exceptional high in 1960 of 39.9 per cent of national income to a low point of 24.3 per cent in 1980 but rose rapidly to 30.2 per cent in 1990. These bald figures are misleading because they are not adjusted for the ratio of employees to the total working population; in 1960 22.8 per cent of the working population were self-employed, whilst only 77.2 per cent were waged or salaried employees. With the structural changes in economic activity – above all the concentration process in agriculture but also in the secondary and tertiary sectors – the ratio of self-employed to working population dropped to just 10.4 per cent by 1990, whilst the employee ratio rose to 89.6 per cent; if one factors in the employee ratio, the result is the adjusted gross wages ratio, shown by the black column in Figure 1, which indicates a return in 1990 to the distribution ratio of 1960, namely 65 per cent. The reversal of the distribution improvements of the 1970s after the *Wende* is, however, clearer if one examines the figures for net disposable income (Figure 1.2). From these it is clear that the growing inequality of market incomes (gross wages and profits) is compounded by the redistribution of fiscal burdens by the state:

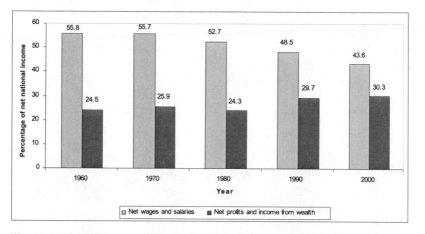

Figure 1.2 Net Wages and Profits Ratio in Germany 1960–2000
Source: Claus Schäfer (2004)

Net wages and salaries (gross income minus income tax and social insurance contributions) as a proportion of disposable household income have declined consistently after 1960, but with a marked drop from 52.7 per cent in 1980 to 48.5 per cent in 1990, while net income from profits and accumulated wealth rose from 24.4 per cent of disposable household income in 1960 to 29.7 per cent in 1990. The political dimension of these changes is evident in the data covering the relative fiscal burdens on employee income and profit income.

The proportions of gross income levied through either taxation or statutory social insurance contributions have, with the exception of a relatively static ratio of social contributions to profit income, moved in opposite directions since 1960, as Table 1.2 shows. Where the (income) tax burden on wages and salaries constituted only 6.3 per cent of gross earnings in 1960, one fifth of all income from profit and accumulated wealth was claimed by Germany's tax authorities; by 1980 the tax burden was roughly equal (15.8 per cent and 15.3 per cent respectively), but by 1990, within the first *Wende* decade, the ratio of profit income paid in taxation was less than half the level of 1960 and 36 per cent less than in 1980. Figure 1.3 shows the development of the combined burden of tax and social levies in an unequivocal manner, demonstrating that the fiscal adjustments of the federal state have provided disproportionate relief to capital income in the last twenty-five years and impose a disproportionate burden on the mass income of wage and salary earners.

Table 1.2 Burden of Taxation and Social Contributions on Gross Wages and Salaries and Profits in Germany 1960–2000

	1960	1970	1980	1990	2000
Tax burden on gross wages and salaries	6.3	11.8	15.8	16.2	19.3
Burden of social contributions on gross wages and salaries	9.4	10.7	12.8	14.2	16
Tax burden on profits and income from wealth	20	16.1	15.3	9.8	7.9
Burden of social contributions on profits and income from wealth	3	2.9	3.9	3	3.5

Source: Schäfer 2004

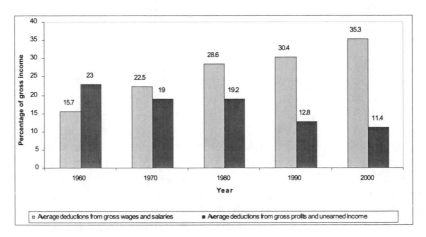

Figure 1.3 Deductions from Gross Wages and Gross Salaries and from Profits in Germany 1960–2000
Source: Claus Schäfer (2004)

The burden on wages rose 131 per cent from 15.7 per cent to 35.3 per cent of gross income in the forty years between 1960 and 2000, while the burden on capital income declined by over 50 per cent, with the sharpest decline of 33 per cent in the first *Wende* decade. There will be further more detailed analysis of fiscal policy in later chapters. The purpose of this brief summary of distribution developments in Germany is to demonstrate the core political dimension of the paradigm shift. Even if one discounts the 1960 figure of a 23 per cent burden on capital income as the result of an otherwise unmatched peak in the rate of profit on gross capital (20.9 per cent) and net capital (34.9 per cent) (Leaman 1988: 205), the development since 1970 indicates a shift, after 1980, in the dominant political attitude towards the concept of equitable and progressive taxation in general and the taxation of capital in particular. The neoliberal paradigm shift, effected under Kohl in the wake of Thatcher and Reagan, involves the normative political prioritisation of the progressive and optimal relief of cost burdens on capital as a means of sustaining the territorial loyalty of businesses and/or promoting new wealth- and job-creating investments. This new supply-side 'capital logic' involves, at the very least, the reduction of marginal rates of taxation and the flattening of the curve of progression; more radical interpretations of the supply-side imperative include the proposition of no progressivity ('flat tax') or even the exemption of capital from taxation altogether. Both these radical propositions have, in the recent context of international tax competition between states, become statutory reality in several European states and have been seriously debated within the CDU in Germany. The disproportionate burdening of mass incomes, as the wellspring of household demand, does not simply reflect the new faith in Say's Law – that demand is generated above all by supply factors (price, quality, utility) – but also the normative abandonment of the principle of distributional justice.

Functional Inequality

A key dimension of the paradigm shift is the implicit (only occasionally explicit) utilisation of inequality as an 'activation' mechanism in a new culture of socioeconomic incentives. It is arguably not far from Arthur Young's comment on the economic necessities of manufacturing: 'every one but an idiot knows that the lower classes must be kept poor, or they will never be industrious ... they must be in poverty or they will not work' (Young 1771: 360) to the twentieth century homilies of the 'enriching mysteries of inequality' (Gilder 1982: 101). According to Gilder, 'welfare fosters a slovenly and improvident way of life ... In a society of rapid social mobility ... the poor know that their condition is to a great degree their own fault or choice' (ibid. 94–95); 'in order to succeed, the poor need most of all the spur of their poverty' (ibid. 118). Galbraith's pithy critique of social relations in contemporary capitalist societies notes the largely unspoken tenet of a necessary functional stratification: 'The underclass is deeply functional; all industrial countries have one in greater or lesser measure and in one form or another. As some of its members escape from deprivation and its associated compulsions, a re-supply becomes essential. But on few matters, it must be added, is even the most sophisticated economic and social comment more reticent' (Galbraith 1992: 31–32).

Galbraith frequently parodied the logic of elitist anti-egalitarianism in terms of the differing incentives that were supposed to apply to rich and poor: 'As the rich needed the incentive of more money, so the poor needed the incentive of less' (Galbraith 1994: 232). The political popularisation of the new inequality in Germany was filtered through the rhetoric of 'partnership' between capital and labour. While Lambsdorff invoked the responsibility of the 'income partners' – employers associations and trade unions – to consider the 'interests of overall economic peace' (1980: 225–26), the weight of his argument is in fact directed against trade unions, as one chapter heading makes clear: 'How many burdens can our market economy bear? What trade unions must consider' (ibid. 254). Lambsdorff recommends in particular that the 'income partners' or 'wage partners' modify the German system of centralised wage bargaining by allowing lower national wage settlements and greater latitude for additional but, of necessity, differentiated settlements at enterprise level (ibid. 257). The CDU in its major economic policy programme of 1984 – the 'Stuttgart Principles' – also recommends basic wage settlements which do not fully reflect the increase in productivity, as a means of boosting company profits and reducing unemployment (CDU 1984a: 12): 'the traditional wage contracts do not offer sufficient possibilities for differentiated wage settlements according to branches and regions, which would be sensible in view of their varying economic positions. New forms of framework agreements between the negotiating parties could create additional latitude for the workforce and management of individual companies to construct wage settlements on an individual basis … In a time of high unemployment, labour law cannot contribute to the splitting of society into those who occupy well secured jobs on the one hand and those without opportunities who are looking for jobs.' (CDU 1984a: 13) Beyond these recommendations for a wider 'wage spreading' (*Lohnspreizung*), neoliberal academics like Meinhard Miegel openly demanded that political leaders should promote the interests of the 'stratum of the rich' upon whose creativity and innovation all society is dependent (Miegel 1983: 130). The active articulation of the need for wealth and greater rewards for the creators of wealth has gone hand in hand with the inversion of the concept of greed such that, '(e)galitarianism in the economy tends to promote greed over giving' (Gilder 1982: 38–39); the questioning of accumulations of wealth as parasitic is dismissed as 'envy' whereas the receipt of social benefits is seen in terms of the parasitism of the underclass, involving a 'fully comprehensive mindset' intent on exploiting/abusing 'the social hammock' of the welfare state to the full. (See Butterwegge 2005: 97ff.) Butterwegge and others chart the popularisation of neoliberalism in the (for some almost conspiratorial) discrediting of the institutions of the social state in Germany's popular print media, effecting a 'social political paradigm shift' in the public imagination (ibid. 98) which can then be exploited by political and economic elites in the key project of redistributing national income, not in the interests of a solidaristic community but in the pursuit of an unproven dogma, namely that the rich have to get richer in order for the poor to escape poverty.

The following chapters will explore in detail the implications of the neoliberal paradigm shift in relation to individual areas of policy and with particular reference to the other great 'change' in Germany's economic circumstances associated with unification in 1990.

THE FALL OF HELMUT SCHMIDT AND THE FORMATION OF THE *WENDE* ADMINISTRATION

Helmut Schmidt's fall from power can be seen both as a reflection of the general crisis of social democracy in Europe (Scharpf 1987) and as a result of the very specific circumstances of West German politics. The SPD had taken over the senior partnership in federal government in 1969 after a (relatively successful) Grand Coalition with the CDU under Chancellor Kurt-Georg Kiesinger (1966–69). The new social–liberal coalition, firstly under Willy Brandt (1969–74) and then under Helmut Schmidt (1974–82), included the smaller FDP as junior partner, a role it had served for thirteen of the seventeen years of the 'CDU-state' under Adenauer and Erhard. The FDP transformed itself gradually from a strident exponent of market liberalism to the right of the CDU at the beginning of the 1950s to a catch-all party which was prepared to coalesce not just with the CDU but also the SPD (e.g., at Land level in Northrhine Westphalia in 1956 and 1966). Under Thomas Dehler and Erich Mende, it moved to occupy the crowded middle-ground of West German politics where it came to stress above all its 'moderating' influence on both the authoritarian conservatism of Adenauer, Erhard and Strauss and the social reformism of Brandt and the SPD. The 1969 coalition agreement between the SPD and FDP, the latter now under the leadership of Walter Scheel, was strongly rooted in foreign policy commitments – *Ostpolitik* – which both Brandt as chancellor and Scheel as foreign minister drove forward; economic and social policy was less prominent. Nevertheless, the perceived 'lurch to the left' of the FDP produced electoral failures in three regions and the defection of key personnel (Mende, Zoglmann and Starke) to the CDU. As a small party, constantly threatened by parliamentary oblivion, by dint of the 5 per cent clause, but also as decisive holder of the parliamentary balance of power, the FDP was obliged to market itself as the reasonable broker between left and right from the outset of the social-liberal coalition in 1969.

The constellation of political forces in the 1970s was, above all, crucially overdetermined by developments in the global and national political economy where many of the established policy assumptions of the Keynesian 'intellectual hegemony' (Scharpf 1987: 23) evaporated. In contrast to the 'miracle' years of high growth and rapidly advancing affluence, the SPD–FDP administrations from 1969 to late 1982 were obliged to cope with exchange rate crises, two oil crises, two severe recessions, the onset of mass unemployment, strong sectoral shifts and much, much more. Under this centre-left alliance the performance of Germany's political economy – i.e., of both the productive trading economy and the state's political crisis management – was arguably better than in most other European OECD countries. An 'object lesson in economic management' (Zweig 1976) no less; the most powerful industrial and exporting apparatus on the continent succeeded firstly in restoring its strong external balances through the recycling of petro-dollars via increased export orders from the Middle East (Leaman 2001: 175) and helped in part to neutralise the effect of imported inflation – which was devastating other European economies – through a strengthening nominal exchange rate against both the U.S. dollar and a basket of OECD currencies (see Table 2.1).

Table 2.1 External Value of the DM and Overall External Balances 1972–1982

1972= 100 Columns 2-4	DM/$ Exchange Rate	DM- ER against 14 currencies	Real ER* against 14 currencies	Balance of Trade (DM Bill)	Balance of Payments (DM Bill)
1972	100	100	100	+20.2	+2.7
1973	121.7	110.4	109.2	+32.9	+12.3
1974	124.7	116.9	108.5	+50.8	26.5
1975	131.3	118.6	103.5	+37.2	+9.9
1976	128.1	125.6	104.0	+34.4	+9.9
1977	138.9	134.6	105.5	+38.4	+9.4
1978	160.7	140.7	105.9	+41.2	+18.1
1979	175.9	147.8	106.5	+22.4	-11.0
1980	177.6	148.2	100.4	+8/9	-28.6
1981	143.1	140.2	91.3	+27.7	-13.1
1982	132.9	147.3	93.0	+51.2	+8.6

Source: Bundesbank, *Monthly Report*, April 1985
*The real exchange rate adjusts the nominal exchange rate by factoring in relative levels of inflation in one country compared (in this case) to 14 other countries

The combination of lower than average inflation and an appreciating nominal exchange rate was, in the circumstances of the high inflation in most other OECD countries, a unique advantage to West Germany's political economy as it enhanced the price competitiveness of German exports. Despite the appreciation of the DM against the dollar of 77.6 per cent between 1972 and 1980 and of 48.2 per cent against a basket of OECD currencies, the real effective exchange rate had appreciated by only 0.4 per cent and, in the repeated bout of stagflation in 1981 and 1982 it actually fell to 91.3 per cent/ 93.0 per cent of 1972 levels. This helped in turn to boost the trade balance to record levels in 1982 and lift the balance of payments out of its temporary deficit in contrast to fifteen out of the then twenty-three members of the OECD, including the United States, France, Italy, Australia, Belgium, Denmark, Sweden and Spain.

However the laurels of this relative success are apportioned – be it to Schmidt's fiscal prudence, the Bundesbank's monetary discipline or (this author's preferred explanation) the prodigious strengths of West Germany's secular economy – in the competitive political and ideological context of Germany in 1981 and 1982 it was processed in a predictably selective and arbitrary manner. Helmut Schmidt's demise was arguably a function of this extreme selectivity. It is incontestable that Germany was severely affected by the second oil crisis, by the doubling of unemployment between 1980 and 1982, by three years of industrial recession (1980–82), by a 9 per cent drop in capacity utilisation, by record bankruptcies and sharp falls in levels of investment (See Table 2.2). However, in the squint-eyed perceptions of the new *Wende*-consensus, the dominant focus was on the deficitary position of federal government finances and those of the regions and local authorities as the primary structural factor behind the stagflationary crisis. The famous 'Lambsdorff-Paper', presented to the last Schmidt cabinet by its liberal Economics Minister, Otto von Lambsdorff (FDP) on 9 Sept 1982 focuses on the negative role of Germany's high state ratio (state expenditure as a proportion of GDP) and the need to make radical cuts in state budgets at federal, regional and local level (Lambsdorff and Tietmeyer 1982: 4–5). The document, produced by Lambsdorff together with the later president of the Bundesbank, Hans Tietmeyer, was indeed described at the time as a 'divorce document' (Stoltenberg 1997: 272), going far beyond any of the reform discussions that had been conducted between the coalition partners in its demand for swingeing cuts in unemployment, housing and maternity benefit and the shifting of the tax burden from direct to indirect taxation (ibid. 8). The Lambsdorff-Paper was reprinted by the weekly *Die Zeit* under the heading of, 'A Manifesto for Secession' (*Die Zeit*, 10 September 1982). It was also understood as such by Schmidt, whose cabinet had already agreed far-reaching budget cuts in July 1982. The SPD leadership decided to dissolve the coalition agreement on 15 September and on 17 September the four ministers of the FDP resigned. The party presidium of the FDP had voted by a narrow majority of eighteen to fifteen to end the social–liberal coalition. The action was also opposed by 40 per cent of the parliamentary party of the FDP in Bonn. Apart from the principled objections of members like Günter Verheugen (Verheugen 1984), Hildegard Hamm-Brücher and Ingrid Matthäus-Mayer, there were tactical worries about the effect of the FDP's defection on the upcoming regional elections in Hessen, worries which proved correct when the party's share of the vote fell below the 5 per cent threshold and disappeared from the Hessen regional assembly. Altogether some 700 left-liberals resigned from the Party, and at the end of November the youth wing, the Young Democrats, severed its links to the parent.

Table 2.2 Consumer Price Inflation in the G7 Countries 1978–1982 (percent change p.a.)

	1978	1979	1980	1981	1982
USA	7.3	8.9	10.4	8.9	5.8
Japan	4.5	3.6	7.5	4.5	2.7
Germany	2.7	4.2	5.8	6.4	5.3
France	9.1	10.7	13.3	13.0	11.5
Italy	13.2	14.4	20.5	18.0	17.1
Britain	9.1	13.6	16.2	11.2	8.7
Canada	7.6	8.5	10.0	11.2	10.2

Source: OECD *Economic Outlook* June 1992

The defection had been clearly prefigured by strident demands for budgetary consolidation at both the FDP's 1981 party conference – articulated in Hans-Dietrich Genscher's so-called 'Wende-Letter' (Jäger 1987: 224f) – by further demands for a restructuring of Germany's *Sozialstaat* at its 1982 conference, by the specific decision of the Hessen party caucus to campaign for a coalition with the opposition CDU at *Land* level in 1982 and by 'mumblings' about Lambsdorff resigning from the Economics Ministry (Jäger 1987: 226). The proximity of the political positions of Free Democrats and Christian Democrats in the autumn of 1982 was marked, as was the contrast between them and the majority opinion within the still welfarist SPD and the trade union movement. The extreme selectivity of the FDP was matched by CDU counterparts, such that Gerhard Stoltenberg (CDU), the later federal Finance Minister under Helmut Kohl from 1982 to 1989, relegated oil crisis, interest rates and exchange rate turbulence to factors of secondary importance behind the critical level of state expenditure and state borrowing in the recession (Stoltenberg 1997: 275). Both Lambsdorff and Tietmeyer (1982: 2) and Stoltenberg (1997: 275 etc) see the decline in the economy's investment ratio (gross investment [predominantly by private enterprises] as a proportion of GDP) as the key deficiency of Germany's recessionary crisis and link this directly with high state borrowing and the upward pressure this borrowing puts on market interest rates. The linkage is the core syllogism of the theory of 'crowding out' – the displacement of private investment through excessive state demand for credit on capital markets – popular in monetarist and neoliberal thinking (e.g., Biedenkopf and Miegel 1979: 64ff) and deployed frequently in the 1970s and 1980s to 'refute' Keynesian theories of anti-cyclical state deficit financing.

In the context of Schmidt's removal from office, the consonance of FDP and CDU views matched the thinking in the Bundesbank concerning the priorities of macroeconomic policy and the need for the fiscal authorities to consolidate their budgetary behaviour (Bundesbank 1983a: 19 etc.).

Next to the growing conflict within the Schmidt cabinet – between Schmidt and his Finance Minister, Matthöfer (SPD) on the one hand and Lambsdorff on the other

– the critical clash between the SPD leadership and the Bundesbank was arguably crucial in deciding the fate of the Schmidt chancellorship. The conflict is well documented (Marsh 1993: 172ff; Kennedy 1991: 40; Leaman 2001: 189ff). While some historians fail even to mention the part played by Germany's central bank in the government crisis of 1981–82 (e.g. Jäger 1987), others are quite explicit. David Marsh speaks of a 'three year battle of attrition' (1992: 174), Kennedy of a clash that 'amounted to a virtual declaration of a state of emergency' (1991: 40). The roots of the conflict were complex, but crucially affected by the structural political rivalry of the autonomous and unanswerable Federal Bank and the electorally answerable federal government. The guiding principles of the Bundesbank, which was statutorily committed to protecting the DM with monetary instruments as an absolute primary goal, differed significantly from those of the U.S. Federal Reserve which, despite its autonomy, is statutorily obliged to consider the effects of monetary policy on growth and employment. The uniquely restrictive statutory position of the Bundesbank in Germany's political economy preprogrammed conflict with the elected authorities, which broke out regularly in relation to both the Adenauer and Erhard chancellorships (Leaman 2001: 125–41). The Bank historically felt obliged to prove its independence by demonstrative acts of opposition to the preferences of the fiscal authorities. However, its power and influence grew considerably in the early 1970s with the collapse of the Bretton Woods system and floating of exchange rates, which effectively passed responsibility for the maintenance of the DM's external value from the federal government to the Federal Bank. The new leverage enjoyed by the Bundesbank produced an effective subordination of fiscal policy to monetary policy in Germany – and indirectly in the political economy of Europe and the rest of the developed world. This new primacy of monetarism in Germany sat uneasily in the SPD's ideological universe of welfarist interventionism, producing tensions within its party programmes between the reform preferences and that which was practically achievable; the celebrated 'economic-political orientation framework for the years 1975–1985' (SPD: 1975) reflected the resigned pragmatism of a party checked both by coalition politics and the supremacy of the Bundesbank but still shielded from public odium by the economy's resilience and relative success in the fight against stagflation. Schmidt's national and international reputation as a crisis manager, as 'fixer' (*Macher*) even allowed the party to fight two elections under the banner of *Modell Deutschland*. However, the reformist propensities of the SPD, or rather its resistance to demands for the reduction in the level of social provision, made a clash with its monetarist rival more likely than not. The hostility of the Bundesbank to the Schmidt administration was increased when the German chancellor, together with Valéry Giscard d'Estaing, negotiated the introduction of the EMS in 1979 in an attempt to bring stability to volatile currency markets, where the system's ERM required the central banks of member states to intervene in currency markets when particular currencies threatened to exceed the predefined limits of fluctuation. In March 1979, the month of the EMS launch, the Bundesbank criticised the tighter banding arrangements of the EMS explicitly: 'Judging from past experience, an attempt to defend exchange rates that have ceased to be credible leads to an increase in interventions and thus to a rapid reduction in the monetary autonomy of the countries with more stable currencies' (Bundesbank Monthly Report, March 1979), i.e. Germany. According to Heisenberg (1999: 54ff), Schmidt had arguably antagonised the Bundesbank in a well-publicised interview in *Business Week* (28 June 1978) where he talks about 'additional instruments of monetary assistance' in macroeconomic management, introducing longer time horizons for monetary policy and – most provocatively – 'sacrificing some of our reserves' and 'expand(ing) our money supply somewhat more rapidly than we have done until now'. Although the Bundesbank was unable to prevent the launch of the EMS, it was able to influence the shape of the new system through correspondence and positional papers. In particular, the plan to introduce the ECU as a pool currency and to establish an EMF along the lines of the international monetary fund (IMF) – with special drawing rights for countries with temporary balance of payments difficulties – was abandoned after opposition from the Bundesbank.

The introduction of the EMS in 1979 coincided with the second oil crisis, as well as with the election of Margaret Thatcher to the premiership in Britain, followed not long after by the election of Ronald Reagan to the presidency of the United States. As Table 2.2 indicates, the trebling of oil prices to over $30 a barrel produced a significant deficit in Germany's balance of payments, albeit only for three years, and more significantly a renewed bout of high inflation; consumer prices rose by 4.1 per cent in 1979, by 5.55 in 1980, 6.3 per cent in 1981 and 5.2 per cent in 1982. However, with the exception of Japan, German inflation rates were low compared to other G7 countries:

Table 2.3 Stagflation in West Germany 1979–1982

	1979	1980	1981	1982
GNP (real growth p.a. in percent)	4.0	1.0	0.1	-1.1
Industrial Production (real growth p.a. in percent) [not construction]	5.2	+0.0	-1.9	-2.5
Production in construction industry (real growth p.a.)	6.7	-2.7	-7.8	-9.0
Gross Investments (real growth p.a. in percent)	0.3	0.5	-9.0	-3.4
State Investment (real growth p.a. in percent)	-0.5	7.7	-3.0	-3.9
Consumer Price Inflation (average change p.a. in percent)	4.2	5.8	6.4	5.3
Unemployment Rate (in percent of Labour Force)	3.8	3.8	5.5	7.5
Productivity (growth in percent)	7.1	4.6	4.4	8.8
Capacity Utilisation in percent	86.7	81.7	77.7	81.7
Bankruptcies	5,515	7,772	9,195	9,362
Notifiable Mergers	243	294	445	453
Central Bank Discount Rate (average p.a. in percent)	4.4	7.2	7.5	7.25

Sources: Bundesbank Monthly Reports, Statistisches Jahrbuch der Bundesrepublik, Bundeskartellamt

The rise in domestic inflation, accelerated by the unavoidable multiplicator effects of primary energy costs, together with strong growth in the money stock necessarily triggered a strong policy reaction by the Bundesbank as it moved to initiate an extended deflationary squeeze, by raising both Discount and Lombard rates through 1979, 1980, 1981 and 1982; given its statutory duties and the structural embeddedness of monetarism in its operational behaviour, it was obliged to deflate. The move to historically high central bank rates in Germany and the rest of Europe could also be justified by the emergence of Reaganomics in the United States, which was a truly hybrid programme of monetary austerity, deficit spending on extravagant arms programmes (e.g., the 'Strategic Defense Initiative' or 'Star Wars' scheme) and capital imports driven by high U.S. real interest rates (Leaman 2001: 184). The two exogenous shocks of imported energy inflation and the 'suction effect' on European finance capital of unprecedented yields on U.S. securities triggered a predictable monetarist response in an ideological environment newly converted to monetarism; 'a sustained monetary loosening'. What was less expected, perhaps, was the intensity and duration of that response which lasted through 1981 – with zero growth and industrial recession – and through the deep recession and record bankruptcies of 1982. By 1981, Bundesbank deflation had become pro-cyclical, as evidenced by the dramatic decline of capacity utilisation and gross investments in that year (–9 per cent).

There was a vigorous debate about Bundesbank policy in Germany, which was arguably not encouraging for Schmidt and the SPD; most of the leading economics research institutes – with the exception of the *Deutsches Institut für Wirtschaftsforschung* in Berlin and the *Wirtschafts- und sozialwissenschaftliches Institut* in Cologne – supported the policy of monetary austerity, as did the Council of Economic Experts (*Sachverständigenrat zur Begutachtung der Wirtschaft*). Nevertheless, the then chairman of the Deutsche Bank Christians was not convinced that higher interest rates would cure stagflation (cited in Kennedy 1991: 45f) and in May 1980 Dieter Hoffmann, head of the *Bank für Gemeinwirtschaft*, expressed the fear that the Bundesbank – as in 1975 – was driving the economy into a recession (*Frankfurter Rundschau*: 6 May 1980). The Bundesbank made life extremely difficult for Schmidt not just by failing to ease the interest rate squeeze when the recession hit home, but also by aligning itself programmatically with the growing opposition consensus within the Bundestag. Helmut Schlesinger, vice-president of the Bundesbank, advocated a wage freeze in 1981 or – given a 6.4 per cent level of consumer price inflation in this year – a real wage cut. Hans Tietmeyer, the later Bundesbank president with strong links to Central Bank Council members, was, in his capacity as head of the Economic Principles department in the Federal Economics Ministry, the co-author of the so-called Lambsdorff-Paper. More culpable, arguably, was the refusal of the Bundesbank to cooperate with the federal government in the case of the Franco-German plan to raise a Saudi Arabian loan in 1981 as an alternative to normal bond-market sources. Schmidt planned to channel the loan through the Credit Agency for Reconstruction (*Kreditanstalt für Wiederaufbau*) and thus – artificially – to ease pressure from the federal budget deficit. It was argued that it would not have a 'crowding-out' effect on capital markets, would be at a favourable rate of interest, provide support for targeted programmes via interest subsidies and consolidate Germany's (and the EU's) bilateral relations with Saudi Arabia, from where the promise of lucrative export deals for armaments, construction and engineering were beckoning. The Bundesbank refused to administer the necessary federal bonds in what was tantamount to a *coup d'état*, seemingly contravening §20 of the Bundesbank Law, which obliges the Bank to issue public securities for the federal government.

It is possible to interpret Bundesbank action in the immediate aftermath of Schmidt's departure as confirmation of its approval over the departure of the SPD from federal office. After a token reduction of fifty basis points (0.5 per cent) in the central bank discount rate from 7.5 per cent to 7 per cent on 27 August 1982, the Bundesbank made two 100-point cuts in the discount rate, the first on 21 October (6 per cent) just three weeks after Kohl's accession, the second on 3 December, when it was lowered to 5 per cent, to be followed by a further reduction to 4 per cent on 17 March 1983.

Die Wende: 'Renewal of the Social Market Economy'?

In the 'constructive' vote of no confidence on 1 October 1982, 256 out of 496 members of the lower house of the federal parliament – the Bundestag – voted for Helmut Kohl, the chairperson of the CDU, as replacement chancellor for Helmut Schmidt; 235, including a sizeable minority of FDP MPs, voted against the motion. Three days later, on 4 October, Kohl announced his new coalition cabinet, comprising eight CDU representatives and four each from the CSU and the FDP. Three of the FDP ministers – Genscher (Foreign Affairs), Lambsdorff (Economics) and Ertl (Agriculture) – had served in Schmidt's cabinet up until 17 September 1982 and with the same portfolios. In his inaugural policy statement before the Bundestag on 13 October, Kohl announced an 'intellectual and ethical change' (*geistig-moralische Wende*) and a 'policy of renewal', as well as an emergency programme to combat the severe recession. Underscoring the government's 'return to the principles of the social market economy', Kohl set as objectives the consolidation of state finances, the stabilisation of contribution rates to the statutory social insurance schemes and the reduction of both the state ratio and inflation.

The invocation of the 'social market economy' is a commonplace in the political rhetoric of the Federal Republic. (It has not only been the CDU, but also the FDP and the SPD that have proposed programmes for the 'renewal of the social market economy', as a cursory search of their recent programme debates reveals.[1]) The

---

1. For example, the website of the parliamentary party of the FDP, in a document entitled 'Renewal of the Social Market Economy Necessary', claims that, '(t)he FDP is the party of the Social Market Economy' (http://www.fdp-fraktion.de). In like manner, the SPD's website presents a 'programme debate' under the title 'Renewal of the Social Market Economy' (http://programmdebatte.spd.de).

CDU's claim to the intellectual property rights over the 'social market' is nevertheless the strongest of all the major parties as the coinage can be traced back to the foundations of the Republic itself. The 'social market economy' was the model propagated by the CDU in its election campaign in 1949, most notably in the Düsseldorf Principles (CDU 1949) and subsequently presented as the key determinant of Germany's 'economic miracle'. The miracle was habitually (and simplistically) ascribed to the management of macroeconomic affairs by Ludwig Erhard – Adenauer's Economics Minister, 'the pioneer of the Social Market Economy' (Mierzejewski 2004) and 'father of the economic miracle' (Encyclopaedia Britannica etc.). While the conception of the SME is a matter of some controversy (Haselbach 1991; Welteke 1976; Leaman 1988: 48–77) and the reasons for West Germany's extraordinary economic success in the 1950s are certainly far more complicated than the paternity metaphor and subsequent CDU propaganda suggest (see, in particular, Abelshauser 1983: 85–102), the party has had the great fortune to have been associated with the blessing of economic recovery and identified with the 'social market economy', whatever it is. The invocation of the SME and the economic success of the 1950s in the politics of the *Wende* had a clear resonance within the West German electorate, as the March 1983 election results would seem to demonstrate, just as the turbulent 1970s, oil shocks, stagflation and two recessions became linked with the hapless SPD in the public imagination and consigned the party to a further sixteen years in opposition.

In the context of the *Wende*, however, and the demonstrable shift to a new market radicalism, the observer must ask: how is the 'social market economy' being renewed? What aspect of the – at best opaque and at worst contradictory – social market theory is to be dusted off and revivified? In order to assess the nature and scale of policy change after 1982 under the CDU, it is useful briefly to outline the intellectual and political pedigree of the 'social market'. Ideologically, the CDU derived the key tenets of its 'social market economy' from the virtually unknown Freiburg school of 'ordoliberals', loosely organised around the economics journal *Ordnung der Wirtschaft* under the intellectual leadership of Walter Eucken (1891–1950), Franz Böhm (1895–1977) and Hans Grossmann-Doerth (1894–1944). Central to ordoliberalism was the explicit limitation of state policy to creating and maintaining the framework of the economic 'order' through '*Ordnungspolitik*' (Eucken 1955), allowing maximum room for manoeuvre to market mechanisms, above all through the rigorous application of *monopoly control*. The very particular self-demarcation of ordoliberals from laissez-faire capitalism, which had tolerated the emergence of monopolies and trusts, and from Wilhelmine 'organised capitalism' (Jäger 1988: 107ff), which had tolerated and even encouraged cartelisation, was replicated in the CDU's *Düsseldorf Principles*:

> The 'social market economy' stands in sharp contrast to the system of the planned economy which we reject, whether the controlling points in such an economy are centralised or decentralised, in state hands or organised via self-administration. ...
> The 'social market economy' also stands in contrast to the so-called 'free economy'

of a liberalistic kind. In order to avoid a relapse into the 'free economy', the independent control of monopolies is necessary to secure competition according to performance competition (*Leistungswettbewerb*). (CDU 1949: 431–32)

In the preamble to the *Düsseldorf Principles*, the CDU provides a definition of the 'social market economy':

> *What does the CDU understand by social market economy?*
> The 'social market economy' is the socially bound constitution of the commercial economy, in which the endeavours of free and able people are set in an order which yields a maximum of economic advantage and social justice for all. This order is created by freedom and obligation, which in the 'social market economy' express themselves through genuine competition and independent monopoly control (ibid. 430).

Monopoly control is then set as the very first of sixteen principles for the 'realisation of the Social Market Economy'; none of the sixteen principles relates to social policy, which is confined to a separate section: the 'social policy principles of the CDU'. While these include welfare provision from public funds in the case of proven need (i.e., when not covered by the statutory social insurance benefits accorded to workers and their dependents), the subordination of social policy to the primacy of economics is made explicit in the concluding remarks of the section:

> It must however be particularly stressed that the basis for a healthy social order is a successful economic policy. The best insurance laws are useless if an inexpert credit policy and fiscal policy reduces or even destroys purchasing power, the level of production, the state of employment, savings. The best social policy is useless, if the economic and the social order do not complement each other reciprocally and promote each other' (ibid. 448).

Together with monetary policy, monopoly control constitutes the key set of state functions in the 'social market'; monopoly control is the only truly innovative element of the CDU programme in 1949 and by implication provides the market with its 'social dimension'. Accordingly, it is mentioned nine times in the course of the CDU's 1949 economic manifesto; it is seen to contribute centrally towards the establishment of social justice by ensuring 'equal opportunities and fair conditions of competition'; the market, freed from the power abuse of cartels and monopolies/oligopolies and trusts, plays the key role in allocating social resources: 'The state is thus freed from the worry of central direction. There remains the task of making and protecting the law, of encouraging competition and organizing monetary affairs' (ibid: 433). Ordoliberalism rightly identifies the concentration and centralisation of capital as anti-pathetic to the efficient functioning of market competition and rightly blames monopolism for the degeneration of German capitalism in Wilhelmine, Weimar and Nazi Germany:

The old-style free economy allowed entrepreneurs to organise themselves into cartels and market associations, in order to dictate prices, arbitrarily to limit production and to conduct the economic struggle with the means of violence, forcing others out of the market and inflicting damage, with blockades, price wars and boycotts. In the process the idea of competition was falsified, blurred and robbed of its dynamic effect. Far too often there was a failure to realise equal and fair conditions for all market participants. Thus in the old-style free economy it often led to the economic exploitation of the weak by the powerful and to economic wars of violence and damage. Those that suffered were the economically and socially weak, in particular the consumers.

Because we wish to avoid the a-social distortions of this kind of 'free' economy, because we see in it a falsified market economy, we demand monopoly control as well as competition based on performance. Only an effective monopoly control prevents private individuals and private associations taking over controlling tasks in the economy. Only monopoly control leads to a situation where the consumer determines indirectly the nature and extent of production and thus becomes master of the economy (ibid. 432–33).

This extensive quotation from the *Düsseldorf Principles* is important not simply because it underscores the centrality of ordoliberal anti-monopoly theory to the electoral programme and the voter appeal of the CDU, but also to allow a differentiated assessment of what has subsequently happened to this – in many respects – bold and radical manifesto. Accordingly, the control of concentrated economic power, of cartels and monopolies is indispensable: 'only an effective monopoly control' can ensure the economically efficient and socially just functioning of the economy.

Combating the abuse of market power is the capstone of the whole social market edifice. The only problem with the strategic design of ordoliberal anti-monopolism is that it is breathtakingly naïve. The subsequent history of competition policy in the Federal Republic demonstrates this beyond doubt (Huffschmid 1972: 150; Leaman 1988: 58ff); the resistance of German industry to the early drafts of the Law against Restraints on Competition was vigorous and effective and driven not just by perceptions of self-interest; it perceived the real danger of radical anti-monopolism for the viability of Germany's political economy. Its application in one single country that was vitally dependent on a global trading economy and whose companies were exposed to competition with companies in other countries which were *not* constrained by such controls would have been disastrous for German exporters and for German recovery. If one pursues the sporting metaphor of 'competition' (*concurrence, concurrenzia, Wettbewerb, Wettkampf*), restraining the market power of German competitors while their Italian, French and British counterparts were still able to enjoy the advantages of collusion and concentrated economies of scale would have been like requiring the German athlete to start from blocks several metres behind the others and to run with his/her running shoe laces tied together. Germany's industrial trade associations were not prepared to be hamstrung by the utopian ordoliberal vision of a state of dynamic equilibrium based on small and medium-sized enterprises, the 'idyll of the petit bourgeoisie' (Welteke 1976: 38) which was, and still is, so attractive to voters. In a seven-year process of attrition German anti-monopolism – that essential ingredient of the social market economy – was effectively scuppered by fierce industrial lobbying, such that the original provisions of a blanket ban on cartels were dropped and capital concentration was left untouched. The 1958 Law on Restraints on Competition was a toothless beast. The ordoliberal theorist and CDU member of the Bundestag, Franz Böhm, acknowledged the defeat of this supposedly core element of the 'social market' and noted sardonically in the latter stages of parliamentary debate that 'if these proposals become law, then industrialists in every single branch of production will be able to sue the general secretary of their trade association for compensation, if he doesn't manage to persuade the cartel authority to allow their cartel' (76th Session of the Bundestag, 24 March 1955). The Law against Restraints on Competition – the supposed 'Magna Carta' of the 'social market economy' – was, according to another liberal historian, so watered down that 'the original idea was barely discernable' (Borchardt 1966: 292f).

Consequently, the trend of capital concentration continued in Germany in line with developments in other countries; many forms of cartel were either subject to Cartel Office approval or automatically permissible (Leaman 1988: 58). The demonopolisation measures of the Allies – involving German heavy industry and German banks – were allowed to lapse by the German authorities. Only the infamous chemical trust, IG-Farben, remained split, in the original three constituent companies: Bayer, Hoechst and BASF. More significantly, perhaps, the three re-merged joint stock banks – *Deutsche Bank, Dresdner Bank* and *Commerzbank* – were permitted to retain their traditional legal form of *universal banks* with their combination of high-street operations and large equity stakes in nonbanks (industrial and commercial corporations). This exceptional bank form – illegal in most other OECD countries because of the demonstrable risk of anti-competitive practice – reinforced the effect of capital concentration qua market share with the element of capital centralisation and the control by banks of the commanding heights of many of Germany's major corporations. By 1967, i.e., within less than ten years of the 1958 Law, the proportion of industrial turnover accruing to the fifty largest industrial companies in West Germany had risen to 42.2 per cent (1954: 25.4 per cent) and continued to rise (Jäger 1988: 230).

Notwithstanding the failure to establish the economic order according to the blueprint of the *Düsseldorf Principles* and their lynchpin control of private market power, the CDU-state – and all subsequent administrations – proceeded to sail under the distinctive banner of the 'social market economy'. The outstanding success of the country's trading economy, the increasing affluence of its voters, the strength of the DM and the resilience of the economy to external shocks rendered the conceptual purity and consistency of the 'social market' idea irrelevant to all but a handful of dissident observers. The 'social market economy' seemed, in the eyes of its most committed high priests, to have neutralised the problem of cyclical economic crises and established stable growth and full employment as a 'permanent condition' (Theodor Blank [CDU] in 1966, cited in: Welteke 1976: 125). Blank was, of course, wrong, as the recession of the winter of 1966/67 demonstrated, but seventeen years of economic performance that outshone all other major Western European countries seemed to justify the faith in a state policy focused on the framework conditions of stable money and free markets and the eschewing of an interventionist fiscal management of the cycle.

What happened at the conceptual level was a quiet redefinition of the 'social market economy', where its distinctiveness was defined not by a rigorous competition policy but by the institutional and regulatory framework of a well-organised capitalist state with high levels of social protection. Government publications frequently defined the 'social component of the economic system' exclusively in terms of the 'dense net of social security surrounding the Federal Republic' (Presse- und Informationsamt der Bundesregierung 1978: 138f etc.). Academic authors, like Karl Thalheim (1978: 13) distinguish the 'social' from the 'free' market economy in terms of state social security, employment protection, worker participation and even counter-cyclical policy but *not* in terms of any competition laws!

Within the CDU, the marginalisation of monopoly control as the central feature of state policy within the 'social market economy' was borne with surprising equanimity; the grumbles of ordoliberals like Böhm were the exception that proved the rule. Ludwig Erhard and Alfred Müller-Armack (the actual author of the concept 'social market economy') certainly made little of the contradiction of the free market vehicle without its steering wheel in their 'manifesto' (Erhard and Müller-Armack 1972), preferring to focus on the 'distortion' of their model at the hands of the ruling social–liberal coalition. Apart from this, the CDU was an ideologically broad church, containing not just committed ordoliberals, but also Christian socialists like Jakob Kaiser, Christian trade unionists organised in the party's Social Committees and committed interventionists; within the sister party, the CSU in Bavaria, Franz Josef Strauss was Keynesian in tooth and claw and collaborated successfully with Karl Schiller in Germany's brief experiment with Keynesianism in the Grand Coalition of 1966–69. Above all, however, the 'Union-Parties' contained pragmatic opportunists who adapted to the necessities of the Cold War, reconstruction and catch-all politics. Adaptation is the indispensable element in the conduct of power politics, arguably much more important than principles.

Nevertheless, the invocation of the spirit of the 'social market economy' in 1982/83 posed some problems for the political architects of the *Wende*. In the context of the conservative (CDU/CSU) and latterly liberal (FDP) critique of the perversion of the 'social market' order by the interventionist SPD (see Hoppmann 1973, Tuchtfeldt 1973, Lambdsorff and Tietmeyer 1982), any 'renewal' would involve reference to the original pure model in one form or another, an examination of the *Urtext* of the *Düsseldorf Principles*. The term *Wende* admittedly allowed some variety in the orientation of the 'renewal', having the sense of both 'return' and 'change of direction' and the theology of economic belief systems is not generally the stuff of weekend constituency surgeries or chats in the works canteen or the bar on a Friday night. However, there must have been some sense of unease in parts of the CDU about the publication of the *Stuttgart Principles* in 1984, submitted as the key motion for the May party conference, in which there is not one single mention of monopoly control or of competition policy as the central feature of the 'social market economy'. Corporate concentration, cartels and mergers are mentioned once, tucked away in Article 30 between SMEs (Art. 29) and company start-ups (Art. 31). The Preamble illustrates the degree to which the 1982 *Wende* is less of a return to basics and more of a change of direction:

> The Social Market Economy is a programme of economic and societal policy for all, because it reconciles *performance with social justice, competition with solidarity* and *self-responsibility with social security* [my emphasis]. The Social Market Economy has its intellectual foundation in the idea of freedom with responsibility which is part of the Christian's image of human beings.
>
> The CDU, the great people's party of the Federal Republic of Germany, was responsible for the political realisation of the Social Market Economy. This was the precondition for the successful economic reconstruction of Germany. It brought us a high standard of living and social security, it promoted social partnership and enabled people to determine their own destinies and to act in their own responsibility. The Social Market Economy combines *the advantages of a free market order with the commitment to social justice*.
>
> New economic and social conditions are making new demands on the adaptability and efficiency of the Social Market Economy. We encounter these demands in societal, economic and technological change as well as in the change of international conditions of competition.
>
> Even in a time of new challenges, such as the Federal Republic of Germany faces in the 1980s, personal freedom, equality of opportunity, property, well-being, work and social progress for all must be ensured. In order to achieve these objectives, the fundamental policy elements of the Social Market Economy relating to the economic order must in future be more strongly emphasised. These include:
>
> * *Competition and personal property which is socially committed*;
> * *Decentralised steering through markets and collective bargaining*;
> * *Control of power through the separation of competences and state monitoring;*
> * Freedom of the consumer, of enterprises and of profession;
> * *Independence and the preparedness to take risks*;
> * Participation by the individual in economic, social and societal progress (CDU 1984a: 3).

The conceptual pairing of the *Düsseldorf Principles* ('freedom and obligation', 'genuine competition and independent monopoly control') is aped in the 1984 characterisation of the 'social market economy', but the substance has changed significantly. The primary focus of the *Stuttgart Principles* is the 'competitiveness' of the German economy in the context of technological developments and changing international trading environment, not 'competition' as an abstract virtue. The objectives of reconstruction, of emergency housing programmes, of redeveloping a merchant fleet and rationalising agriculture, are replaced by the need to maintain the market position of Germany's major export industries (ibid. 5–7), the need to extend Germany's powerful tradition of innovation and patenting into the growth areas of semiconductors, microprocessing and biotechnology (ibid. 7–12), the need to reform the labour market and working times (ibid. 12–14) and to protect the environment (ibid. 14–15). The accompanying 'materials for the discussion of the Stuttgart Principles' (CDU 1984b) focus predominantly on the potential effects of new technologies on production/productivity and the labour market.

Germany's strong international position is seen to have been politically jeopardised above all by the 'disastrous development' of the 1970s, when:

> (a)s a result of social democratic policy … the state's share of gross national product grew too strongly, state expenditure and state debt rose in an unacceptable manner, bureaucratisation and state regulation increased. The partial paralysing of private initiative in state and society, the obstructing of structural economic change, the decline of investments were the result, which in turn helped to cause unemployment' (CDU 1984a: 5).

The diagnosis of the 'wrong developments in the seventies' (CDU 1984b: 9ff) is extraordinarily selective in that it neglects to mention the turbulent global economic conditions during this decade at any stage; no currency crises, no oil crises, no imported inflation, no imported recession. The reader is presented with a grotesquely monocausal explanation of the ills of the German political economy, which to a large degree reverses the causal chain; while undoubtedly political mistakes were made during the brief period of Keynesian demand management and while there was evidence of overheating in the domestic economy before the first oil crisis, any comparison of oil-importing OECD countries in this crisis decade will show that the German economy and the German state fared better than most. Apart from Japan, Germany had the lowest level of unemployment in 1982 (5.9 per cent) out of all the G7 countries, with their average of 7.7 per cent; its average PSBR between 1973 and 1982 was third best at -2.6 per cent behind the United States (-1.2 per cent) and France (-1.1 per cent) but rising to only -3.3 per cent in 1982 ahead of the United States (-3.4 per cent), Japan (-3.6 per cent), Canada (-5.9 per cent) and Italy (-11.3 per cent); its current account balances (at 0.8 per cent of GDP) were better than all other G7 countries except for the temporarily oil-rich United Kingdom (+1.7 per cent); the undeniable decline in investment (nonresidential fixed capital formation) was no worse over the same period than the G7 average (average decline for FRG: -1.46 per cent, G7: -1.47 per cent); its average rate of inflation over the decade of stagflation (1973–82) was only 5.15 per cent compared to 8.97 per cent for G7 and 8.28 per cent for Japan; with Japan, Germany was the only other G7 country to show an effective exchange rate (OECD definition) above 1970 levels through to 1982. (All figures from OECD *Economic Outlook*, June 1992.)

The CDU critique of 'wrong developments' under the SPD was at best disingenuous, at worst a dishonest hatchet-job. It was above all dishonest because it referred (in part accurately) to the changing conditions of international competition but not the relative performance of other major economies and polities in that environment during the same crisis period, nor to the plaudits brought to bear on Germany's 'object-lesson in economic management' (Zweig 1976). It is disingenuous because it ignores the sharp rise in both the state ratio and state borrowing under Ronald Reagan and Margaret Thatcher in the early 1980s, whose neoliberal policies were supposedly the model for the Kohl *Wende*.

What the CDU's selective diagnosis of course allowed was a conclusion which matched the prejudices of mainstream economics institutes that had abandoned Keynesianism with lemming-like haste in the 1970s, as well as the political preferences of corporate interests that saw in supply-sidism, monetarism, privatisation and deregulation key vehicles for improving returns on capital, for maximising revenue and minimising cost. The *Stuttgart Principles* accordingly presented a set of policy proposals which were aimed at increasing the 'preparedness to work and to take risks' (CDU 1984a: 3) and to improve 'the conditions for the formation of risk capital' (ibid. 10). There were three main categories of measures proposed, itemised in numbered paragraphs of the *Stuttgart Principles*:

Framework Conditions

26. Budgetary consolidation and the reduction of the share of GDP deployed by the state (the state ratio) is the first named measure, to be achieved by reducing subsidies; implied are older industries, notably coal mining, shipbuilding, (housing) construction. Lower state borrowing brings fiscal policy into line with monetary policy and serves to 'promote private investment' – presumably by neutralising the 'crowding-out effect' on interest rates.

27. It is proposed to reform both PAYE and assessed income tax, reducing direct tax burdens but also tax allowances – in line with Conservative taxation reform in the UK: 'Better to have lower tax rates and fewer exceptions than high tax rates and many exceptions' (9)

28. The core thrust of tax reform is to increase the ratio of company capital (to turnover and/or credit capital) and thus to reduce the disincentives for self-financing. The capital ratio will rise again above all, if company revenues exceed revenues on risk-free money holdings.

29. SMEs are to be helped with the formation of risk capital by reducing the obstacles to stock-market listing, to capital transfers and venture capital stakes as well as reducing/abolishing some taxes on capital (company tax, stock exchange tax).

30. As noted above, paragraph 30 provides the token nod in the direction of competition policy, with its commitment to apply existing cartel legislation

consistently and to improve the Law on Unfair Competition. Its opening sentence refers to 'an efficient *Mittelstand*' as 'a fundamental precondition for competition' inveighs against 'excessive concentration' as being 'hostile to competition' (*wettbewerbsfeindlich*).

31. Existing programmes promoting company formation are to be improved through coordination, in particular between central and regional governments.

32. 'Measures for the de-bureaucratization of the economy and our living conditions (*sic*)' are to be aimed at building regulations, commerce, food retailing and the production of statistics (*sic*).

33. The privatisation of state commercial holdings and service enterprises at central, regional and local level will 'extend the scope for private initiative' and 'strengthen competition'.

Framework for Research and Technology

34. The 'de-bureaucratization of university research' at central and regional level is intended to improve the interchange of university and company personnel and is to be backed by increased state funding.

35. The coordinated promotion of technology transfer is intended to assist SMEs in particular, for example with the development of techno-parks close to higher education institutes.

36. High-tech basic university and private research in key technologies (e.g. semi-conductors, biotechnology).

37. The state practice of direct research project funding is to give way to less prescriptive, indirect funding, allowing a stronger input from private business. Private research funding is to be favoured by special tax allowances and state research grants for researchers in SMEs.

38. State enterprises, like the Bundespost [post and telecommunications], are to be encouraged to cooperate with private companies – for example in micro-electronics and fibre-optics – in the establishment of local broadband networks.

Restructuring of the Labour Market and Working Time

39. 'An important precondition for the maintenance of existing and the creation of new jobs is that the ratio of revenues to costs is improved for enterprises. This also depends essentially on the way in which labour costs develop'. The primacy of free collective bargaining allows the document simply to appeal to the 'wage partners' to consider the consequences of wage negotiations for 'growth, employment and international competitiveness'. However, the reduction of indirect labour costs – the text singles out the health service/health insurance – is accessible to statutory reform, allowing both a reduction in the contributions burden and in the long term the reconsideration of which 'social tasks' should be borne by the para-public social insurance system and which by the state.

40. This paragraph again appeals to the 'wage parties' (*sic*) to create greater flexibility in wage bargaining, allowing greater scope for regional and enterprise-based variations, in particular paving the way for individualised wage contracts.

41. The liberalisation of 'much too inflexible' labour regulations will encourage new employment by promoting individual short-term and part-time contracts, with public sector employment acting as a model.

42. The flexibilisation of working times is made easier by new technologies and provides citizens with greater choice. The paragraph applauds the government's promotion of early retirement as a means of reducing unemployment but rejects the general introduction of the thirty-five-hour week.

43. The adaptation of the 'dual' system of industrial and commercial training to the changes in sectoral employment structures and to new technologies is essential, such that both central and regional governments are called upon to institute the appropriate reforms and to consider the particular requirements of continuing education.
(CDU 1984a: 9–14)

The results of this *Wende* programme will be examined in the following chapters. At this stage it is important to underscore that the core objectives are – in sum and implicitly rather than explicitly – to alter the macroeconomic distribution of social resources, such that the state renounces a proportion of its share, wage earners forego a proportion of general or specific productivity gains and corporate and unincorporated companies maximise margins between revenue and costs and retain capital for re-channelling according to private preferences rather than public prescription (qua Keynesian demand management). The logic of this neoliberal programme is, in the first instance, that the relationship between the four major categories of demand (private consumption, state consumption, private investment and export demand) is modified in favour of the latter two and at the expense of the first two. Thus, in its *Economic Survey* of Germany for 1984/85, the OECD summarised the 'focal points of the new policy orientation' succinctly and accurately as the 'restructuring of national product away from consumption to investment, supported by a rise in profits' (OECD 1985: 9).

Germany's traditional and increasingly high export dependency must be nurtured and protected by minimising costs and domestic inflation, allowing a competitive advantage for high-grade finished goods despite the habitual strength of the DM against other world currencies; private investment, notably in high-tech equipment that maximises productivity growth, has to be encouraged as the foundation for the future growth of the productive economy. Private consumption and state consumption can grow but at a lower rate. The programme of export- and investment-led growth thus resembles that of the 'miracle' years of the 1950s when Germany achieved a higher investment ratio, a lower consumption ratio and a higher contribution of exports to growth than any of its European neighbours (Leaman 1988: 109).

While the CDU clearly had no illusions about the significant differences in the global economic environment between the 1950s and the 1980s – the *Stuttgart Principles* are, after all, predominantly about adaptation to changed circumstances – the prioritisation of international competitiveness and the accumulation of (investment) capital over household and state consumption betokens a belief in the efficacy of export-led growth as a prescription for politico-economic survival in the post-Bretton Woods system of globalised competition, in which the prioritisation generates the multiplicator effects which help to reconnect the ruptured circle of profits, investment and higher capacity, growth, employment and demand, capacity utilisation, profits etc., within the domestic economy. The robustness of this hypothesis was questioned by few economists at the outset of the *Wende* experiment. Werner Glastetter, Rüdiger Paulert and Ulrich Spörel, in their historical conspectus of German economic development from 1950 to 1980, published in 1983, expressed strong suspicions that the 'forcing of exports' would soon come up against the limits determined by the absorption capacity of global markets and by currency issues. Their analysis, they add, 'ought to have demonstrated that an offensive strategy that rests on the belief that these limits can be extended arbitrarily by the improvement of supply-side conditions could all too easily turn out to be a dangerous speculation' (Glastetter et al. 1983: 551; see also Arbeitsgruppe Alternative Wirtschaftspolitik 1984: 272ff).

The sceptics were right. The marked shift in policy preferences under Kohl which sought to constrain household and state demand and favour exports and investment produced both a dysfunctional imbalance in the overall dynamics of Germany's economy and, more dangerously, the increasing conviction that the imbalance was still not sufficient to generate strong and sustained growth via the supply side. The enterprise was, as this book is seeking to demonstrate, based more on faith and doctrinaire conviction than on any empirical evidence.

The first article of neoliberal faith concerns the reliability of private economic decision makers (qua enterprises) to deliver choices and decisions that would in sum benefit the macroeconomy; that – in the highly complex division of labour in the global economy of the late twentieth century – the 'invisible hand' would restore the dynamic equilibrium that ensures growth and employment, in particular in a period in which the demand for human labour was being significantly reduced by mechanical and electronic devices. These devices also had the additional and distinct advantage – in employers' eyes – of being nonunionised!

The second article of faith concerns the belief in Say's Law that supply would *ceteris paribus* generate demand for the product or service provided. Within the environment of developed nations all pursuing policies that sought to moderate wage costs as a supply factor, the relative reduction in disposable household income would, it might be expected, create severe limits on the capacity of the domestic market to respond to the allure of the supply-side, however beautified and perfumed. This would also seem to apply more obviously in developed economies where the absence of severe need increases the potential elasticity of demand for nonessential goods.

A third article of faith transfers the first two articles to the international level where the ability of the (German) state to influence developments on foreign markets is virtually nonexistent (AAW 1984: 274). There are few, if any, supply-side inducements that a state can deploy in order to influence the private decisions of foreign economic actors beyond export credit guarantees and benign trade diplomacy.

The orientation of the *Stuttgart Principles* towards the issue of 'our international competitiveness', i.e. the competitiveness of German corporations on global markets, exposes firstly the contradictions of the earlier conception of the 'social market' underpinned by independent monopoly control and secondly the continuing tension between the market power of the large (German) corporation on international, regional, national and local markets. Competitiveness on international markets – a rule precondition which also applied in the 1950s – requires not just high-quality products/services and high-quality marketing and after-sales service but, above all, *economies of scale*. There are proven advantages of vertical and/or horizontal concentration for the successful mastery of international trade. Controlling several stages of production from primary goods through to preproducts and finished goods in a large corporation (vertical concentration) allows cost efficiencies which generally elude smaller, territorially limited companies which operate fewer or just one stage of production; controlling a significant share of an international market for one group of products (oil, gas, copper, bauxite etc.) allows the advantage of oligopolistic or monopolistic supply (horizontal concentration). The history of capitalism charts a process of inexorable concentration within locations, nations, regions and finally internationally. The geographical compass of markets has grown over time, interrupted only by war and occasional severe recessions; over the last sixty years the volume of international trade – i.e., activity on world markets – has expanded consistently faster than world GDP and parallel to this increased trade intensity, the companies operating on world markets have grown in size as they sought to increase market share. The transnational corporation does not conduct mergers and acquisitions to increase competition but to reduce the effects of competition. Immanuel Wallerstein's assertion that 'all capitalists seek to monopolize' (Wallerstein 1983: 142) is difficult to refute when one looks at the recent waves of merger and acquisition activity both nationally and internationally.

The commitment of the CDU (albeit confined to a quiet corner of the *Stuttgart Principles*) to combat 'excessive company concentrations' because they 'are antipathetic to competition' (CDU 1984a: 9) is at best disingenuous, at worst mendacious, because the maintenance of German competitiveness depends on the particular fitness of German oligopolies (in the chemical, electrotechnical, engineering and automotive industries) to compete with American, Japanese and other European oligopolies. Their operation within global markets may reflect intense competition at this level. At national or local level the power of these 'national champions' as both suppliers but also as monopsony customers (for smaller suppliers and local labour) is prodigious and demonstrably 'antipathetic to competition'. If one adds to this trading power the value of their export trade to the national external balances, the increasing mobility of industrial producers between national locations of production and their ability to 'outsource' labour-intensive areas of production and servicing, the powerlessness of national competition policy is all too apparent, as the following chapters will show.

THE KOHL ERA: CDU SUPPLY-SIDISM IN PRACTICE

Helmut Kohl took office at a cyclically favourable time, i.e., at the very end of the severe recession of 1982 and the beginning of a general European recovery. Industrial orders, in particular in investment goods, began to recover, in particular in the fourth quarter of 1982, along with foreign orders for manufacturing goods (Bundesbank 1983a: 6). The improvement in order books for commercial property and equipment can in part be ascribed to the special depreciation allowances and investment grants for commercial building introduced in 'Operation '82'. Domestic orders for investment goods rose markedly from September through to December when they reached a level 25 per cent higher year-on-year. Orders for consumer goods, on the other hand, were only 5 per cent higher year-on-year. The final quarter improvement in investment goods orders could also have been encouraged by the Bundesbank's sudden series of interest rate cuts after a twenty-three-month credit squeeze; the rates set on 19 September 1980 (discount rate: 7.5 per cent, Lombard rate: 9 per cent) were only marginally relaxed on 27 August 1982 during the death throes of the social–liberal coalition (discount rate: 7 per cent; Lombard rate: 8 per cent) but then, following the formation of the centre-right coalition (CDU/CSU and FDP) and a meeting between the new Finance Minister Stoltenberg and Karl-Otto Pöhl, president of the Bundesbank, and Helmut Schlesinger, vice-president, on 5 October (Stoltenberg 1997: 282) the bank reduced both rates by a full percentage point, firstly on 22 October (discount rate: 6 per cent; Lombard rate: 7 per cent) and then again on 3 December 1982 (to 5 per cent and 6 per cent respectively). The Bundesbank also relaxed its minimum reserve ratios for commercial bank deposits in all categories – short-, medium- and long-term holdings as well as the savings deposits of non-nationals – on 1 October. Monetary policy suddenly became relatively benign, therefore, as the new administration embarked on its reform programmes. Additionally the dangers of imported inflation were in part neutralised by the appreciation of the DM against most other currencies but, in particular, against the US dollar throughout the course of 1982. While it took industrial production longer to recover from the 1982 recession – at the height of which (July 1982) it had fallen by seventeen percentage points compared to 1980 levels – retailing turnover accelerated in the last quarter of 1982 and continued growing strongly through 1983.

The reform agenda was spearheaded by Gerhard Stoltenberg (CDU) as Finance Minister and Otto von Lambsdorff (FDP) as Economics Minister. The delivery of supply-side improvements for producers/service providers/employers proceeded along three tracks, the one providing quantitative changes (reductions) in the proportion of business income that was levied by the state through taxation, social insurance contributions and other charges; the second providing changes to the regulatory framework relating to the labour market, capital markets, retailing, telecommunications and other utilities; the third providing targeted support for companies, notably SMEs, in relation to research and development, training, credit, exporting etc. Additionally, the privatisation of state enterprises or of state equity holdings in private corporations would provide opportunities for private investors to invest accumulated reserves or cheap credit in predominantly key utilities with a monopolistic or oligopolistic profile. A further and significant channel of government policy lay in *inaction and nondecisions*, i.e., in the role to which neoliberal roll-back theories (and the old ordoliberal model) proposed that states should return: no more planning, 'global steering', no more intervention: 'The state is thus freed from the worry of central direction. There remains the task of making and protecting the law, of encouraging competition and organizing monetary affairs' (CDU 1949: 433). When factor markets are liberalised and driven extensively by the market mechanisms of supply and demand, inaction by the state is essentially the new condition of supply-side bliss. That such inaction has consequences for the nature and conduct of democracy will be considered later in this analysis.

Taxation Reform

The Federal Republic has a remarkable taxation system in many respects. Over the past half-century and more it has developed to a level of complexity that makes it a veritable paradise for tax advisers, solicitors and academic tax specialists. According to a German acquaintance who works as a tax adviser, over 70 per cent of all the academic literature written in the world on taxation is concerned with the German system. The core reason for this mountain of tax wisdom is the accumulation of taxation legislation which developed after the foundation of the FRG as Federal and Regional finance and economics ministries sought ways to neutralise the effect of punitively high marginal rates of tax imposed on Germany by the Allied Occupation Statute (Leaman 1988: 117ff). The Control Council Law of 1946 had a top rate of 93 per cent and, above all, a steep curve of progression. The reforms in the 1950s, after numerous changes to top rates (e.g., 1951: 80 per cent; 1952: 55 per cent; 1953: 70 per cent), frequently contested and/or vetoed by the occupying powers, concentrated less on marginal rates and more on devising methods – above all for companies, both unincorporated and joint stock – for reducing the tax base via standard allowances for costs and special allowances (for accelerated or degressive depreciation, for example). Through the Investment Aid Law of 1951 firms could write off up to 50 per cent of the appropriation and running costs of moveable assets in the first three years and up to 30 per cent of the purchase cost of fixed assets (buildings and plant). Such legislation sought to give priority to capital formation within companies as well as a source of self-financing in the context of an initially weak capital market. And it worked very well. Publicly visible high marginal rates – which remained high while other European countries reduced them – concealed effective rates of business taxation which put Germany in the middle ground of European states, because German companies were able to offset a much higher proportion of their costs (the chauffeur, the car, the chauffeur's uniform, etc.) than their European counterparts. With persistently high investment ratios – the recycling of profits for the extension, improvement and rationalisation of capacity – there was little pressure to change. When signs of serious macroeconomic fragility emerged in the late 1960s, plans for a 'great tax reform' were announced – the first by Franz Josef Strauss as Finance Minister in the Grand Coalition in 1968 – but this and subsequent attempts in the 1970s came to nothing. Against the background of a rising state ratio in the Brandt and Schmidt eras, the Kohl *Wende* made taxation reform a key policy priority.

In December 1982, the 1983 Budget Law was passed together with a Supplementary Budget Law (*Haushaltsbegleitgesetz* 16 December1982). The latter contained the raising of VAT on nonessential items from 13 per cent to 14 per cent and from 6.5 per cent to 7 per cent for essential items; Finance Minister Stoltenberg stated explicitly that the VAT increase was intended directly to finance corporate tax relief. The rise would come into force on 1 July 1983 and was expected to increase revenues from VAT by some 7.5 per cent in a full year (Stoltenberg 1997: 280). The Supplementary Budget Law also introduced tax allowances applying to income tax, corporation tax and local business tax for a limited period relating to the acquisition of companies threatened by insolvency, as well as temporary facilities for offsetting long-term debts against company tax liabilities. Together with the tax relief measures from the Schmidt government's Employment Promotion Law of July 1982, the Federal Finance Ministry thus provided company relief of DM

1.89 billion in 1983. The Tax Relief Law of 22 December 1983 saw a reduction of the wealth tax rate from 0.7 per cent to 0.6 per cent on commercial assets and a rise in the basic allowance on this tax to DM 125,000. With special depreciation allowances for SMEs and for research and development and the extension of (the now notorious) special depreciation allowances for ships and aircraft, and other minor changes, fiscal relief – i.e., taxation foregone – totalled DM 6.48 billion in 1984, DM 5.65 billion in 1985 and DM 5.75 billion in 1986 (calculations from AAW 1986: 158–59).

As part of the emergency measures adopted in the winter of 1982/83, the Kohl government also instituted a repayable Investment Aid Levy on high earners, amounting to 5 per cent of their tax liabilities for the two years 1983 and 1984, with the primary aim of providing particular assistance for housing construction projects. Just before the emergency levy lapsed, the Federal Constitutional Court declared it to be unconstitutional and insisted on its immediate repayment. Less controversially, in April 1984 the government raised basic allowances for farmers to compensate for losses deriving from increased VAT payments. In the winter of 1984/85, the Kohl administration embarked on its so-called 'great tax reform' affecting income and corporation tax. The Tax Reduction Law was presented to the Bundestag in December 1984 and passed with minor amendments on 24 May 1985. Initially, the Law envisaged a two-stage process, coming into force on 1 January 1986 and 1 January 1988, but in 1987 a third stage was agreed for implementation in 1990. In the first stage, the child tax allowance was raised significantly from 432 DM to 2,484 DM, providing relief of some 5.2 billion DM; basic allowances for income tax were raised by 324/648 DM to 4,536/9,072 DM (single person, married couple), amounting to 2.1 billion DM; the steep curve of progression would be partially flattened out, providing 3.6 billion DM relief.

The second stage (1 January 1988) was to involve a further and more extensive flattening out of the curve of progression (8.5 billion DM) but it was supplemented by measures from a third stage, initiated by the Tax Reduction Extension Law of 14 July 1987, involving a rise in basic allowances to 4,752/9,504 DM, an allowance for skills training and improvements in special depreciation allowances for SMEs allowing 20 per cent of acquisition or production costs to be set against tax over three years. Total tax relief for this stage amounted to 13.7 billion DM.

The bulk of the measures from the Tax Reduction Extension Law came into force on 1 January 1990 and represented the most incisive of all three stages, both quantitatively and qualitatively. The third stage involved, above all, a reduction in marginal tax rates for income tax, with the top rate falling from 56 per cent to 53 per cent and the entry rate falling from 22 per cent to 19 per cent, but most significantly it introduced linear progression from 19 per cent to 53 per cent at a cost of 23.7 billion DM; basic allowances were again raised (to 5,616/11,232 DM) and the child tax allowance was increased to 3,024 DM. Corporation tax was reduced for retained profits from 56 per cent to 50 per cent. The total cost of stage three to the public purse was 44 billion DM, including the element brought forward two years. However, the net relief effect was 'only' 20 billion DM as a result of the removal of some 19 billion DM worth of company allowances.

Income tax relief measures were also financed out of increases in a number of federal and regional indirect taxes; petroleum tax was increased, such that its share of total tax revenue rose from 6.3 per cent to 6.8 per cent between 1980 and 1990; tobacco tax was increased less markedly and its share remained unchanged at the end of the decade at 3.4 per cent (1970: 4.6 per cent). Vehicle licences (an exclusive Land tax) were subject to new legislation in 1985, favouring low-emission vehicles and penalising high-emission vehicles. While the revenue from the licences rose, its share of total revenue still fell from 1.9 per cent in 1980 to 1.6 per cent in 1990.

Stoltenberg's income tax relief measures were only fractionally financed by increases in indirect taxation. Most of them were funded by cuts in expenditure by both territorial authorities and state agencies like the *Bundesanstalt für Arbeit* (Federal Agency for Labour).

- The 1983 Supplementary Budget Law saw reductions in Child Benefit of 20 DM for the second (down to 100 DM per month) and the third (200 DM) child.
- With the new federal coalition 'accepting' unemployment levels of 2.35 million for 1983 (Stoltenberg 1997: 280), contribution rates to the Unemployment Insurance Funds were raised from 4 per cent to 4.6 per cent of gross earnings, while federal grants to the Federal Agency for Labour were cut by 1.3 billion DM.
- The revised Federal Law for the Promotion of Training (*BaföG*) came into force on 1 August 1984, removing state grants for students in higher education and replacing them with interest-free student loans; financial support for schoolchildren through *BaföG* was almost completely removed.
- Civil servants' salary increases were delayed by six months to 1 July 1983 and capped at 2 per cent.
- Health insurance contributions for pensioners, scrapped in 1977, were reintroduced.
- Indexed pension and social benefit increases were postponed for six months.
- On 1 January 1984 unemployment benefit (*Arbeitslosengeld*) for those without children was cut from 68 per cent of the last net wage packet to 63 per cent; unemployment assistance (*Arbeitslosenunterstützung*) was cut by two percentage points to 56 per cent of the last net wage. Holiday and Christmas pay were incorporated into the income base from which social insurance contributions are calculated.
- In the same year, patient contributions to health costs were increased.

- On 19 April 1985, pensions contributions rates were raised by 0.5 percentage points to 19.2 per cent, starting in June 1985; however, unemployment contributions were lowered to 4.1 per cent of gross wages/salaries. Pensioner contributions to health insurance funds were raised to 4.5 per cent of gross income, with the view to increasing this gradually to 5.9 per cent.

A common assertion of the neoliberal proponents of tax relief, in particular the flattening of the line of progression, was that the effect on net state revenue would be less significant – or even positive – because tax reform would remove many of the reasons for tax evasion and/or escape into the cash-based shadow economy. In defence of the 'great tax reform', Finance Minister Stoltenberg in 1986 calculated that the extent of the 'black and underground economy' amounted to some 10 per cent of annual GDP (Stoltenberg, cited in: Eissel 1997: 136), with a corresponding loss of taxes and social insurance contributions. The claimed correlation between higher marginal tax rates and lower marginal tax revenue was popularised by the American economist Arthur Laffer and is superficially persuasive:

- The black economy is generated by a primary desire to avoid paying taxes.
- The preparedness to pay tax or to declare taxable income declines with a rising marginal rate and increases as the marginal rate falls.
- Employing tax advisors to devise sophisticated tax avoidance schemes is only worthwhile when marginal rates are high and the saving is considerable. There would be less incentive to 'invest' in expensive accountants' fees if the 'return' on the investment (i.e., the resulting increase in income) were relatively modest.
- Tax revenue rises as marginal rates fall. 'The higher the rates the less the revenue' (Gilder 1982: 178).

The empirical evidence to support the hypothesis of improved revenue from lower marginal rates is, however, pretty unconvincing. If one looks at the development of tax revenues in Germany from the main capital taxes (assessed income tax and corporation tax), one can see a clear declining trend since the early 1980s *despite* lower rates, or, of course, *because* of them.

Eissel is clearly right when he suggests that, as long as the tax system continues to contain tax loopholes that can be exploited to reduce tax liabilities, they will be exploited (Eissel 1997: 137ff). Tax honesty is not triggered by the simple decision to flatten or indeed abolish the curve of progression. Tax honesty is rather the function of a social culture and the normative patterns of social responsibility that have evolved within it. In Germany's case 'tax morality' has, on the one hand, been underpinned by the postwar accommodation between the 'social partners' in a period of growth and plenty, and by the solidaristic ideology of both social democracy and the catholic social theory in Christian democracy; the 'social committees' of the Union Parties and the Christian trade union movement played a significant role within the broader movement supporting this accommodation between capital and labour, certainly up until the 1980s. On the other hand, the West German state arguably undermined the solidaristic potential of the tax regime by maintaining the original structures (high top rate of income tax, high rate of corporation yax – both at 56 per cent) but providing the myriad offset opportunities that characterise the German system. If legal tax avoidance facilities are reduced less fast than marginal rates, it is arguably inevitable that revenue will decline rather than grow. However, it is more persuasive to assert that, in a tax culture like that of Germany, raising rates will reinforce avoidance.

Stoltenberg's memoirs contain an interesting concession about the seductive charm of Laffer-logic: 'The extensive initiatives of the Reagan administration to reduce tax burdens and the partly illusory expectations of a self-financing enterprise via stronger growth impressed many circles in Germany before a more sober appreciation set in in the USA' (Stoltenberg 1997: 290). One significant indicator of the extent of German tax morality was revealed by the fiasco of the withholding tax (*Quellensteuer*) which came into force on 1 January 1989 to tax interest income on bank savings accounts at source. The 10 per cent tax on interest income was a token initial tax payment beyond which all account holders would be expected to declare all interest income in annual tax returns. 1988 saw a significant flight of capital out of German bank accounts to accounts (often within the same bank) in neighbouring countries like Luxembourg where bank secrecy remained. In its Annual Report for 1988, the Bundesbank stated unequivocally that the withholding tax, 'led ... to massive shifts of domestic long-term money holdings into cash and (to a lesser extent) into liquid bank deposits that were exempt from withholding tax, but also into foreign securities' (Bundesbank 1989: 45). Only 43 billion DM were put into domestic bank deposit accounts in 1988, compared to 70 billion in both the previous years (ibid.). In contrast 'private investors and enterprises *suddenly* [my emphasis] expanded their long-term money deposits abroad' (Bundesbank 1989: 50), doubling the 1987 figure of 43 billion DM (itself a record) to 88 billion. German demand for foreign bonds more than doubled to 55 billion DM and investment funds enjoyed some 19 billion DM in extra business. In a language free of irony, the Bundesbank stated that it was above all 'subsidiaries of German banks that ... took advantage of the lively demand for DM-deposits that were free of withholding tax' (ibid. 56).

The haemorrhage of capital was so great that the Kohl cabinet decided less than five months after the tax came into force (on 10 May 1989) to revoke the law, as of 1 July, after which many of the depleted savings accounts were miraculously restored to pre-tax health. The Bundesbank's subsequent commentary on the extraordinary events surrounding the withholding tax is staggeringly unshocked by the monumental demonstration of tax dishonesty on the part of individual German account holders, German enterprises and German financial institutions: 'With the removal of the uncertainties (sic!) surrounding the taxation of interest income, the preparedness of non-banks to make long-term domestic money deposits suddenly increased' (Bundesbank 1990: 42). It is noteworthy that the authors of the 1988 and 1989 reports employ the same word ('*sprunghaft*') to describe first the flight and then the return of billions of DM and the extraordinary euphemism 'removal of uncertainties' to describe the capitulation of the Kohl government to the economic power of cheats. Given that Stoltenberg estimated that almost half of all interest income remained undeclared in German tax returns (Stoltenberg 1997: 301), the revocation of the withholding tax was certainly panicky and arguably craven, when set against the background of six years of tax relief on business incomes which reduced the average tax burden on incorporated companies from 29.3 per cent in 1982 to 21.1 per cent in 1990 (Schäfer 2004: 586). The glibness of the Bundesbank, the supposed overseer of bank probity in Germany, suggests tacit approval of tax evasion at the very least. In June 1991 the German Federal Constitutional Court, however, declared the revocation of the withholding tax to be contrary to the principle of equality of treatment in tax affairs (Article 3.1 Basic Law) and demanded the introduction of appropriate legislation by January 1993 (Bundesverfassungsgericht 1991).

Whatever else the *Quellensteuer* episode demonstrated, it certainly was not the Laffer hypothesis of tax honesty rising as top marginal rates fall! Beck and Meine (1998: 177) quote the frequently cited statistic contrasting the generally high 'declaration ratio' of wage and salary earners of over 90 per cent with the 55 per cent of income from profit that is revealed to German tax authorities (see also Eissel 1997: 137). To rectify this anomaly would need either a surprising conversion of profit-maximising individuals and companies to a new tax ethic, or action on the part of the state to widen the tax base and to increase the power of the regional tax offices to pursue tax evasion. However, as several authors have pointed out, Germany's Länder reduced the numbers of tax inspectors from the 1980s onwards and consequently the number of tax inspections. Eissel (1997: 144) cites Federal Finance Ministry figures, showing the increasing irregularity of inspections for large companies (every 5.4 years), medium-sized companies (every 14.5) and small enterprises (every 63.1 years) (figures for 1995).

Regulatory Reform up to 1990

The second pillar of *Wende* politics between 1983 and 1990 concerned regulatory reform, which in turn was based on the neoliberal perception of the supposed stifling effect of much state regulation on the optimal operation of the secular economy: 'Superfluous statutes and laws hinder structural change and individual initiative in the economy and limit unnecessarily the freedom of the citizen. Thus further measures for the de-bureaucratisation of the economy and our conditions of life are essential' (CDU 1984a: 11). The CDU identified the particular problems associated with building regulations, commercial law, grocery retailing and rules governing the production of statistics (*sic!*) (ibid.). The problems associated with planning law, most notably the comparatively slow pace of planning applications and their associated costs, and the comparatively restrictive rules governing shop opening hours were well chosen targets for criticism in the 1980s. West Germany was well known for its highly juridified, rules-based social and economic culture. The centrality of the Federal Constitutional Court as guardian of the German *Rechtsstaat* (the state based on the rule of law) was a critical feature of German political culture after the calamitous abuses of law under the Nazi *Unrechtsstaat*. However, the preference for statute in German social culture goes back to the traditions of the Prussian and then the imperial state and is reflected in the professional separation of branches of law – Labour Law, Administrative Law, Social Law, Criminal Law, Commercial Law – with separate courts, judges and lawyers and distinct appeal pathways. The German long-standing predilection for rules has been the frequent butt of jokes: Lenin, for example, famously remarked that, if German Social Democrats were called upon to storm a railway station as part of a popular uprising, they would all buy platform tickets beforehand! A further and more significant feature of Germany's regulatory culture, in particular as it evolved after the First World War, is that it covered a wide range of utility providers that were already in private hands – in contrast to the other major economies of Italy, France and Great Britain. Germany's political economy, even before the foundation of the Federal Republic, was characterised by a relatively low level of central or regional state ownership of either industrial or infrastructural holdings: 'the West German state holds a smaller share of the nation's business than some other European states where strong working-class movements brought about the nationalisation of important key sectors' (Esser 1989: 62).

The origins of German nationalisation were almost exclusively mercantilist in nature, i.e., driven by the preferences of the state for modernisation and adaptation of the domestic economy to changing international conditions. Apart from major equity holdings in the energy concern VEBA, the Salzgitter steelworks, Volkswagen, Lufthansa and the conglomerate VIAG, the federal state was only directly responsible for the federal railways and the federal postal and telephone service. The electricity and gas utilities were already private, commercial enterprises; coal, steel and shipbuilding were likewise privately run (albeit with considerable direct and indirect subsidies by central, regional and local authorities). Significantly, in this context, these key economic sectors – partly or wholly owned by the state in Britain, France and Italy – were already subject to distinct regulatory regimes in the Federal Republic, regimes that were specifically designed to counteract the abuse of natural monopoly power, to maintain security of production and supply or – as in the case of much postwar legislation – to create organisational checks and balances, including workforce participation and employment protection.

The energy sector and the iron and steel sector are notable examples of such regimes. Laws governing the state policing of the private 'electricity economy' (1919), the 'coal economy' (1919) and the 'energy economy' (1935), the later 'codetermination' legislation governing industrial relations in the West German coal and steel sectors (1951) and the parallel integration of the German coal and steel industries into the European Community for Steel and Coal (ECSC) (1951), represented highly complex regulatory systems involving public and private bureaucracies. The complexity reflected the absence of direct state control over monopolistic suppliers (electricity, gas) and oligopolies (coal, steel) and the corresponding need for indirect control.

With the exception of publicly owned regional and local banks, the structure of asset ownership in the Federal Republic in 1982 thus corresponded in large measure to the kind of minimal state share aspired to by proponents of privatisation in other European countries. Its regulatory culture was, to a considerable extent, determined by the dominant position of private capital in key economic sectors. It also conformed to the ordoliberal model of state–market relations which formed the basis for the CDU's 'social market economy', the 'third way' between capitalism and socialism, as it was presented in 1949.

The roll-back of the state in Germany was destined, therefore, to be quantitatively and qualitatively different to developments in other EU member states. Setting aside the unique privatisation activity associated with the absorption of the German Democratic Republic (GDR) into the FRG, the proceeds from the sale of central and regional state assets in the 1980s and 1990s were dwarfed by those of Italy, Britain, France, Japan, Australia and even Sweden (Huffschmid 2002: 80). Some re-regulation of the regimes governing utilities would be necessary as a result of the Single Market Act (1985) and of EU directives aimed at harmonising national legislation and establishing the proverbial 'level playing field' between national 'players', but it was only telecommunications that faced the upheaval of both privatisation and a brand new national/international regulatory framework.

It is possible (and important) to distinguish between three categories of structural (regulatory) reform: the first and central category concerned the liberalisation of labour market statutes and the reduction of labour cost burdens for all employers within Germany; the second concerned the reform of specific sectors of the domestic German economy where the pressure for reform was driven by domestic political preferences (predominantly retailing and health); the third category concerns those areas of the economy that were critically affected by the development of new technologies and by international market pressures like telecommunications and financial markets (see Woolcock et al. 1991).

Labour market reform figured most strongly in the *Wende* manifestos of both coalition parties (CDU 1984a; FDP 1985). In the 1980s the German economy was – in comparison to other OECD countries – marked by generally high wage levels, high levels of professional training and skill, high labour productivity, the shortest working year, highly juridified industrial relations, mandatory social insurance against sickness, old age, unemployment and industrial accidents, high levels of employment protection and low levels of industrial unrest. The statutes of employment law had been accumulated over more than a century of reforming legislation. There had been three waves of reforms, the first in the latter stages of the Bismarckian era (health, pension, accident insurance 1883–89), the second in the 'Weimar' Republic after the First World War (eight-hour day, unemployment insurance), the third after the Second World War (workers' participation, employment protection, enhanced social insurance benefits). The expense of the German system is reflected in the high ratio of marginal wage costs to direct labour costs (84 per cent in 1987), in the extensive state-funded system of labour courts, in the jointly funded 'dual system' of industrial and professional training and the various institutions of workers' codetermination – through Works Councils and employee representation on the boards of corporations.

The standard justification for extensive regulation of labour markets is their unique character compared to other commodity markets; it is in the mutual interest of employers and employees to maintain continuity of both production/service provision and of labour incomes as the primary source of domestic demand for the goods and services provided. Some proponents of deregulation deny the distinction between labour and other 'factors of production' (Keuchel 1989; Besters 1990) and argue strongly for the market regulation of the supply of/demand for labour power on the grounds that political regulation of the labour market 'largely suspends competition' and establishes 'cartel agreements' between employers and employees as the rule (Deregulierungskommission 1991: 136). The 'encrustation', 'ossification' (ibid. 1) or 'sclerosis' (Merklein 1985) of labour relations in juridified norms needed to be combated, according to proponents of deregulation, as a means of both encouraging investment and generating employment.

The Federal Republic as a location for production and investment will be enhanced in international competition because, with a more efficient labour market, mobile capital can reckon on a more attractive rate of return. It is not true that employees need be acutely concerned about their chances of employment through deregulation and re-regulation; if increasing numbers of workers are dismissed, the chances of re-employment in a well functioning labour market are greater than in one which is excessively regulated.' (Deregulierungskommission 1991: 157)

The first wave of labour market reforms was significantly accompanied by the persistence of mass unemployment despite the cyclical recovery of 1983 and 1984. Mass unemployment weakened the bargaining and lobbying power of organised labour in the following two decades, and lubricated the parliamentary passage and subsequent implementation of the structural reforms. While the 1984–89 series of measures were certainly less radical than the swingeing changes in the United Kingdom in the 1980s and indeed in unified Germany in the 1990s and the new millennium, the combined effect of liberalised labour statutes and high unemployment in the 1980s was entirely as intended: downward pressure on wage settlements and unit wage costs.

- The Early Retirement Law (29 March 1984), which came into force on 1 July 1984, provided grants from the Federal Institute for Labour (funded by the federal government) towards early retirement packages for older workers, such that younger entrants to the labour market would have the chance of employment; workers aged fifty-seven were offered the chance of receiving at least 65 per cent of their last gross monthly income, if they retired early – where normal full-term pensions were paid at a rate of 69 per cent. The Federal Institute for Labour provided a grant equivalent to 35 per cent of the early retirement pension to an employer on condition that the retiring worker was replaced by an unemployed individual or a young person seeking a job. Several hundred thousand older workers took advantage of the scheme which was extended beyond the original term of 1988 – at some considerable cost to the federal budget, as acknowledged ruefully by Stoltenberg later (1997: 286). The Early Retirement Law was opposed by the SPD in opposition and by most of the trade unions; the latter regarded a shorter working week as a more effective means of redistributing labour time among the workforce and, led by the metal workers' union *IG Metall*, campaigned for the introduction of a thirty-five-hour week without loss of gross earnings. In contrast, the Christian Trade Unions, the Social Committees of the CDU, but also the leaders of the Catering Workers' Union (IGNGG) and the Textile Workers (GTB) supported the early retirement route.
- The 1984 revision of the Youth Employment Protection Law modified certain requirements governing the deployment of apprentices, giving employers greater flexibility, in particular in relation to working time (AAW 1989: 69).

- The 1985 law governing The Social Plan in Bankruptcy and Insolvency Proceedings on the one hand confirmed the primacy of the 'social plan' (applying to company agreements on severance pay etc.) before other creditors' claims, but it limited individual compensation to the equivalent of only 2.5 months wages/salaries and the total volume of social plan funds to one third of residual assets.
- The deepest inroads into labour law were made by the 1986 Employment Promotion Law: a) opportunities for short-term contracts of employment were increased by extending the maximum contract period from six to eighteen months (twenty-four months in new businesses); b) subcontracted labour regulations were modified, allowing six-month contracts instead of the previous three; c) the trigger threshold of the number of redundancies at which Works Councils had the right to insist on social plan arrangements was almost doubled.
- The Employment Promotion Law (§116) also made significant changes to statutes governing strike action, removing benefit entitlement from third parties in a union affected by the regional strike action of union colleagues. This measure generated widespread opposition among the union movement and within the SPD and Green Party. On 6 March 1986, over a million workers took part in more than 250 mass meetings, mostly during working hours, to protest against §116.
- Again in 1986, the Law for the Disabled removed the six-month special protection from dismissal for newly employed disabled workers.
- In 1986 the restrictive Shop Closing Act was liberalised, extending potential working hours for certain shop workers.
- Maritime law was altered in 1989, allowing German registered ships to employ foreign sailors at rates of pay obtaining in their country of origin.

There is considerable disagreement about the quantitative impact of the above changes to labour law in the 1990s. Stoltenberg claimed that the reforms, in particular the revisions to the Employment Promotion Law, produced 150,000 additional jobs between 1984 and 1989. Economists close to the German trade unions, however, stressed the broader effect of the 'enormous redistribution in favour of profits in the course of the 1980s' resulting from the combined effect of mass unemployment, increases in productivity and (comparatively limited) labour deregulation compared to the United Kingdom and the United States (Müller and Seifert 1991: 499); Müller and Seifert argue that any increase in employment had been less a result of the cyclical recovery of growth at the end of the 1980s than of the technology-driven trend in productivity growth and the growth of overall economic capacity (ibid. 491). Wolfgang Däubler noted the 'erosion of the normal labour relationship' with the advantages of flexibilisation accruing to employers (Däubler 1988), while Carola Möller underscores the specific effects of short-term contracts on employment in the expanding service sector, such that over 50 per cent of all employment had become 'unprotected' by standard provisions of employment protection (Möller 1988), a situation which was particularly threatening to the position of women in the labour market.

Setting aside the issue of specific causal linkages, notably between labour market deregulation and macroeconomic outcomes, it is instructive to review the development of wages and salaries in relation to prices and productivity growth, but also in relation to income from capital. As Table 3.1 shows, negotiated wage rates grew modestly in the period 1983–89, averaging 3.2 per cent per annum in nominal terms over the seven years; gross wages and salaries per employee correspondingly grew by an average of 3.1 per cent, indicating a slight fall in average annual working time per employee and/or an increase in part-time employment. More significant are the modest rises in real gross income (averaging 1.5 per cent per annum) and real net income (0.9 per cent) per employee. These contrast with the marked rises in real gross income from business activity and wealth, which averaged 7.2 per cent in the same period and – with the effect of tax relief on business income – real net income from capital which averaged 7.9 per cent (Sources: Schäfer 1990; Bispinck 1990; own calculations). The evident weakening of organised labour as a result of a decade of severe structural unemployment is unmistakable in the significant fall in the wages ratio (see Table 3.1) and the consistent widening of the disparity between the incomes of employees and employers.

Table 3.1 Development of Wages, Prices and Productivity in Germany 1983–1989

	1983	1984	1985	1986	1987	1988	1989
Productivity	3.1	2.7	1.3	1.3	1.2	3	2.1
Cost of living	3.2	2.4	2.1	-0.2	0.1	1	2.8
Wage Rates (monthly)	3.3	2.9	3.8	3.5	3.4	2.9	2.8
Gross Wages & Salaries per employee (nominal)	3.2	3	2.9	3.8	3	3.1	3.1
Gross Wages & Salaries per employee (real)	0	0.6	0.8	4	2.9	2.1	0.3
Net Wages & Salaries per employee (nominal)	3.2	1.8	1.6	-4.2	1.8	3.4	2
Net Wages & Salaries per employee (real)	-1	-0.6	0.5	4.4	1.7	2.4	-0.8
*Gross Wages Ratio (adjusted)**	68.7	67.5	66.8	65.9	66	65	64.1

Source: Bispinck (1990) * Wages and salaries as a proportion of Gross National Income

Table 3.2 Average Duration of New Wage Agreements in Germany in 1989

Branch of the Economy	Average Length of New Wage Contracts in months
Agriculture, Horticulture and Forestry	18.9
Energy, Water and Mining	17.2
Basic Materials	20.2
Investment Goods	29.1
Consumer Goods	21.5
Food Processing	17.1
Construction	12.6
Retailing and Wholesaling	19.4
Transport and Communications	14.3
Financial Institutions	14.3
Private Services	15.9
State Authorities, Social Insurance Funds	12.0
Whole Economy	19.1

Source: Bispinck (1990)

It was also evident in the increasing number of wage agreements which were negotiated to apply for more than a year. By 1989 the average duration of new wage agreements had risen to 19.1 months for the economy as a whole but with significant variations between individual branches of the economy (see Table 3.2). It is significant that key branches of the economy had the longest staged pay deals, like investment goods (average duration: 29.1 months), consumer goods (21.5) and basic materials (20.2). This compared to all 108 public sector pay deals that maintained a strict annual cycle of negotiations. Over half of the 1989 wage agreements within the investment goods sector (389 out of 740) had three-year deals and thirty-six agreements were between forty-four and forty-eight months. A key feature of the bargaining position of most of Germany's trade unions in the 1980s was the inclusion of shorter working hours in most negotiation strategies, deriving from solidaristic commitments on the part of the labour movement towards the reduction of unemployment, whereby minor reductions in working hours were conceded by employers in exchange for moderate rises in hourly/monthly pay rates. Between 1984 and 1989 the average collectively agreed working week in Germany fell from 39.6 to 38.1 hours; these average figures do conceal significant differences, for example, whereas in 1984 three quarters of all workers were covered by working week agreements of forty hours or more, by 1989 the proportion had fallen to just 11 per cent, while 29 per cent of workers in 1989 were already on thirty-seven-hour contracts. Contractually agreed working years varied in length from 1,601.6 hours in the iron and steel industry, to 1,796.8 hours in agriculture and 1,788.4 hours in hotels and catering. Practically all the newer labour contracts contained provisions for the variation of weekly working times to cope with commercial fluctuations in demand and supply; Bispinck notes that the number of branches with flexible working week arrangements rose from eight to eighteen out of twenty between 1986 and 1989 (Bispinck 1990: 1356) with equalisation periods of between one week and a whole year; within the metal-working industry, the equalisation period rose from just one week in 1984 to six months by 1989 after the introduction of the thirty-seven-hour week. Similar concessions to employers' concerns over seasonal/periodic market fluctuations were agreed regarding overtime and flexi-time.

Despite the wave of trade union action in 1984 by both the metal-workers' union *IG-Metall* and the print-workers *IG Druck und Papier*, the labour movement gained relatively little in the 1980s. Technological change, notably the development of semiconductors, computer electronics and robotics provided enterprises with the means for replacing living labour with machines and for increasing productivity; the print unions in Germany and other European countries were among the first to experience the marginalisation of century-old typesetting skills. Additionally, the 1980s saw several branches of the economy affected by severe structural crises; the shipbuilding industry in the north and the coal mines and steel plants in the Ruhr region and in Saarland were above all affected by weak global demand and by the strength of Japanese and South Korean competitors. In 1983, the new Kohl administration agreed to crisis support of 83 billion DM to salvage the Saar steel company, *Arbed-Saarstahl*, but – while maintaining existing indirect subsidies for shipbuilding – did not intervene to prevent the closure of the *AG-Weser* yard with the loss of 1,200 jobs. In 1987, the continuing crisis of overcapacity in the steel industry was the subject of tripartite talks between employers, trade unions and both regional and federal ministries, which ended with an agreement to cut 34,900 jobs across the industry; similar discussions in the same year concerning Germany's coal mines produced a timetable of cuts in production and manpower to be completed by 1995; 30,000 job losses and a reduction in production capacity of between 13 and 15 million tons a year was the target. It is noteworthy that the German federal and regional governments maintained the so-called *Kohlepfennig*, the special coal levy on electricity bills introduced in 1974, until it was ruled illegal in 1994 by the Federal Constitutional Court and abolished the following year. The coal levy was nevertheless replaced by generous subsidies for the extraction of hard coal and the production of coking coal to assist both electricity production and steel-making; the annual subsidy in 1998 was still 7.8 billion DM. This public subsidy for private companies contrasts with the withdrawal of UK support for its privatised coal industry in the 1990s and a correspondingly brutal reduction in UK coal and steel capacity. It also reflects the strong residual mercantilist preferences of the Kohl administration, as well as the persisting corporatist culture as applied to both industrial and regional policy in Germany. As Peter Humphreys rightly noted: 'In 1985 ... finance minister Gerhard Stoltenberg (CDU) had promised to reduce them [state subsidies] by 6.9 per cent and in 1986 he aimed to cut them back by 6.5 per cent. Yet, the lobbies prevailed and by 1988 the level of subsidies – including tax allowances – was no less than 30 per cent higher than when he came to office' (Humphreys 1989: 132). To this extent, the incorporation of trade unions in the macroeconomic policy architecture in Germany can be seen to have influenced the neoliberal rhetoric of the CDU's 1984 programme, which declared that the 'subsidising of industrial branches that are in crisis must therefore be of limited duration and – while considering social requirements – be gradually reduced or adapted (sic)' (CDU 1984a: 7).

The influence of the German trade union movement in the 1980s should not, however, be exaggerated, as the erosion of real wages and the wages ratio (Table 3.1) clearly demonstrates. Additionally, the bargaining power of organised labour was arguably also weakened in the two years of above average GDP growth (1988: +3.7 per cent; 1989: +3.8 per cent) by the exceptional influx of ethnic Germans (*Aussiedler*) from the Soviet Union, Romania and Poland – 202,673 in 1988, 377,055 in 1989 – in the wake of negotiations between the Gorbachev and Kohl administrations. *Aussiedler* had the automatic right to German citizenship, even if their families had established themselves in Russia 250 years earlier, or in Romania even 600 years before. Thus, while the working population rose by 576,000 between 1987 and 1989, the number of unemployed only fell by 191,000. The effect of the influx of *Aussiedler* and of *Übersiedler* (immigrants from the GDR after November 1989) would continue to compound the weakening position of trade unions and ease the realisation of further structural reforms of German labour law in the remainder of the Kohl era and after the accession of the Red–Green coalition in 1998.

Branch-specific Re-regulation

In a ten-year retrospective study of deregulation in the first part of the Kohl era, Douglas Webber (1992) identified four branches of the German economy, in which significant efforts of re-regulation were made. Two of these fall into the category of 'endogenous' problem areas in need of domestic attention: retail opening hours and health care. The other two were more clearly determined by both technological developments and by the influence of international markets, notably telecommunications and financial services.

The issue of shop opening hours had a quaint parochial feel about it in the 1980s. It was certainly not high on the policy agenda of the CDU but was promoted vigorously by its junior coalition partner, the FDP, particularly after the federal elections of 1987 when it had increased its Bundestag representation as against CDU/CSU losses. The limiting of shop opening hours went back to 1956 and involved a general ban on Sunday trading and, with the exception of petrol stations, kiosks, railway station outlets and chemists, limited weekday opening to 7.00 until 18.30 and Saturday hours from 7.00 until 14.00. In the case of the reform initiated (reluctantly) by the Kohl cabinet, a clear majority (some 70 per cent) of retail employers represented by the Chief Community of German Retailing (*Hauptgemeinschaft des Deutschen Einzelhandels*) together with the shopworkers' union and elements within the CDU opposed the extension of opening hours. The main business thrust for reform came from the minority of big grocery chains and self-service department stores (Webber 1992: 156); with lower labour costs, the latter were confident that they could generate sufficient additional turnover to cover extended opening hours. The 1989 compromise deal had a Clochemerle quality to it, since overall weekly opening hours were kept the same but Thursday evenings could be extended by two hours from 18.30 to 20.30, balanced out by bringing forward Saturday closing from 18.00 to 16.00. There have been further revisions to German opening hours since 1989, in 2003 and 2006, but there is still considerable controversy about the macroeconomic efficacy of extending the time available to consumers for shopping, particularly given the relative stagnation in the growth of disposable income in the majority of German households (Table 3.1).

The issues surrounding health care reform were, and remain more complex, essentially because they involve considerably more groups of actors, operating at different levels and driven by varied material and other interests. Again, health reform did not figure in the CDU's 1984 programme, nor in the public debates of the early 1980s. However, contribution rates to the Health Insurance Funds continued to rise, partly because the growth of incomes subject to social insurance levies was growing less dynamically than GDP and partly because health related rates of inflation exceeded those of the cost of living index. The particular debate about the suitability of Germany as a location for investment (*Standortdebatte*), which intensified in 1987, focused among other things on the development of marginal wage costs and the key elements of employer contributions to employees' social insurance funds. It rendered health sector management politically relevant, particularly in the context of the new supply-side orthodoxy; hitherto the sector had been managed internally by the health insurance funds and the other stakeholder providers. The policymaking process was rendered complicated firstly by differences within the coalition, but secondly by the key regional responsibilities for the country's hospital service where particular states, notably Bavaria, were strongly opposed to radical changes in the structure of health care provision.

Germany's health system was certainly comprehensive in its preparedness to fund not just acute and ambulatory care, but also generous recuperative care in spa- and other sanitoria. Minor attempts at reducing health care costs had been included in Schmidt's 'Operation '82' which increased patient fees for prescription costs and recuperative 'cures'. More swingeing increases in patient fees were included in the 1987 health reform initiative but were abandoned after opposition from the CDU Social Committees. The rising cost of prescription drugs produced proposals for the medium-term regulation of drugs prices but, in the short term, resulted in a controversial proposal to extract a 1.5 billion DM levy from the pharmaceutical companies; the levy proposal was also abandoned after strong pressure by the latter. Doctors' interest groups put up stiff resistance to proposals to increase the intervention powers of the health insurance funds, monitoring the appropriateness of treatments and doctors' accounts, and were supported by the FDP, who also campaigned against proposals for the political fixing of dentists' fees through the Labour Ministry. The final shape of the Health Reform Bill, passed in November 1988, made few changes to the governance of health care but produced annual cost savings of around 14 billion DM. Higher patient fees for hospital stays (10 DM per day) for spectacles, dentures (50 per cent of total cost) and prescriptions (10 per cent), and a reduction in death grants were the main vehicles for cost savings. New arrangements were also introduced involving price capping for generic drugs and the listing of drugs considered less effective and therefore not eligible for statutory prescription payments. (For further details see Bandelow and Schubert 1998.)

The two examples of domestically driven supply-side reforms – retail opening hours and health care – would seem to confirm the underwhelming verdict of the OECD as avid promoter of supply-sidism when it noted 'comparatively little progress' in structural reforms in Germany (OECD 1988). The transformation of telecommunications, however, and the marked changes in both the practice and the governance of financial institutions, provide a valuable contrast to retail and health care reform, indicating the potent influence of both technological factors and global competition.

The CDU's 1984 economic manifesto is dominated by the urgent priority of promoting the development of new technologies as a primary vehicle for maintaining the international competitiveness of German companies and of German scientific research. (CDU 1984a; CDU 1984b). The urgency was in part determined by the fact that Germany's share of world exports in high technology products had fallen from 16.8 per cent to 14.5 per cent between 1970 and 1984 while Japan's had doubled from 10.9 per cent to 20.2 per cent and the United States maintained its share of around a quarter (Sharp and Shearman, cited in: Humphreys 1989: 129). The perception of an overcommitment in the branches of the first and second industrial revolutions (heavy industry, chemicals, electrotechnology, mechanical engineering, automotive) was widespread and there were clear worries about the capacity of Germany's political economy to react appropriately to the demands of the new electronic and communications revolution. Humphreys notes the obstacles embedded in the hitherto successful institutional arrangements:

- A fragmented system for the promotion of industrial innovation, in the shape of regional economics and education ministries driving separate and largely uncoordinated programmes of technology development designed to enhance regional and local locations for investment.
- A separation of federal competences for research and development promotion in IT and telecoms where policy preferences varied from the active promotion of industrial policy (Ministry of Posts and Telecommunications, Ministry for Research and Technology) to the eschewing of structural policies and the promotion of private, market-based approaches (Economics Ministry, Finance Ministry).
- An all too cosy 'symbiotic' relationship between the state monopoly of the Bundespost (combining postal services, telecommunications and banking) with big suppliers of technological goods, like Siemens. (Humphreys 1989).

Despite these obstacles, significant pressures were building on telecommunications providers worldwide. New technologies – in cable networks, in fibre optics and satellite communications and computerisation – indicated enormous potential for the expansion of individual communications services. The break-up of AT&T in the United States in 1982 and the reform of the UK postal and telecommunications monopoly, culminating in the majority privatisation of the newly formed British Telecom in 1984, encouraged the European Commission, in conjunction with the Single Market Programme, to recommend the deregulation of some state utilities, notably the telecommunications sector. More than a dozen consulting committees advised DG XIII on telecoms issues in 1985, leading to the commissioning of a green paper on the reform of the sector. Together with the Netherlands and France, the German federal government commissioned consultations within the sector; in 1981 the Monopoly Commission had already made recommendations for the liberalisation of equipment provision in telephone services, and this became an important feature of the domestic debate after 1984. The Kohl administration appointed a special commission under Professor Eberhard Witte which submitted its report in 1988, a year after the publication of the EC's Green Paper. The Witte Commission shied away from the radical reform of the sector as represented by the UK case which had imposed a partial reduction of British Telecom's monopoly in telephony. Rather, it made two recommendations which would prove crucial for the subsequent privatisation process, namely the separation of the three operational pillars of the Bundespost into separate, organisationally independent units – telephony, postal services and banking – and, secondly, the separation of entrepreneurial activity from regulatory activity within the sectors. The Commission's report disappointed the more radical lobbies within the FDP, the banking system and the Federation of German Industry, which had urged the abolition of both the postal and telephone monopolies and aggravated both the postal workers' union, the opposition parties within the Bundestag and some representatives of the CDU left. However, by drawing closely on the EC's green paper and insisting on the maintenance of the services' social responsibilities – notably for comprehensive geographical coverage – the bulk of the Commission's recommendations were incorporated in the 1989 Law on the Structure of the Postal Services. The Law contained the introduction of some competition, notably in the marketing of terminal equipment and in the provision of 'new' services, based on satellite and mobile telephony. Webber comes to sanguine conclusions on the efficacy of this first stage of telecoms reform: while it did not match 'the bolder steps taken in the USA, Japan and Britain ... in contrast to the Labour Minister's health insurance reform project, the telecommunications reform was not shredded to pieces on its way through the decision-making process. And, as well as ushering in the first comprehensive organisational reform of the Bundespost, it pierced the first substantial holes in the monopoly of the "Fortress on the Rhine"' (Webber 1992: 168).

There is, nevertheless, a common feature in the Christian-Liberal administration's initiatives in the structural reform of retailing, health services and telecommunications, notably the maintenance of a consociational dimension in both the decision-making processes and in the institutional architecture of the re-regulated sectors; the inclusion of a variety of 'stakeholders' – notably of workers' representatives – in the three sectors that were all highly labour intensive betokened a political concern for the consensual resolution of reform processes or, at the very least, the perils of legitimacy in a federal system. As Humphreys noted, Kohl was dogged by the 'constant need to take account of Land elections' meaning 'that policies have to be designed to appease a multitude of interests' (Humphreys 1989: 132).

The 'consociational' dimension was less obviously apparent in the reform of Germany's financial services, most notably of its stock markets. The latter were neither active recruiting territory for white collar unions nor, in contrast to other economies, institutions which attracted the interest of ordinary householders. In the 1980s only 5 per cent of the German population owned shares, compared to 18 per cent in the United States and between 15 and 17 per cent in Britain. Share ownership by private households as a proportion of share capital had in fact fallen from 27 per cent in 1960 to 16 per cent in 1982, the bulk (49 per cent) being in the hands of other enterprises, banks and insurance companies (Moran 1989). Stock exchanges and other securities exchanges in Germany are dominated by Germany's universal banks. Apart from their own extensive equity holdings – illegal in most other OECD countries – the universal banks assisted in the flotation of shares and bonds and controlled four-fifths of all share trading (Moran 1989) and deployed their depositors' shares (qua votes) as proxies in company annual general meetings. As a result, the volume of trading on the nine major provincial stock markets in Germany was far lower than in the major financial centres of the world such as London and New York. The trading of commodity and other 'futures' was virtually nonexistent, the bulk of German trading in commodity futures being done through London, Rotterdam, the United States or the Far East; trading in the more recent innovations of financial futures remained largely illegal.

As a result, German securities markets were disdained by their foreign counterparts as backward and provincial, a judgement which in large measure ignored the historically stable and reliable function of German financial institutions in the country's uniquely integrated productive economy (Leaman 1994: 23). There were problems but no evident 'crisis' of Germany's financial institutions in terms of their ability to service the operational needs of larger corporations, SMEs or private households. The pressure for the reform of securities exchanges thus derived from other factors. Webber rightly notes the increasing trade in financial futures in London and Paris in the 1980s as a determinant factor in encouraging the abolition of the ban on financial futures trading in Germany (Webber 1992: 170), but he leaves unclear the driving force behind the pressure to reform. This was arguably not simply the (correct perception) of the threat of foreign securities markets as lures for the expatriation of German finance capital; rather, the dynamic thrust came from the qualitative shift in the mode of capital accumulation, above all from the generation of vast liquid reserves within Germany's industrial and commercial corporations in the wake of the supply-side reforms of the 1980s and the associated growth in company profitability. The expectations of the supply-side policymakers were of a virtuous circle of high profits generating higher productive investments, higher growth and higher employment. The reality was quite different. The price of the supply-side revolution, which deliberately favoured capital, was the combined pressure on gross wages from mass unemployment and reduced union bargaining power, and on real net disposable income from the increased fiscal burden on wage incomes through income tax and indirect taxation (see above). This in turn reduced the relative strength of the domestic demand of private households. If domestic demand for a range of products stagnates – as it did in the 1980s – the pressure to increase the capacity to satisfy that demand, i.e., to invest in additional machinery to increase production, evaporates. The virtuous circle of supply-side economics is thus neutralised after the first stage, i.e., after the generation of additional profits. In the absence of investments to extend capacity, the options for the deployment of corporate reserves are limited.'Rationalisation' investments aimed at modernising production methods and increasing labour productivity were one common option, as were moves to extend market share through mergers and acquisitions (see below). However, increasingly financial investments, not just in equities but in new 'products' such as commodity and currency futures, attracted corporate reserves because during this period and beyond they promised considerably higher returns on capital than standard productive investments.

The accumulation of vast corporate reserves was the catalyst for the reform of Germany's securities markets and the evidence both of the failure of supply-sidism to reshape the country's productive trading economy and the rapid degenerative decline of German capitalism into the anarchy of 'casino capitalism' and monetary accumulation (Leaman 2001: 193).

Privatisation

As noted above, the scope for privatisation was by no means as great in Germany as in the other core economies of the EU. The country's political economy had never been subject to successful campaigns for nationalisation as a vehicle for the collectivisation and democratisation of economic assets. State ownership of particular utilities (water, transport, telecommunications) was determined by both scale economies and by the strategic desire to control natural monopolies; state ownership or part-ownership of other branches of the economy was strongly influenced by mercantilist principles of nurturing local, regional and national champions (e.g., Volkswagen, Lufthansa), promoting new enterprises through a specific holding company (VIAG) or protecting weakened branches of the economy (Salzgitter and Maxhütte steelworks and the coal pits of the Saarbergwerke) as a function of structural economic policies, be they industrial or regional in strategic terms.

In 1983 the capital value of federal holdings amounted to some 8.5 billion DM (Esser 1989: 64); the federal authorities had exclusive control of the federal railways (*Bundesbahn*) with around 350,000 employees and the telecommunications network of the Bundespost with about 550,000 employees as well as 74.3 per cent of Lufthansa. Esser cites comparative figures for state holdings in the 269 largest Western European companies, in which West Germany with just 3.9 per cent of German holdings contrasted with France (24.9 per cent), Britain (12.5 per cent), Italy (51.8 per cent) and Austria (82 per cent). However, these shares varied from one branch to another (Table 3.3).

Table 3.3 Federal Share of Industrial Assets in Selected Industries in per cent in 1983

Branch	Share	Branch	Share
Hard Coal	12.2	Lignite (brown coal)	5.4
Crude Steel	8.7	Rolled Steel	10.2
Aluminium	50.3	Petroleum	9.9
Electricity	28.9	Motor vehicles	36.3
Shipbuilding	14.1	Bottle Glass	21.3

Source: Esser 1989

Federal ownership of the loss-making steel mills of the Salzgitter works dates back to the 1930s; through the majority share of the federal holding companies *Vereinigte Industrieunternehmungen AG [VIAG]* and *Industrieverwaltungs-GmbH*, the state had significant interests in aluminium production, oil production, property and transport equipment. With its minority shares in the energy utility VEBA (43.8 per cent) and Volkswagen (20 per cent), the federal authorities had indirect influence on a considerable proportion of electricity production (28.9 per cent) and motor vehicles (36.3 per cent). The VEBA holding was reduced to 30 per cent in 1984, which fell in turn to 25.6 per cent after a rights issue, in which the federation, through VIAG, did not participate; the final holding was disposed of in 1987. Apart from the extensive local and regional ownership of banking assets – through the *Sparkassen* and *Landesbanken* – the federal authorities had significant strategic holdings in special purpose banks: the *Kreditanstalt für Wiederaufbau* (80 per cent federal holding; Länder: 20 per cent) was originally designed to co-finance postwar reconstruction. It now contributes to domestic economic development through housing loans, student loans, as well as loans and export credits to SMEs, and to developing and transition countries through funding for both state-sponsored and privately sponsored programmes. The banking assets of the *Kreditanstalt für Wiederaufbau* in 1982 totalled some 66 billion DM, but it has never been considered a legitimate subject for privatisation. The other two major federal holdings, however, in the *Deutsche Pfandbriefanstalt* (housing and local authority finance: 46.7 billion DM) and the *Deutsche Siedlungs- und Landeskreditbank* (agricultural finance: 27.7 billion DM) were, however, included in the draft list of privatisation candidates published by Finance Minister Stoltenberg in 1985.

The 1985 list of thirteen holdings set for privatisation included the major assets of VIAG, Volkswagen, Lufthansa, the *Deutsche Pfandbriefanstalt* and the *Deutsche Siedlungs- und Landeskreditbank*. In the course of the almost two-year consultation period, the plan to dispose of the 74.3 per cent stake in Lufthansa was dropped after particular pressure from the Bavarian government under Franz Josef Strauss. Strauss argued both in terms of

Table 3.4 Federal Privatisation Measures 1984–1989

Year	Company	Federal Holding		Size of holding sold		Remaining Share	
		DM mill	percent	DM mill	percent	DM mill	percent
1984	VEBA AG	737.1	43.8	232.0	13.8	505.1	30.0
1985	VEBA AG	Rights issue and workforce share issue. Federal stake drops to 25.5 percent					
1986	VIAG AG	507.1	87.4	232.0	40.0	2751	47.4
	Volkswagen AG	Federal share falls from 20.0 percent to 16 percent after rights issue					
	IVG AG	110.0	100	49.5	45.0	60.5	55.0
1987	VEBA AG	505.1	25.5	505.1	25.5	–	–
	Treuarbeit	9.3	45.0	3.0	14.5	6.3	30.5
1988	Volkswagen	240.0	16.0	240.0	16.0	–	–
	Deutsche Verkehrs-Kredit-Bank	75.0	100.0	18.7	24.9	56.3	75.1
	VIAG AG	348.0	60.0	348.0	60	–	–
	Schenker & Co GmbH	230.0	100.0	51.8	22.5	178.3	77.5
	Deutsche Lufthansa	Federal share falls from 65 percent to 51.6 percent as a result of a rights issue					
1989	Treuarbeit AG	6.3	30.5	1.0	5.0	5.3	29.5
	DSL-Bank	253.4	99.0	140.7	48.5	112.7	51.5
	Salzgitter AG	425.0	100.0	425.0	100.0	–	–

Source: Bundesfinanzministerium 1996

protecting a national airline from foreign takeover and in terms of the strategic importance of Lufthansa's fleet in times of conflict. Esser argues more plausibly that it was Bavarian mercantilist preferences which dominated the debate, most notably because Bavaria was the location for significant elements of Germany's aerospace industry which benefited significantly from state procurement contracts (Esser 1989: 69).

The first major wave of privatisations in West Germany in 1986–89 was thus less comprehensive than expected. The federal state's large holdings in VEBA, VIAG, Salzgitter and Volkswagen were entirely liquidated. Other holdings of smaller value – in Transport Bank, the IVG holding company, Treuarbeit, the Bundesbahn subsidiary Schenker and the DSL-Bank were reduced, but with sizeable minority holdings still in place. No significant regional or local enterprises were sold off in this period. Rather, the mindset of regional economics ministries remained dominated by strategic considerations of industrial policy. The retention of strategic holdings by the federal state also suggested a stronger element of industrial policy than was typical of neoliberal regimes like the British. Nevertheless, while one undeniable dimension of privatisation sales was the fiscal desire to increase revenue to offset tax concessions (Esser 1989: 68 etc.) the pattern of future, more radical privatisations had been set and the foundations for the disposal of both the state telephone network and of Lufthansa had been laid, firstly by the separation of the Bundespost into three discreet units, secondly by the decision not to participate in the Lufthansa rights issue, and thus to promote 'passive privatisation' (Esser 1989: 69).

One dimension of privatisation that needs to be mentioned in passing is the attempt by the federal government to popularise share ownership by limiting the allocation of all or some of the privatisation issues to members of a company workforce or to ordinary members of the public as part of a programme of 'wealth formation' (*Vermögensbildung*). So-called 'people's shares' (*Volksaktien*) had been issued in conjunction with the 1959 privatisation of Preussag and the part-privatisation of Volkswagen and VEBA in 1965, but in all three cases a large percentage of the issued shares were soon resold. Mimicking the policies of Margaret Thatcher's Britain, the Kohl government sought to revive the fortunes of 'popular capitalism' with the 1984 flotation of 4.6 million VEBA shares; however, only 1.5 per cent of the flotation (70,000 shares) was channelled through the revised *Vermögensbeteiligungsgesetz* (Esser 1989: 67). The aversion of German savers to the risks associated with the stock market disasters of the late 1920s and early 1930s was arguably reinforced by the sharp drop in equity values in October 1987, the year the final tranche of VEBA shares was sold and a year before the disposal of the Bund's share of Volkswagen. In contrast to Britain and the United States, the allure of the share-owning democracy continued to elude most ordinary Germans.

The picture that emerges from a brief survey of privatisation in the first part of the Kohl era is of a lack of urgency, certainly compared to the helter-skelter of state sales of the social housing stock and of the major gas, electricity and telecommunications utilities in the United Kingdom. Apart from the FDP, there were few strong political proponents of radical privatisation à la Thatcher. With the consistent trading success of Germany's productive economy (in contrast to the marked industrial decline of the UK), external surpluses generated increasing levels of gold and currency reserves, as well as a national currency which rapidly became the anchor of the EMS and against which most other EMS currencies were obliged to depreciate. In 1987, briefly but significantly, Germany overtook the United States as the strongest global exporter in absolute terms. Healthy corporate profitability also meant that there was not, as yet, strong pressure from the corporate sector for a sell-off of state assets as a new source for valorising capital. The corporate sector was also generally well served by Germany's financial institutions – as lenders and stakeholders – and, in any case, well provided with financial reserves. Finally, Germany's regional and local state authorities manifested a strong traditional profile as promoters and co-funders of enterprises in their territory, such that both local savers and business borrowers trusted and valued the *Sparkassen* and the bigger regional banks; the perceived problems of Germany's subnational authorities were not, in the main, associated with their transport and other services but with the growing burden of social welfare, as more and more unemployed fell outside the traditional system of the state social insurance system (Huster 1985: 199 etc).

Josef Esser has asserted convincingly that the 'key factors in the coalition (CDU/CSU/FDP) government's privatisation policy have sprung from a combination of symbolism ('we are privatisers too') and fiscal considerations' (Esser 1998: 120). After the upheavals of unification in 1989–90 and the acceleration of an increasingly unfettered global capitalism, there would be growing pressure to loosen the direct mercantilist bonds between state enterprises and the private economy, both from within Germany's beleaguered political economy and from key political developments within Europe, most notably the Single Market and EMU.

Conclusion

Supply-sidism in Germany – in the form of taxation reform, deregulation and privatisation – was credited by its proponents with the ability to reverse the mistakes of the 1970s (CDU 1984b: 9f). The neoliberal diagnosis of the 'wrong developments' made a fundamental link between the decline in investments, employment and growth and the rise in the state's share of national income and the extension of the state's regulatory activity. By marginalising the effects of two oil crises and the collapse of the trading and payments system underwritten by the dollar, the neoliberal diagnosis generated the crudest of syllogisms which concluded that the removal or loosening of state controls would restore a dynamism to investments, growth and employment, which had been repressed and frustrated by state interference. The primary catalyst of this process of restoration would be the facilitation of higher gross returns on capital – through reduced costs – and a lower tax-take on income from capital. The easing of cost and tax burdens on capital would allow the accumulation of corporate reserves which would then be deployed in a virtuous circle of reinvestment, production, wealth creation, job creation and growth at both micro and macro levels. 'Investing has to be made worthwhile again' (CDU 1984b: 12); 'The conditions for the formation of risk capital have to be improved' (CDU 1984a: 10). Higher profitability is the key, therefore, to removing the obstacles to the operation of the virtuous circle.

Table 3.5 Profit Ratio, Investment Ratio, Growth and Employment in selected European Countries 1980–1988

	Profit Ratio Change in percentage points	Growth of real GDP (annual ave)	Growth of Gross Investments (annual ave)	Investments Ratio 1980	Investments Ratio 1988	Investments Ratio (+/-)	1980–88Growth of employment (annual ave)
Belgium	+6.9	1.6	0.3	22.3	18.6	-3.7	-0.2
Denmark	+1.1	2.0	1.8	21.6	22.3	+0.7	0.8
Germany (W)	+5.0	1.8	0.6	23.9	20.9	-3.0	-0.1
France	+4.7	1.9	1.1	24.2	21.0	-3.2	-0.1
Ireland	+5.2	2.5	-2.6	32.0	18.4	-11.6	-1.4
Italy	+1.1	2.2	1.2	24.5	20.4	-4.1	0.7
Netherlands	+6.7	1.4	2.0	22.2	21.3	-0.9	0.0
Portugal	+4.3	2.2	2.0	27.7	22.7	-5.0	-0.9
Britain	+5.8	2.8	4.5	18.4	18.1	-0.3	0.1

Source: Eurostat National Accounts, Luxembourg 1991; own calculations; calculations on ECU basis

The 1980s were indeed years in which profitability improved not just in Germany, but in most other European economies, and the share of profit income (the profit ratio) in national income rose by an historically unprecedented amount (see Table 3.5, Column 2); Denmark and Italy, with a modest rise of just 1.1 percentage points, are the exceptions that prove the rule. While Table 3.5 does not allow particularly refined conclusions about the influence of macroeconomic determinants, what it does nevertheless demonstrate is that the *chain reaction promised by the neoliberal reformers did not occur*. The massive redistribution of national income in favour of businesses and the self-employed did not act as a catalyst for higher investment and higher growth. With the exception of Denmark, every one of the countries included in the Table 3.5 saw a decline in the investment ratio – the proportion of GDP reinvested in the economy – between 1980 and 1988. In Germany, despite a 5 percentage point rise in the profit ratio, there was a 3 percentage point fall in the investment ratio; in turn, there was no growth in employment, but rather an average annual decline of 0.1 per cent, according to Eurostat figures. If the table were to represent the test results of an engineering innovation – in this instance of the neoliberal turbocharger – there would be little hesitation in pronouncing the performance to have been dismally disappointing. However, as so frequently occurs within the inexact science of economics, the failure of the profit-fuelled turbocharger could be blamed on other factors, most notably the continuing and excessive burdens maintained on capital in the form of taxation, social levies and regulations. Not too much supply-sidism, but too little was the repeated syllogistic conclusion of the unrepentant market zealots.

The reasons for the failure of 1980s supply-sidism were, however, less to do with exogenous variables qua state, bureaucracy and trade unions, and much more to do with the monstrous illogicalities of the new market theology itself. The neoliberal model was, above all, based on the perception of the superiority of 'market forces' over political institutions in the allocation of all factors of production and service provision. The perception was flawed, as Keynesians, Marxists and even ordoliberals had recognised: 'the' market – any market – was potentially dysfunctional, both in terms of extreme fluctuations (cyclical weaknesses) and in terms of market dominance and the neutralisation of the very mechanisms of supply and demand that are supposed to provide balance in the dynamic process of growth. The reality which confronts the neoliberal faith in the efficiency and efficacy of the market is that 'the' market does not exist, neither as an historical constant which operates with the predictability of a machine or the tides or the seasons, nor as an identically ordered arrangement of forces at a particular point in time where the process and the outcome is roughly the same and where there is consequently little need for external, political interference. Local, regional, national, continental and global markets manifest colossal differences. Oligopolistic markets trading scarce or geographically limited commodities (diamonds, bauxite, tungsten) operate differently from oligopolistic markets characterised by overcapacity (motor vehicles, aircraft). Monopolised markets (crude oil, water) function quite differently from labour markets in areas of high unemployment. Monopsonies – firms like supermarkets controlling large proportions of market demand – enjoy better market conditions in relation to their suppliers than small customers of large suppliers. The list could be extended ad nauseam. In the context of this review of economic policy in Germany since the beginning of the 1980s it suffices to state that it was these many differences in the operational arrangements of different markets that prevented the expected revival of the virtuous circle of profits and productive investments. The circle was broken by the emergence and expansion of other, new and quite distinct markets which yielded high returns but which bypassed the old productive economy. The next chapter looks at some of the new markets developed by 'casino' capitalism, notably financial speculation and merger mania.

LIBERALISATION AND MONETARY ACCUMULATION

In the 1980s structural unemployment worsened markedly. Unemployment more than doubled between 1980 (889,000) and 1982 (1,833,000), the year of stagflationary recession, when GDP fell by –1.1 and inflation rose to 5.3 per cent. It continued to rise during the recovery, reaching a peak of 2,304,000 in 1985. While registered unemployment fell by almost 300,000 up until 1989 to 2,037,000, the pattern of incremental rises in the baseline of structural unemployment, begun in the 1970s, continued. The next recession in West Germany (1993) would begin with a far higher initial level than the 1981/82 crisis, notwithstanding the colossal challenge of Germany's unification crisis and the collapse of employment in the East. For the West, the era of 'jobless growth' had taken a firm hold. A simple comparison of the figures for job vacancies and total unemployment shows the ever widening disparity between the demand for work and the supply of jobs (Table 4.1).

This disparity can be explained in a variety of ways: (i) by reference to the 'prohibitive' cost of labour in Germany (the dominant view of German employers); (ii) by reference to the rationalisation of production, the replacement of living labour by machinery and the corresponding rise in productivity; the increasing 'capital intensity' of companies means that production (and production capacity) can rise while the payroll falls; (iii) by reference to the decline in the level of growth which, in combination with (ii), means that unemployment only begins to fall when rates of real growth exceed a certain level (current wisdom suggests levels of between 2 and 2.5 per cent); (iv) by reference to the failure to distribute the available labour time appropriately such that all who want to work can work (the dominant argument of trade unions and others).

These explanations are to a greater or lesser degree persuasive and valid. However, one key factor has to be added to any halfway adequate account

Table 4.1 Official Unemployment, Unregistered Reserve and Vacancies in West Germany 1980–1989

	Registered Unemployed	Official Rate of Unemployment*	Unregistered Reserve	Total Unemploy-ment	Vacancies
1980	889,000	3.8	622,000	1,511,000	308,000
1981	1,272,000	5.5	748,000	2,020,000	208,000
1982	1,833,000	7.5	950,000	2,783,000	105,000
1983	2,258,000	9.1	1,085,000	3,343,000	76,000
1984	2,266,000	9.1	1,207,000	3,473,000	88,000
1985	2,304,000	9.3	1,289,000	3,593,000	110,000
1986	2,228,000	9.0	1,350,000	3,578,000	154,000
1987	2,229,000	8.9	1,338,000	3,567,000	171,000
1988	2,242,000	8.7	1,372,000	3,614,000	189,000
1989	2,037,000	7.9	1,427,000	3,464,000	251,000

Source: Federal Institute of Labour. * Ratio of registered unemployed to total employed population

of German (and European) economic history in the last twenty-five years to explain the permanence of structural unemployment and the failure of supply-side remedies to restore the 'magic square' of stable growth, stable prices, stable employment and healthy external balances. That factor is the shift to a new form of capitalist accumulation that does not require the normal process of circulation in the production and distribution of commodities, in the provision of services to individuals, households and commercial enterprises and the employment of living labour. This new form of *monetary accumulation* operates alongside the traditional spheres of production/service provision; it feeds off the financial surpluses of these spheres but does not need the material foundations of social need and social consumption to achieve a return on the financial investment (see Altvater 1992: 143ff; Leaman 2001: 193–219). The autonomous sphere of monetary accumulation is characterised above all by the separation of financial investments from the process of producing and selling goods. One common illustration of this is the decoupling of international trade from the international flow of money. Up until the early 1970s, currency transactions – the international exchange and conversion of one currency to another – more or less matched the value of internationally traded goods and services; apart from the exchange controls managed by nation states to prevent the disruption of the supply of money within the domestic economy, trading enterprises operated in conjunction with financial institutions to do little more than ensure that supply contracts were fulfilled.

After the floating of exchange rates in 1971–72 and the gradual suspension of exchange controls, the unpredictability of currency movements produced both extensive forward trading of currencies and the development of an increasingly active currency futures market. While annual global trade grew from $1,005 billion in 1976 to $2,147 billion in 1986 (UNCTAD 2006), currency transactions multiplied to an estimated $188 billion daily by 1986 (Bank for International Settlements). Assuming that there are 250 working days in the year, the annual currency transactions would thus have been sufficient to finance global trade twenty-two times over. By 1995 the disparity between trade and currency flows had grown to 1:25. By 1998 the Federation of German Investment Banks (BVI) could state plainly in its Annual Report:

> Capital worldwide is on the search for the best returns. In particular international capital flows have become much more significant – on average 1,230 billion dollars a day circle the world. Only three percent of that serves the completion of trade in goods. The other 97 per cent are pure financial transfers, capital that above all is in search of short- and long-term investment opportunities. (BVI 1998: 41, cited in: Huffschmid 2002)

There was – and there still is – a commercial logic to forward trading in currencies, namely to create some kind of predictability in the conduct of the trade in goods and services, a predictability that was severely weakened by the end of Bretton Woods and damaged further by regular speculative attacks on individual currencies. However, as Huffschmid suggests:

> even if one considers that every exchange deal is often associated with several safeguard deals and secondly that a certain surplus supply is a requirement for the smooth functioning of currency markets – as a kind of liquidity reserve – there is a crass mismatch between the extent of currency trading and real trade in goods and services. Here too the motive of speculation is decisive.' (Huffschmid 2002: 43–4)

The shift to speculative currency dealing – with a tenfold increase in the daily volume of transactions between 1979 and 2001 (see Table 4.2) – has run parallel to the rapid expansion of traditional spheres of financial speculation, namely stock markets and commodity markets, and to the emergence of a wide variety of new financial 'products', including so-called 'derivatives' and 'option futures'.

Table 4.2 Global Currency Transactions 1979–2001 (Daily Turnover in US$ Billion)

1979	1989	1992	1995	1998	2001
120	590	820	1,190	1,490	1,210

Source: Bank for International Settlements

Stock markets that deal in the shares or equities of listed companies fulfil several roles, including the mobilisation of large volumes of finance from institutions and individuals as stakeholders through initial 'flotations' and additional 'rights issues', and secondly the trading of shares between individuals and institutions. Holders of shares derive potential benefits from the apportionment of profits through dividends and from the sale of holdings at a price higher than the initial purchase price. The speculative trade in equities played a significant role in the major stock exchanges of the world – New York, London, Paris, Tokyo, Hong Kong – in the postwar period, but the speed with which share holdings changed hands was relatively modest. Up until 1980, stocks were held for an average of at least ten years; the traded volume of shares worldwide in 1980 was just one-tenth of the market capitalisation of all listed shares (World Federation of Exchanges 1981). In Germany, with its unique system of banking, the universal banks dominated the business of share flotations, held large stakes in most major companies and acted as proxies for smaller investors at company AGMs. Share trading was conducted via several provincial stock exchanges that traded a modest number of shares in a comparatively small number of public limited companies elegible for listing. The structure of share ownership in West Germany showed a significant reduction even in the proportion of shares in private hands in the years before the *Wende*. It fell from 27 per cent in 1960 to just 19 per cent in 1980 and 16 per cent in 1982, while enterprises (nonbanks) increased their portfolio holdings to 40 per cent of all German stock, nonresidents to 21 per cent and financial institutions (banks and insurance companies) to 15 per cent. (Moran 1989: 115) Even by 1987, West German stock exchanges listed only 673 out of more than 2000 registered public limited companies (PLCs), compared to the United Kingdom with 2,685 listed companies and the United States with 1,575.

Over the last two-and-a-half decades, global equity markets have been transformed, taking Germany's stock exchanges with them. Above all, their function has altered from one which predominantly mobilises capital through initial and supplementary flotations of shares to one which trades equities more intensively, for increasingly speculative purposes and with much shorter time horizons (Figure 4.1).

While global merchandise trade grew five-fold from $2 trillion in 1980 to $10.4 trillion in 2005, the value of global trade in equities increased nineteen-fold in just ten years between 1980 and 1990 from $300 billion to $5.9 trillion and a further nine-fold from 1990 to 2000 to $56.2 trillion. After the slump in share prices and in share trading in 2001–2002, the trade volume recovered to reach $51 trillion in 2005. In 1980, equity trade was equivalent to one-tenth of the share value of all listed companies in the world. This meant that equities were held for an average of ten years before being sold on. By 1990 the timespan of shareholdings had dropped to just

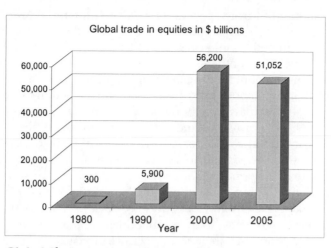

Figure 4.1 Global Share Transactions 1980–2005
Source: World Federation of Exchanges, *Annual Reports*

nineteen months and by 2000 to little more than six months (Huffschmid 2002: 40). The primary function of equities as sources of regular income in the form of dividends over extended periods of 'tenure' had given way to the trade function of a rapid capital gain derived from speculative short-term holdings. In Germany, while major shareholders like universal banks and insurance companies continue to maintain long-term holdings in most German blue-chip companies, the rate of turnover in German and foreign stock on Germany's stock markets has grown significantly, such that the *Deutsche Börse* (figures for 2005) now processes some 87 million share transactions annually with a total value of $1.9 trillion, a third of the London Stock Exchange (LSE), not much less than the pan-European Euronext group ($2.9 trillion), but certainly a long way from Germany's 'pygmy' status in the 1980s (Moran 1989: 112). Huffschmid notes that the Frankfurt stock exchange now has a higher rate of turnover – each share changes hands on average 1.4 times a year – than the LSE (1.7).

The trade in so-called 'derivatives' only began to have an impact on the German economy after 1990 and the establishment of the *Deutsche Terminbörse* in 1990, and will be dealt with in later chapters. Derivatives are nevertheless symptomatic of the marked shift towards financial investments that started in the 1980s, notably in London, and which represented a further incremental step away from real accumulation to trading with essentially fictitious values.

Collectively, the new financial markets have developed into a formidable sector of the global economy, which derives its added value not from the satisfaction of the fundamental need of economic agents (households, enterprises, public authorities) to consume products and services generated by human labour but from speculative bets on immaterial processes. This truly extraordinary sphere of autonomous accumulation was, at an early stage, rightly dubbed 'casino capitalism' by Susan Strange (1986), Elmar Altvater (1992: 157) and others.

How does one account for the emergence of this extraordinary and highly controversial phenomenon? Davidson asserts correctly that for mainstream economists, 'all speculative activities in efficient markets are stabilizing' (Davidson 1999: 92), providing real benefits in contrast to the real costs of government interference. The shift away from the fixed exchange rate regime of Bretton Woods is thus seen as a rational choice of the more efficient mode of economic management: 'the' market. In stark contrast, Keynesians, like Tobin, Eichengreen and Wyplosz (1995), socialist economists like Huffschmid (2002) and eco-socialists like Altvater (1992) strongly assert that the new international financial markets are potentially highly destructive and that their emergence has more to do with crises in the global political economy than with rational reform. Both Altvater and Huffschmid identify not simply a fundamental crisis of the global trading and payments system in the early 1970s, reinforced by the first oil crisis of 1973–75, but above all a crisis of capitalist accumulation. The postwar boom, which brought both high returns on capital and significant welfare gains for the mass of the population in the developed countries of the North, began to wane in the United States in the 1960s and in Europe and the rest of the OECD in the 1970s. Initially high profits and strong growth had allowed significant increases in real wages and, with labour shortages, an increase in the share of wages and salaries in national income; this in turn had generated strong consumer demand and increased economic capacity to satisfy that demand both directly through consumer goods production and indirectly through the production of investment goods. As global growth rates weakened, the pressure on profits increased – the rate of profit fell – and the virtuous symmetry of strong domestic demand and strong external demand began to break down. Above all, the incentive to extend capacity was reduced by lower marginal returns on investments and by the cost and productivity advantages of rationalisation investments, which allow reductions in labour force; capacity utilisation in Germany had fallen from a peak of 92 in 1970 to 86 in 1972, i.e., even before the oil crisis when it fell even further to 83 (1974) and 76 (1975) (Leaman 1988: 206).

The pressure on national economies had also increased by the growing disparities between countries with trade surpluses, like Japan and Germany, and those with trade deficits, like the United States and, after the temporary respite of North Sea oil, the United Kingdom. This in turn put greater pressure on the external value of national currencies, on domestic inflation – through the import price effects of re- or devaluations – and on the internal factors affecting the competitiveness of domestically produced goods and services. The oil crises certainly reinforced these structural problems and accelerated the structural crisis of accumulation, but they also underscored retrospectively the enormous advantages that developed economies had derived from the exploitation of cheap oil from less developed regions of the world. The oil crises also made it extremely difficult to manage the structural crisis of accumulation by means of restoring the symmetry of domestic and external demand, i.e., allowing real wages to increase to sustain high levels of consumer spending; the increased cost of imported energy made it more urgent to increase the volume of exports to restore external balances, which in turn demanded increased cost and quality competitiveness on the part of national domestic producers. At the microlevel, at the level of the company, reducing wage costs – above all unit wage costs – was a rational strategy, even if at the macrolevel of the national economy the relative reduction in wages as a proportion of national income would reduce the contribution of household demand to overall growth. Despite this macroeconomic cost, Helmut Kohl's neoliberal *Wende* was driven in large measure by the conviction that Germany could export its way out of stagnation by improving the supply-side conditions of German businesses.

The connection between the neoliberal export-led growth strategy and the dramatic expansion of national and global financial markets is to be found, firstly, in the alteration of the balance of demand factors driving the engine of German economic growth. Table 4.3 shows private consumption rising to over 56 per cent of GDP in the early 1980s but falling to below 1970 levels in 1990, to just 53.6 per cent. State consumption peaks in 1980 at the height of the social–liberal coalition but falls gradually to 18.3 per cent in 1990, still 2.6 percentage points above 1970 levels but reflecting above all the difference between the full employment years of 1970–73 and the persistent structural unemployment of the 1980s and beyond (see Table 4.1). Gross investments, together with increases in company inventories, fell from 27.6 per cent of GDP in 1970 to 23.5 per cent in 1980 and to 19.5 per cent in 1985, recovering to 21.8 per cent in the economic boom year of 1990. Between 1980 and 1990 therefore, the ratio of domestic demand to GDP declined from 100.3 to 93.6; the key difference was made by the increase in the ratio of exports to GDP to 36 per cent in 1990 and the rise in net exports (exports minus imports) from -0.3 to 6.4 per cent of GDP in the same period, which was significantly higher than in the first three decades of postwar growth (Glastetter et al. 1983: 482). West Germany in the 1980s became much more dependent on exports for the utilisation of domestic capacity and the maintenance of domestic employment, but also in terms of its contribution to growth. It was both a mark of the prodigious commercial success of Germany's major trading corporations but, as Abelshauser has pointed out, the 'chronic trade surplus' involved the 'transfer of real goods to foreign countries, leaving the Federal Republic with mere claims and currency reserves that could not be deployed productively' (Abelshauser

1983: 162). The shift in the balance of demand away from private consumption and investments to exports was above all supported by the supply-side reforms of the 1980s (see Chapter Three) which increased the fiscal burden on mass incomes and relieved business incomes, and in consequence produced a key precondition for the accumulation, in the 1980s and beyond, of very high corporate financial reserves.

Table 4.3 Balance of Demand Factors in West Germany 1970–1990

Demand Factors as Proportion of GDP in %	1970	1980	1985	1990
Private Consumption	54.6	56.2	56.5	53.6
State Consumption	15.7	20.1	19.8	18.3
Gross Investments	25.5	22.7	19.6	21.0
Inventories	2.1	1.2	-0.1	0.8
Exports	22.6	29.1	35.2	36.0
Imports	20.5	29.4	31.1	29.6
Net Exports	2.1	-0.3	4.2	6.4

Source: Bundesbank, Monthly Reports (various)

As Table 4.4 shows in 1970, German enterprises had a comfortable cushion of financial assets, equivalent to two-thirds of their tangible assets, sufficient to finance substantial programmes of investment in new plants and machinery. By 1980 this had risen to three-quarters, and by 1990 reached virtual parity with fixed assets. In the manufacturing sector, significantly, the rise was even more marked, such that by 1995 financial assets were over a fifth higher than fixed assets; in motor manufacturing the ratio stood at 1.57 in 1995, in the electrotechnical sector at 1.76 and in the chemical sector the sum of bank deposits, government stock, industrial bonds, currencies and other securities was double the value of the fixed assets of a highly capital-intensive industrial sector. This shift in the balance of asset ratios had, among other things, strong relevance for the conduct of monetary policy (see below). In this context, it is sufficient to underline the correlation between a higher profit ratio, a lower investment ratio and a higher ratio of financial assets to real assets in the core sectors of Germany's highly successful trading economy. The anecdotal quips about Daimler-Benz and Siemens being banks with industrial subsidiaries were not far wide of the mark. They and other big corporations were increasingly sitting on huge financial reserves which could be and were deployed, both to fund a wave of mergers and acquisitions, and to play the high-yielding financial markets.

There were two further significant sources of large accumulations of liquid reserves in the economies of the North: firstly, OPEC countries predominantly used the banking and finance system of OECD countries to recycle their so-called petro-dollars; these amounted to some $450 billion between 1974 and 1981 alone. Secondly, after the second oil crisis and the

Table 4.4 Asset Ratios in Selected Branches of the German Economy 1970–1997 (Ratio of Financial to Fixed Assets)

	1970	1980	1985	1990	1995	1997
All Enterprises	0.66	0.75	0.84	0.99	1.03	1.11
Manufacturing (All)	0.64	0.77	0.96	1.01	1.22	
Chemicals	0.76	0.87	1.21	1.41	2.0	
Engineering	0.87	0.93	1.07	0.95	1.12	
Motor Vehicles	0.47	0.85	1.04	1.02	1.57	
Electro-technical	0.95	1.30	1.59	1.53	1.76	
Retailing	0.42	0.41	0.41	0.46	0.54	

Source: Bundesbank 'Ertragslage und Finanzierungsverhältnisse westdeutscher Unternehmer' (Article series in Monthly Report, annually October/ November)

rise in real interest rates in the early 1980s, the increasing debt burden of developing countries produced a reversal of the capital flows; whereas between the mid-1950s and 1980 'the annual flow of funds into the Third World had averaged about $40 billion …(a)fter 1982 the flow of funds *out of* the Third World averaged about $35 billion a year, amounting to nearly 10 per cent of the value of the Third World's total exports' (Barratt Brown 1993: 43). Again, these funds were processed through the banking system of developed countries.

Together, the corporate reserves of First World enterprises, the petro-dollars of the Organization of Petroleum Exporting Countries (OPEC) and the debt-servicing transfers from poorer developing countries provided the financial systems of the OECD with the seed corn for the extraordinary expansion of financial speculation witnessed since the 1980s. An important stimulus to the feverish carousel of financial speculation was the demand for money from debtors, most notably national states in both the developed and the less developed world. As Figure 4.2 clearly shows, government balances in Germany were comfortably in surplus between 1950 and 1964; the drift into recession in 1966–67 was accompanied by modest state deficits, followed by a recovery of surplus to 1973, after which the state borrowing requirement remains steadfastly high; the brief and extraordinary annual budget surplus in 1989 stands out as the exception that proves the rule. In the second half of the 1970s the German state was obliged to borrow an average of DM 40 billion a year to cover its additional expenditure. Germany's borrowing requirement as a percentage of nominal GDP between 1973 and 1982 was some 2.64 per cent, roughly the same as the average for the whole of the OECD countries (2.6 per cent). The financial markets of the developed countries in the 1970s were well enough stocked both to fulfil the requirements of European and other developed states and to provide developing countries with credit, both to

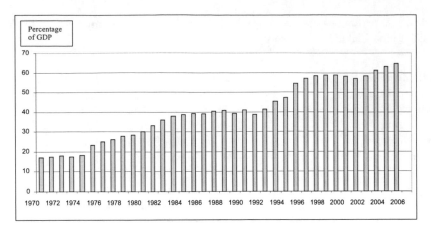

Figure 4.2 State Debt Ratio in Germany 1970–2005
Source: Statistisches Bundesamt, Lange Reihen

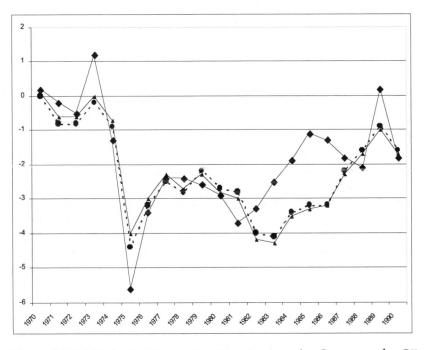

Figure 4.3 Public Sector Borrowing Requirement for Germany, the G7
and the OECD 1970–1990
Source: OECD *Economic Outlook* Nrs 47 and 51

import expensive oil and to finance ambitious development programmes. The level of liquidity in financial markets was so high that, even with strong price inflation, real interest rates (market interest rates adjusted for inflation) remained seductively low for borrowers.

The relatively comfortable position of debtors changed rapidly in the wake, firstly, of the second wave of oil price rises in 1979, secondly, as a result of the massive programme of rearmament initiated by the Reagan administration, which took office in 1980, and, thirdly, as a result of the severe application of monetarism by the major banks of Europe (Bundesbank) and the United States (Federal Reserve) involving a long and intense programme of high central bank rates for refinancing debt.

The richer states of the North were able in the 1980s to reduce budget deficits through austerity measures, as a result of the decline in the price of crude oil and through rises in the relative value of European manufactured goods compared to imported basic materials ('rising terms of trade'). The poorer developing states, however, became trapped in a cycle of increasingly bad debt, where old outstanding debts were rescheduled using new, short-term loans with very high and variable real rates of interest and against the background of falling commodity prices as they attempted to pay for debt through cash-cropping and increased production for an increasingly saturated market. 'For some of the Third World countries the flow of debt payments took as much as 50 per cent of the earnings from their annual exports. Out of the $1,200 billion which the Third World owed in 1990, only $400 billion constituted the original borrowing. The rest consisted of accrued interest and capital liabilities' (Barratt Brown 1993: 43). The trebling of developing countries' debt burden indicates not simply the catastrophic results of the grim decade of excessively high real interest rates but, in this context, the extent to which financial markets in the North were provided with increased liquidity derived from the rape of natural resources and the exploitation of poorer sections of global society. The debt crisis involved, above all, the stalling or abandonment of development programmes in less developed countries, initiated in the 1970s and now rendered unviable by the charges levied by banks and other financial institutions in the North. The redistribution of income and wealth within the developed economies at the expense of poorer sections of society was thus matched by the redistribution of global wealth at the expense of the developing world and for the benefit of creditor banks and enterprises in the developed world. Moreover, the impoverishment of large sections of the population in the developing world produced analogous effects on global demand, as neoliberal redistribution measures were having in the national economies of the North. Households and businesses in the South were relatively less able to buy the North's manufactured consumer goods and the investment goods that were vital for the modernisation of their economies. This rendered the strategy of export-led growth pursued by most OECD countries less promising and the logic of supply-sidism even less plausible. There was no point in extending the production capacities of Northern goods manufacturers if the disposable income of poorer countries was curtailed. The profits accrued by exporting companies whose costs had been reduced by domestic policy measures (see Chapter Three) and by rising terms of trade were thus channelled into the new and increasingly frenetic financial markets.

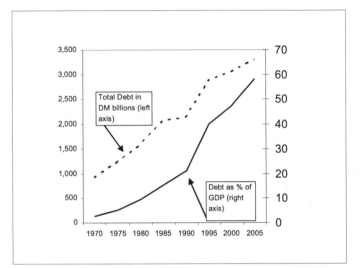

Figure 4.4 State Debt in Germany in DM Billions and as a Percentage of GDP 1970–2005
Source: Bundesbank Monthly Reports (various)

The Policy Context of Monetary Accumulation: the Hegemony of the Bundesbank

While Germany's elected federal government was promoting neoliberalism by jettisoning many of the instruments of macroeconomic control through privatisation, regulatory reform, tax relief on capital and budgetary austerity, the other major institution of the German state was consolidating both its domestic influence and its influence over other European states: namely, the Bundesbank. With this extended power, Germany's central bank was more decisively promoting both neoliberal supply-sidism and the revolution of speculative monetary accumulation. As noted previously, the Bundesbank enjoyed the considerable advantage of not being answerable to any superior authority. Its statutory independence did not simply render it safe from the political influence of electorally answerable governments, but implicitly demanded a publicly articulated resistance to and self-demarcation from external influences. The floating of exchange rates in 1973 thrust the Bundesbank into the forefront of German and European macroeconomic policy. In the context of stagflation, the Bundesbank was not troubled by the dilemma confronting most other OECD states with dependent central banks – of whether to prioritise the fight against inflation or against unemployment – because its statutory duty was to ensure the stability of the DM (§3 Bundesbank Law); this duty was even more unequivocal than that of the US Federal Reserve Board which, while free to pursue an autonomous monetary policy, was (and is) obliged to consider the effects of monetary policy on the overall health of the macroeconomy. The Bundesbank's power to focus on counterinflation and monetary stability was enhanced by the transition to flexible exchange rates; the constitutional monopoly of the federal government in questions of the external value of the currency was effectively suspended by the end of Bretton Woods; the external value of the DM was henceforth determined primarily by the strength of the country's trading economy and its external balances but secondarily by the policy decisions of the Bundesbank relating to interest rates and to interventions in the currency markets.

'From the beginning of the 1980s the German Bundesbank had become the factual centre of German economic policy' (Huffschmid 2002: 154). The weakening of German democracy that necessarily accompanies the roll-back of the (elected) state and its ceding of control to the market mechanisms, notably those of international financial markets, corresponded to the strengthening of the democratically untouchable institution of the independent central bank. The reputation of the Bundesbank was at its most illustrious in the 1980s, as it reaped the laurels of Germany's relative success in combating stagflation; the fact that this success was predominantly the result of the supreme international competitiveness of Germany's industrial corporations did not prevent observers from committing the crude syllogism which rendered the Bundesbank the primary architect of German success and consequently recommended the model of central bank autonomy as the cure-all for economic ills. The Bundesbank myth (Leaman 2001) was deeply rooted in a German social culture which had been traumatised by two hyperinflations (1921–23 and 1945–48) and a history of the political abuse of the bank of issue. The acceptance of the autonomy first of the Bank deutscher Länder and, after 1957, of the Bundesbank, however, was promoted on the back of a lie: that it was the democratic institutions of the Weimar Republic that had ruined the Reichsmark and that therefore monetary policy had to be rendered inaccessible to the potential abuse of postwar democratic forces. In fact, the hyperinflation of 1922–23 was presided over by an autonomous Reichsbank, made independent in May 1922 at the insistence of the French and the British, and the 1945–48 currency chaos was the result of the Nazis' flagrant deployment of the printing presses to feed the machine of war, leaving a massive overhang of liquidity in a situation of extreme scarcity.

The myth of the unimpeachable guardian of the German's badge of pride, the DM, was nevertheless a potent one, as numerous opinion polls attested. It was stylised sycophantically into a latter-day order of noble and selfless servants of the nation who did 'the right thing' by Germany. Balkhausen, in his hagiography of the Bundesbank (1992), quotes a long passage from Wilhelm Röpke, one of the pioneers of ordoliberalism, which had in turn been used by Hans Tietmeyer, Bundesbank president from 1993 to 1999, and reflects the perception – and implicitly the self-perception – of social elites:

> It is of decisive importance – and this is increasingly a generally held conviction – that there is in society a group of leaders, however small, that sets the tone and feels a responsibility in the name of the whole of society for the inviolable norms and values of society and which lives up to this responsibility in the strictest fashion. What we need at any time and what we need all the more urgently today, when so much is crumbling and tottering, is a genuine *nobilitas naturalis* with its authority comfortably acknowledged by the people of their own free will; an elite which derives its aristocratic title only from the most supreme achievements and from an unsurpassable moral example and which is cloaked in the natural dignity of such a life ... To belong to this stratum of moral notables has to become the highest and most desirable goal, against which all life's other triumphs pale into insignificance. (Röpke 1966: 192)

The Bundesbank's approval rating was above all reinforced by the apparent failure of elected politicians (German or otherwise) to maintain economic prosperity and full employment, and by the new experience of price inflation in the 1970s and early 1980s; the preparedness to tolerate strong doses of deflationary monetarism was correspondingly high (Huffschmid 2002: 140). The level of resistance to the new 'extremist religion' of 'central bankism' (Luttwak 1997: 226) was minimal and dangerously so. The Bundesbank and its American counterpart, the Federal Reserve Board, were arguably coresponsible for the political chaos of global economic governance in the 1980s and beyond and reinforced the shift towards monetary accumulation. The primary charge that can be laid against these two independent institutions – and the other central banks in their thrall – is that they prioritised the fight against inflation at the expense of other economic policy goals. Luttwak sees a, 'simple explanation for the rise of central bankism', which is institutional: 'while the value of money is protected with fierce determination by the central bankers, industry and labour have no such exalted defenders' (Luttwak 1997: 225). Huffschmid takes the argument further by asserting persuasively that the new monetarism was not simply indifferent to the effects of counterinflationary policies on employment, but rather saw unemployment as a necessary instrument in the pursuit of low inflation, as exemplified by the popularisation of the notion of NAIRU (the non-accelerating inflation rate of unemployment) (Huffschmid 2002: 141). The Bundesbank did not need to espouse the NAIRU hypothesis, asserting instead its statutory duty of ensuring currency stability and referring in orthodox fashion to the linkage with the money stock and the need, in times of high demand for liquidity, to reduce that demand through raising the cost of credit. Accordingly, it pursued a rigorous credit squeeze between 1979 and 1983 in an attempt to counter the renewed threat of (imported) inflation.

The Bundesbank's problem did not simply involve the weakness of monetarist theory, but above all the changed national and global context of economic policymaking in the late twentieth century. The abandonment of exchange controls within the OECD between 1974 and 1994 (Germany got rid of its remaining controls by 1981) exposed the increasing divergence in economic performance between economies, manifested both in the external balances and in the exchange rates of their currencies. As Figure 4.5 indicates, the current account balances of OECD countries were relatively stable up until the early 1970s. The divergence between the chronic deficit of countries like the United States and chronic surplus countries like Germany then become apparent in the 1980s. The asymmetry in the external balances of individual countries has a direct effect on the external value of

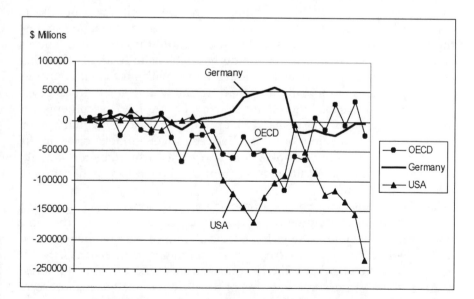

Figure 4.5 Current Balances, OECD, Germany, USA 1963–1998 in $ Millions

the national currency; deficits inclining currencies to devalue, surpluses producing the pressure to revalue. Devaluation brings both advantages for exporters in reducing the relative price of exported goods, but also obvious disadvantages in the form of high cost imports. Within a system of managed exchange rates like that of Bretton Woods, current account problems could be resolved with relative ease. With the advent of flexible exchange rates and free capital movements, however, these problems are less easily managed. The speculative flows of vagabond capital increase the urgency for deficit countries to secure capital inflows to offset the current account deficit. The primary vehicle for attracting such inflows is the level of interest offered by bank and other securities in the deficit country, which are strongly influenced by central bank discount rates.

As Table 4.5 demonstrates, the need to attract capital inflows is reflected in the differences between the central bank discount rates of individual countries, where the disparities are also amplified over time. In 1970, all the countries in the sample had positive current account balances and central bank discount rates, mostly in the narrow band of 5.5 to 7.5 per cent; Portugal was the exception with 3.5 per cent, but this clearly correlates with the healthiest external position. In 1982, after a decade of floating exchange rates, stagflation and major changes in the trading positions of individual countries, the disparities in monetary conditions were dramatically altered. Portugal, with a colossal current account deficit of 11.8 per cent of GDP (and inflation of 20 per cent) had a discount rate of 19 per cent. The two countries with the lowest discount rates (Germany and Japan) had positive external balances. The United Kingdom, while North Sea oil ensured temporary external surpluses, had higher inflation (8.7 per cent) than the OECD average (7.3 per cent) and a currency that was slowly depreciating against the DM; the only way to ensure sufficient capital inflows to London's securities markets was to provide high real returns to holders of sterling bonds. Similar disparities are evident in 1990 with all deficit countries showing higher central bank rates than Germany and Japan. In all cases, however, central bank interest rates had become key instruments for influencing not simply the demand for and supply of money within a given territory, but also the flow of capital between sovereign territories. In the case of Europe, the Bundesbank's dominance was ensured by the strength of Germany's external position, its currency and the policy architecture of the EMS (see below).

The key points in the context of the analysis of monetary accumulation are that the extreme asymmetries of the global economy created a dynamic which raised real interest rates to historically unprecedented heights, and that the political process was driven by two dominant central banks, the US Federal Reserve Board and the German Bundesbank. While real interest rates – generally measured in terms of the difference between short-term yields on government stock and the rate of consumer price inflation – were

Table 4.5 The Asymmetry of International Interest Rates: Current Account Balances and Central Bank Discount Rates in Selected Countries 1970–1990

Category / Country	US	J	G	F	It	UK	P	Sp
Current Account Balance as % of GDP 1970	0.2	1.0	0.6	0.1	1.2	1.3	1.9	0.2
Discount Rates 12/70 %	5½	6	6	7	5½	7	3½	6½
Current Account Balances as % of GDP 1982	-0.4	0.6	0.8	-2.2	-1.8	1.7	-11.8	-2.5
Discount Rates 12/82 %	9	5½	5	9½	18	12[a]	19	8
Current Account Balances as % of GDP 1990	-1.6	1.5	3.3	-0.8	-1.6	-3.5	-0.3	-3.7
Discount Rates 12/90 %	7	6	6	9¼	12½	13¾	14½	8

Source: OECD Economic Observer (various), Bundesbank Monthly Report (various)
[a] Publication of Minimum Lending Rate suspended by Bank of England in August 1991; figure in column relates to MLR of March to August 1991

Table 4.6 Real Interest Rates in G7 Economies 1990

	Market Interest Rates on short-term (3-month) securities	Rate of Inflation	Real Interest Rate (Column A – Column B)
United States	7.5	5.1	2.4
Japan	7.7	2.6	5.1
Germany	8.5	2.6	5.9
France	10.3	3.0	7.3
Italy	12.1	6.3	5.8
United Kingdom	14.8	5.6	9.2
Canada	13.0	4.2	8.8

Source: OECD *Economic Outlook 51* June 1992

minimal in the 1970s (they averaged –0.27 in the United States; see Leaman 2001: 209), they rose sharply in the early 1980s. As Table 4.6 shows, the real yields (Column C) on three-month government securities in 1990 were very high by historical comparison; a relatively comfortable rentier return would be 2.5 per cent (Brittan 2005). With the temporary exception of the United States, all other G7 countries were offering stunningly attractive resting places for capital.

The emergence of high real interest rates coincided with significant shifts in the deployment of national economic resources in Germany and other European countries:

- Net household saving as a proportion of disposable household income rose from an already high level of 12.2 per cent in 1980 to 13.9 per cent in 1990 (OECD figures).
- The reliance of German enterprises on external financing fell significantly in the 1980s. After the relatively high 'gearing' in the period 1950 to 1975, when the ratio of external finances to total company funds averaged over 29 per cent, the slight fall in the 1975–82 cycle to an average of 24 per cent was followed by a dramatic decline between 1983 and 1989 to just 10.6 per cent (Glastetter et al. 1991: 128). This was despite the fact that German enterprises increased the proportion of distributed net profits from two thirds of total net profits to some 97 per cent in the period 1983–89 (ibid. 131, fn.49). At the same time the contribution of depreciation – the declared loss of value of existing plant and equipment set against tax liabilities – to company finances continued to rise to almost two thirds (65.8 per cent) between 1983 and 1989; this reflected both the real process of technological modernisation in the manufacturing and the service sectors and the supply-side stimuli of the Kohl government in the form of special depreciation arrangements in its tax reforms. The low average ratio of external financing of 10.6 per cent for the first period of the Kohl era actually conceals a truly dramatic decline from 32 per cent in 1980 to just 4 per cent in 1988.
- Public sector finances, despite economic growth and expenditure cutbacks, were in deficit for every financial year except for 1989 as a result of persistently high unemployment and generous tax relief measures. The proportion of public expenditure devoted to investments fell from 12.2 per cent in 1980 to 8.8 per cent in 1990, while interest payments on government debt rose from 5.8 per cent to total expenditure to 8.6 per cent in the same period.

A number of authors draw a direct causal link between the latter developments and the 'regime-change' to monetarism. Stephan Schulmeister describes the shift in terms of 'primary economic balances':

> The transition – caused essentially by central banks – to a system in which the rate of interest remains permanently above the rate of growth, generated the following 'systemic' problem: since the sum of all primary balances (of income and expenditure) is equal to zero, the state was quite unable to achieve primary surpluses, given the constant primary surpluses of the enterprise and household sectors. It therefore 'suffered' virtually permanent primary deficits: the investment weakness of enterprises depressed tax revenues and led to increases in payments to the unemployed and other social transfers. (Schulmeister 1997: 303)

The breakdown of the classical accumulation system driven by private credit from private savings for private real investments left the state to maintain an increasing proportion of both social consumption and social investment. Additionally, the competition between states (both developed and developing) for credit from private capital markets, in particular for capital imports to offset current account deficits, put upward pressure on market interest rates. The rise in the public sector share of global debt had nothing to do with any 'crowding out' of private enterprises from capital markets; the decline in the gearing ratios of enterprises was not caused by a decline in investments, 'but above all by an enormous increase in the financial assets (*Eigenmittel*)' of private companies (Glastetter et al. 1991: 130). There was no need for real investments to be stymied by any lack of capital, since, 'measured by the available financial means, a far higher volume of investments would have been possible – given different financial behaviour' (ibid. 130).

The financial 'behaviour' of German and other enterprises was determined in large measure by the new framework, established by the major central banks of the world, which used high (real) interest rates *over extended periods of time* to combat inflation. A crucial difference between the 1970s and the 1980s is that real interest rates remained permanently above the rate of real GDP growth. In such a position debtors *in toto* have to prevent overall expenditure growing faster than turnover/GDP, in other words compensating for the increased cost of interest by reducing other expenditures. Companies in the 1980s – particularly larger corporations with high levels of financial assets – were far less exposed to this pressure than states, indeed *they were increasingly able not just to avoid debt burdens but to become net creditors* by the fact that they, 'turned their primary balance into a permanent surplus' (Schulmeister 1997: 303). States became the predominant debtors to financial institutions and industrial corporations, as the latter bought increasingly large portfolios of high-yielding financial assets offered by governments.

The duration of monetary deflation is as important as the intensity of monetary squeezes. The longer the squeeze is maintained, the greater is the tendency for the formation of real capital to be depressed (ibid: 302) and with it the future growth in the production of goods and supply of services. This is clearly evident in the case of West Germany. If one takes periods in which the Bundesbank's discount rate was 4.5 per cent or higher as a benchmark for a phase of restrictive monetary policy, the 1972–75 squeeze was accompanied by reductions in commercial fixed investments in every year averaging -4.1 per cent; residential investments fell markedly in 1974 (–14.8 per cent) and 1975 (-10.5 per cent). In the next big squeeze (1979–83) nonresidential fixed investments declined by -3.7 per cent in 1981 and -4.5 per cent in 1982 (residential: -5 per cent and -4.9 per cent respectively). Both periods included recessions: 1975 when GDP growth was -1.3 per cent and 1982 when it fell by -1.1 per cent. Notwithstanding the hitherto unknown phenomenon of stagflation, several authors see strong evidence for the Bundesbank having at least reinforced recessionary tendencies by maintaining a squeeze too long, i.e., pro-cyclically, exacerbating the downturn (Schulmeister 1997: 302; Leaman 2001: 182ff).

A restrictive monetary policy is thus seen to be dysfunctional when, by maintaining high real interest rates over time, it makes life more difficult for the state as a whole, which is obliged to provide welfare support for the unemployed and their dependents while revenues are limited by low or negative growth and borrowing is more expensive. The counter-productiveness of monetary policy is compounded by its undiscriminating quality. Increasing the cost to banks of refinancing credit through higher central bank rates is supposed to reduce the demand for credit from private enterprises and households. However, if the large corporations, through the accumulation of large financial reserves, become net creditors, they are not simply immune to the restrictive force of higher discount rates but rather benefit from higher rates through higher bond and other market yields. It is predominantly the small and medium-sized enterprises that are affected by higher short-term interest rates as they are historically more heavily dependent on external financing (Roedl 2003: 12). (This is quite separate from the fact that larger companies have bigger time horizons where strategic investment and financing decisions are made on the basis of expected returns over many years, making short-term rate fluctuations far less relevant.) Higher real interest rates thus have a discriminatory effect on smaller enterprises with higher gearing and a higher dependency on short-term loans. The danger of insolvency – when banks foreclose on loans, for example – is thus much greater for SMEs, as is the danger of takeover by a larger competitor when SMEs are weakened by debt or other cost burdens. There are a small number of examples of failure and bankruptcy among larger corporations, but these are the exceptions that prove the rule. The acceleration of merger and acquisition activity in the 1980s (See Figure 4.7) is evidence both of the vulnerability of weaker, smaller companies and the financial power of the asset-rich larger companies. Strictly speaking, the acronym should be reversed to A&M, given that most of the mergers involve takeovers of the equity of one company by the major shareholders of another; there are very few examples of genuine mergers where shareholders of two companies agree to acquire reciprocal holdings in each other. An examination of the biannual reports of the Berlin Cartel Office shows a consistent pattern of big fish (with turnovers in excess of €1 billion) swallowing small fish (with annual turnovers of up to €500 million).[1]

---

1. Taking the years 1995–2004, 69.7 per cent of the takeover agents had turnovers of €1 billion or more, 93 per cent of the companies taken over had turnovers of €500 million or less. Source: Bundeskartellamt, *Tätigkeitsberichte*, 1996, 1998, 2000, 2002, 2004 (own calculations).

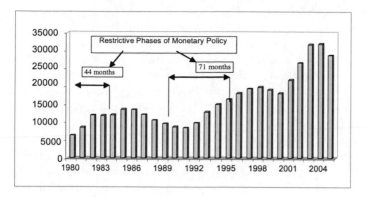

Figure 4.6 Company Insolvencies and Monetary Policy in Germany 1980–2005
Source: Creditreform

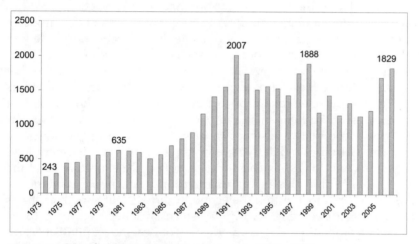

Figure 4.7 Notifiable Mergers in Germany 1973–2006
Source: Bundeskartellamt, *Tätigkeitsherichte*, (various)

The policy architecture of neoliberalism and monetarism was crucially coresponsible for the mayhem of the Third World debt crisis, reinforcing the secular problems of the advanced industrial economies that were unable to maintain the benign dynamic of growth that allowed wages and profits, consumption and investment to rise in concert. By maintaining high real interest rates for most of the decade of the 1980s, the Bundesbank helped to immobilise that benign dynamic, to increase the attractiveness of financial speculation, repress consumption and reduce the attractiveness of credit-financed investments. By ignoring the relative immunity of corporations with large reserves to monetarist changes in short-term interest rates and the far greater elasticity of SME demand for credit, the Bundesbank contributed to a demonstrable wave of economic concentration. With other central banks it contributed very significantly to the exacerbation of the debt crisis of developing countries and to the deterioration of state finances in developed countries. Above all, it allowed a system of financial speculation and monetary accumulation to take root in the political economies of the richest regions of the world, a system which is based on the generation and augmentation of essentially fictitious values.

This in turn has given rise to an economic mindset which is redolent of delusion and self-delusion, akin to the case of Hans Christian Andersen's naked emperor, who is persuaded by two outrageous swindlers that the fine suit of (invisible) clothes they design and sell him is only visible to clever observers and not to the dim-witted. Both the dim-witted emperor and his sycophantic subjects are not prepared to admit to their stupidity and defiantly deny the evidence of their senses when the emperor walks stark naked through the streets. The delusion (conspiracy of silence) is only broken when a boy in the crowd shouts out that the emperor has no clothes on. The chief difference between the Andersen fairy tale and the 'modern' world of monetary accumulation is that the crowd in the fairy tale had nothing to lose; today the process of social reproduction has become perversely dependent on the growth dynamic of fictitious values so that the 'crowd' is deaf to the cries of sceptics. Not just individual shareholders and creditors but whole sections of society are affected by the investment strategies of insurance companies and pension funds, which valorise their capital – the accumulated funds of contributors – in large part through equity, currency, futures and derivatives trading whose value is determined not by the demand for goods and services but by the expectations of the gambling den. Within this nexus of interdependence, no insiders are seemingly prepared to question the economic, intellectual or ethical basis of fictional wealth creation. Within Western societies, we seem to be increasingly trapped in the convenience of 'casino capitalism' and unwilling to doubt its efficacy or wisdom. Orthodox discourse on the subject is often extraordinary. For example, on 5 December 1996 Alan Greenspan, former chairman of the Federal Reserve Board, mused about the phenomenon of stock market speculation: 'How do we know when irrational exuberance has unduly escalated asset values, which then become subject to unexpected and prolonged corrections' (cited in Wolf 1999: 25). Greenspan's implied answer to his rhetorical question would be: 'We don't'. The vague talk of 'corrections' or 'consolidation' certainly does not amount to an explanation of what happened on 19 October 1987, when the Dow Jones index fell 22.6 per cent, the FTSE 26.4 per cent, the Hang Seng (Hong Kong index) by 45.8 per cent and the DAX by 24 per cent, or similarly in the summer of 1998. Whereas monetarists bring the full weight of their intellectual rigour to bear on the structural causes of inflation and on the transmission mechanisms, circuitry and time lags of corrective monetary policy, the phenomenon of financial asset inflation is given scant attention; the exceptions (see Wolf 1999) proving the rule. For example the DAX index of German share value changes rose by 30.3 per cent between December 1982 and December 1983 in a year in which the value of domestic production and service provision (nominal GDP) rose by just 4.1 per cent. The disparity in 1985 was even greater, when the DAX rose by 72 per cent and nominal GDP grew by 4.3 per cent. There was barely a murmur from the guardians of price stability in the Bundesbank; rather the potential for strong share price rises is seen as, 'very attractive for foreign investors' (Bundesbank 1986: 30). Two years later the year-on-year drop of over one-third in the DAX was described as, 'a correction of the preceding speculative exaggerations' (*Monatsbericht* December 1987) and explained above all with reference to the high volume of activity by 'foreign institutional investor groups' on Germany's equity markets (Bundesbank 1988: 54f). The account of the 1987 crash in the Bundesbank's annual report for the year is disingenuous, both in terms of its apportioning of blame on exogenous factors, including a sideways swipe at other 'monetary authorities of the big industrial countries' (ibid. 54) for issuing 'considerable quantities of liquidity', and in terms of the evident contradictions in the bank's analysis, which sees the desirability of 'strengthening the weight of long-term investors in the equity market' against short-term (foreign) speculation but welcomed the liberalisation of exchange controls and the ongoing modernisation of German stock exchanges: 'The German economy deserved the stock exchange in the Federal Republic achieving the standard which it has had for a long time in other larger industrial countries' allowing the, 'increasingly large company units access to an appropriate source of risk capital' (Bundesbank 1988: 56–57). It is precisely the combination of the exchange liberalisation, vast reserves of vagabond capital and 'modernised' stock and currency markets – promoted directly or indirectly by the Bundesbank – that was responsible for the disruptive speculation that hit Germany in 1987. The bank's comforting words in December 1987 sum up the contradictoriness of its position: 'the financial sector will in general produce hardly any negative effects worth mentioning on the real (*sic*) sphere of the economy' (*Monatsbericht* December 1987: 22ff). The real economy can therefore take credit for the share price boom between 1985 and early 1987 (seventeen times the growth rate of nominal GDP!) but remains untarnished and unaffected by the share price slump.

The policy context of the mayhem in financial markets in the 1980s cannot be understood without reference to the development of the EMS and the role played in that system by the Bundesbank. The EMS was a political construction promoted by Helmut Schmidt and Valéry Giscard d'Estaing in 1979 – in the face of opposition from the Bundesbank – as a more effective means of stabilising the currencies of EC economies than the previous 'snake' or 'snake in the tunnel'. It established not simply a system which allowed currencies to fluctuate in value within narrow bands (+/– 2.5 per cent), but which also obliged the individual central banks of member states to intervene when one or more currencies was in danger of either falling below the 'floor' or rising above the 'ceiling' of the fluctuation bands. This so-called 'exchange rate mechanism' was supposed to be automatically triggered, with the extreme option of realigning currencies if central bank interventions failed. It was supposed to function as a cooperative venture, solidly founded on the Franco–German partnership, and to develop into a currency union based around the basket of currencies which made up the fictitious European Currency Unit (ECU). The fundamental problem of the plan was, firstly, that it assumed some kind of symmetry in the progress of both the French and the German economies and, secondly, that it sat very uneasily with the policy autonomy of the Bundesbank. It was statutorily 'independent of instructions from the Federal Government' (§12 Bundesbank Law) and, as a monetarist institution, viewed the strident fiscalism of the new Mitterand administration of 1981 with some hostility. The maintenance of high interest rates by the Bundesbank and its European satellite central banks in a year which saw recessions in five EC countries (United Kingdom, Denmark, Belgium, Netherlands, Luxembourg) and two other European countries (Spain and Austria) can be seen both as the product of 'insular monetarism' (Kennedy 1992: 63) and as an indirect means of bringing the Schmidt and Mitterand administrations to heel; the success of this policy can be seen in the major realignment of EMS currencies in October 1981 when the DM and the Dutch Guilder were revalued by 5.5 per cent against the other EMS currencies, and the French Franc and the Italian Lira were devalued within the EMS by 3 per cent (see Table 4.7). In the eleven years from 1979 to the eve of German unification in 1990, the DM was revalued six times, gaining 39 per cent in value against the other currencies within the EMS. Both the French Franc and the Italian Lira were devalued five times. With the structural power of Germany's political economy within the EC, the Bundesbank was able to dominate the EMS by maintaining relatively high real interest rates in Germany, which necessitated much higher rates in those EMS countries which, in part because of devaluation, were suffering both higher rates of inflation and a negative balance of payments for most of the 1980s (see Table 4.5 above). France and Italy, after current account surpluses in 1979 ($5.2 billion and $5.89 billion respectively), slipped into deficit after the oil price shock which grew to $–14.91 and $–14.45 respectively (Figures: OECD). Germany, on the other hand, after a CA deficit of $–5.41 in 1979, enjoyed constant and rising surpluses, ending up with $47.08 billion in 1990. The only economy to enjoy consistent external surpluses alongside Germany was the

Netherlands; the only EMS currency to appreciate against the DM was the Guilder – by 15 per cent between 1979 and 1990. The EMS, having been envisaged by the French as a vehicle for neutralising the leverage of the Bundesbank and the growing hegemony of the DM in the 1970s, became a Bundesbank show. France, despite strong government preferences for a fiscalist approach to combating unemployment, was forced to adopt 'the norms of disinflation and austerity' (Heisenberg 1999: 86). The next decade – with the challenges of postcommunism and the major political programmes of German unification, the Single Market and European Monetary Union – would bring much more of the same.

Table 4.7 Developments within the European Monetary System 1979–1990

Date	EMS Realignments and other developments
1979 (24.9)	Revaluation of the DM by 2%, devaluation of Danish Krone by 2.9%
1979 (30.11)	Devaluation of Danish Krone by 4.8%
1981 (23.3)	Devaluation of Italian Lira by 6%
1981 (5.10)	Revaluation of the DM and the Dutch Guilder by 5.5%, devaluation of French Franc and Italian Lira by 3%
1982 (22.2)	Devaluation of the Belgian Franc by 8.5% and of the Danish Krone by 3%
1982 (14.6)	Revaluation of the DM and the Dutch Guilder by 4.25%, devaluation of the Italian Lira by 2.75% and of the French Franc by 5.75%
1983 (21.3)	Revaluation of the DM by 5.5%, the Dutch Guilder by 3.5%, the Danish Krone by 2.5% and the Belgian Franc by 1.5%; Devaluation of the French Franc and the Italian Lira by 2.5% and of the Irish Punt by 3.5%
1985 (20.7)	Devaluation of the Italian Lira by 6%; revaluation of all other EMS currencies by 2%
1986 (7.4)	Revaluation of the DM and the Dutch Guilder by 3%, the Danish Krone by 2.5% and the Belgian Franc by 1%; devaluation of the FF by 3%
1986 (4.8)	Devaluation of the Irish Punt by 8%
1987 (12.1)	Revaluation of the DM and the Dutch Guilder by 3% and of the Belgian Franc by 2%
1989 (19.6)	Entry of Spanish Peseta into EMS (within fluctuation bands of ± 6%)
1990 (8.1)	Devaluation of Italian Lira by 3.7% while it enters narrow bands (± 2.25%)
1990 (5.10)	Entry of British Pound into EMS (within wider band of ± 6%)

GERMAN UNIFICATION AND THE UNRAVELLING OF NEOLIBERALISM

There is no doubt that the unification of Germany was a political triumph for Chancellor Helmut Kohl. It fulfilled Adenauer's ambition of removing the GDR from the political map and uniting East and West Germans under the constitutional provisions of the Federal Republic's Basic Law. Economic and social union, which took place on 1 July 1990, thus involved the absorption of the territory and population of the former GDR into the social and economic system of the West; jaundiced eyes regarded it as colonisation (Christ 1991), an *Anschluss* (Roth 1990) which saw the 'destruction' (Nick 1995) or 'slaughtering' (Suhr 1990) of East Germany. In any event, the population of the East, their social organisations and their intellectual elites had very little say in the strategy for restructuring East German society after currency union or after full political unification on 3 October 1990. The political, administrative, entrepreneurial, managerial, professional and academic expertise deployed in the unification process came almost exclusively from the West, including other Western countries; there was 'no endogenous transformation' (Reissig 2000b: 29). Technically, this was the logical thing to do, given the disparity of the two socio-economic systems of the GDR and the FRG and the need to achieve a rapid transformation of the East's institutions. Politically, however, it reveals a central irony of the unification process: that it was driven and accelerated by the political pressure of the mass of East Germans in early 1990 whose views were subsequently rarely counselled by their West German controllers, dubbed unforgettably '*Besserwessis*' (a pun on the German for 'know-all': '*Besserwisser*'). Unification would certainly have taken place at a much more leisurely pace if the Kohl cabinet, its economic advisers and the Bundesbank had been able to pursue their original preferences: gradual marketisation of the eastern economy, coaxing the Ost-Mark towards convertibility and alignment with the DM, privatisation of state assets and convergence of fiscal regimes. These preferences were rendered utterly irrelevant by the threat of mass migration, explicit in the protest slogan: 'If the DM comes to us, we'll stay, if it doesn't, we will go to it'. Kohl was one of the first to recognise the unstoppable dynamic of rapid unification, when in February 1990 he suddenly offered East Germans currency union at the earliest possible date.[1]

German unification in 1990 was an extraordinary and unique event in modern world history. The end of the Cold War brought with it the rapid transformation of the bulk of the Soviet empire and its satellite states in Eastern and central Europe, including the GDR. None of the other CEECs – Poland, Hungary, Czechoslovakia, the Baltic States etc., – underwent the transition from state socialism (back) to capitalism through absorption into an existing capitalist economy. 'Transition was nowhere more abrupt than in East Germany' (ibid. 24). In addition, the capitalist economy into which the GDR was absorbed happened to be the strongest in Europe and the second strongest trading economy in the world: the economy of the FRG. The structural political and structural economic conditions under which the GDR was transformed were, probably inevitably, radically more inflexible, less open to modification, deceleration, deintensification than for any of the other transition countries. Once the decision had been reached on 18 May 1990, just 190 days after the collapse of the Berlin Wall, for the regions of Brandenburg, Mecklenburg-Western Pomerania, Saxony, Saxony Anhalt and Thuringia to be admitted into the constitutional framework of the West German Basic Law (using §23 of the same), and for the citizens, enterprises and territorial authorities in the East to adopt the DM as common currency forty-three days later (1 July 1990), the radicalness and speed of transformation was a given. In theory at least, the other CEECs had the advantage of being able to pursue mercantilist transition strategies that were more or less attuned to the economic needs of their national social economies; judgements on economic policy could be made with reference to the normal macroeconomic indicators applying to sovereign territories: to growth, investment, employment, consumer price inflation, money supply, capacity utilisation etc. In the case of East Germany, however, economic policy was governed with reference to the whole national German economy and its main indicators. Of course, special consideration was given to the monumental task of adapting the economic institutions in the East to the requirements of Western markets, and vast sums of money were spent in the process, but the adaptation took place crucially within the context of a common hard currency and a business environment which was now characterised by crass disparities. These disparities exposed

---

1. By 1990 Germany had already received hundreds of thousands of ethnic Germans from Romania, Poland and the Soviet Union and was also the destination for many thousands of political and economic refugees from the developing world (see Chapter 3).

East German enterprises and East German workers to market pressures that were in part spared the other CEECs, which could or were obliged to use exchange rate devaluation to improve the economies' export competitiveness or could exploit the extremely low wage costs of their skilled workforces to attract inward investment and outsourcing contracts. Their transitions, although fraught with hardship for large sections of the population, were 'organic' in the sense that they were informed by the endogenous potential and weaknesses of a unitary body of economic agents, all operating on new territory according to new rules. East Germany joined its Western counterpart in a market already dominated by seasoned international 'champions', operating to often highly complex, Byzantine rules of taxation and corporate governance with which Eastern enterprises were barely acquainted.

The view advanced here clearly enjoys the benefit of hindsight and is now shared by many observers within the business community, within political elites and within academics, but it is a view which was much less in evidence at the beginning of the process of unification. The judgement of the majority of observers – both German and foreign – at the end of 1989 and throughout 1990 was much more upbeat. After all, the unification of Western Germany with 'middle Germany'[2] brought together the dominant industrial power of the EC and the most advanced economy of COMECON. Like its Western counterpart, the GDR supplied its Eastern partners with much of their high-tech requirements, with electronics and precision tools. Like its Western neighbour, East Germany had been credited with its own kind of 'economic miracle' in the first three decades of its existence, building up both a heavy engineering sector from scratch and developing electrotechnical and chemical research infrastructures that were some of the best in the Eastern bloc. From this kind of banner headline perspective, the marriage of these two industrial giants at the heart of a post-Cold War Europe represented less of a worrisome economic problem and more of an economic and political challenge to the other nations within the EC. Accordingly, Margaret Thatcher referred to the perceived need in 1990 to 'check the German juggernaut' (Thatcher 1993: 797).

Domestically, the political euphoria over the dismantling of the gruesome Berlin Wall was accompanied in certain quarters by confident

---

2. The GDR occupied the central swathe of Bismarck's 1871 Reich, which was finally dismembered in 1945 when Silesia, Eastern Pomerania and part of East Prussia were ceded to Poland and the rest of East Prussia to the Soviet Union. The West German reunification programmes of the 1950s and 1960s involved the reuniting of all the 'occupied' territories of 'middle Germany' (the GDR) and the 'East' under the constitution of the Federal Republic. German maps of central Europe thus differed significantly from those of the victorious Allies and other European states. 'East Germany' only became common parlance in the Federal Republic in the wake of Brandt's *Ostpolitik* and the recognition of the Oder-Neisse line as the eastern border of the German 'nation'.

predictions of a new united prosperity, evoking above all the myths of the postwar 'miracle'. Chancellor Kohl in a Bundestag debate in June 1990 asserted that '(w)e will do it if we focus on the skills with which we built up the FRG more than forty years ago out of the rubble of our destroyed towns and landscapes' (*Verhandlungen des deutschen Bundestages, Stenographische Berichte*. Vol. 154, p. 17,142). Ingrid Matthäus-Maier, the SPD finance policy spokesperson, predicted that currency union would generate 'an economic miracle in the GDR' (ibid. 14,857), a view shared by the otherwise hard-nosed pragmatist, FDP chair and former Economics Minister Otto von Lambsdorff: 'What we achieved in 1948, the GDR will achieve in 1990' (ibid. 16,412). The international investment bank Goldmann Sachs confidently forecast that the East would effectively reach Western levels of productivity within ten years of unification; that is, by the year 2000. (Goldman Sachs 1992). This extreme confidence was based on a very selective perception of the strengths of the GDR economy, on the mythology of 'economic miracles' and on the supposed triumph of neoliberalism over Keynesianism and socialism.

The selective assessment of the GDR economy accentuated the positive and eliminated the negative; it was rightly stressed that East Germany had the highest labour productivity of all COMECON partners, that the quality of its capital stock (its plant and machinery) was also high by eastern standards, that the GDR had a highly trained industrial workforce, a strong tradition of academic and industrial research, the highest standard of living in the East, a sectoral structure not dissimilar to that of the FRG, a high export ratio, high levels of private savings and a significantly higher investment ratio than its Western neighbour (see Table 5.1). Even critical Western observers acknowledged the strengths of the East German welfare state, and their much vaunted 'social achievements' (Bust-Bartels 1986; Abelshauser 2005: 397; Jäger 1988: 259f).

Table 5.1 Selected Economic Indicators for East and West Germany 1980–1989

Indicator	GDR	FRG
GDP Growth p.a. (average 1980–89)	3.8 percent	1.9 percent
Private Consumption Growth p.a. (1980–89)	3.2 percent	1.5 percent
Gross Investments Growth p.a. (1980–89)	1.9 percent	1.2 percent
Investment ratio (as percentage of GDP) 1989	25.6 percent	22.5 percent
(1980)	(31.1 percent)	(23.5 percent)
Trade Surplus as percentage of GDP 1989	2.9 percent	4.1 percent
GDP per head of population	21 539 Mark	35 827 DM
GDP per member of workforce	36 796 mark	80 588 DM

Source: Priewe & Hickel, *Der Preis der Einheit*

Notwithstanding the problems associated with official East German statistics, the indicators included in Table 5.1 would suggest that the relative performance of the GDR economy in gross investments, private consumption and real GDP growth outshone that of the FRG. Even if per capita GDP is markedly lower in the East, the comparative growth trend also suggests that there could be convergence of East and West if the East–West disparity of 1.9 per cent were maintained or even increased. However, what such a selective presentation neglects above all is the macroeconomic and macropolitical context of the GDR's progress; it was rooted in the artificial and protected environment of bloc membership and the strict governance of the command economy. The provision of goods and services was determined by centralised political authorities, prices and wages were fixed by ministers and civil servants, the priorities of research, development and investment were set according to political perceptions of the needs of enterprises, households and the barely legitimised state, within the parameters of commitments to COMECON and the Warsaw Pact. Even if this command economy provided a material standard of living to its citizens that in 1989 exceeded that of several OECD countries and the vast majority of other nations in the world, the alteration or indeed the destruction of its protected international environment was always going to threaten not just the operation of a politically determined system for allocating social resources but above all its viability in a new market environment.

In the world-historical context of the end of the Cold War, the rebirth of 'national self-determination', the promise of a restored nationhood in Germany and of a 'common European house' (Gorbachev), negative assessments of the feasibility of economic unification were at least downgraded, even if they were not entirely set aside. The deficiencies of the GDR economy, scorned and lampooned by Western critics right up until the autumn of 1989, were in part set aside in the politically perilous months after 9 November 1989. The backwardness of the East when compared to the quality of West Germany's economic infrastructure, its transport and communications systems, the world-beating quality of its investment and consumer goods was played down; the farcical waiting times for consumer durables – up to ten years for a family car, such that secondhand car prices generally exceeded those of new cars – this and other glaring deficiencies were allowed not to matter in the strategic pursuit of national unity which accelerated in January and February 1990.

The mythology of west Germany's 'economic miracle' in the 1950s, already deployed in Kohl's neoliberal *Wende* in 1982, was invoked once more in relation to the economic potential of a united Germany. Abelshauser (2005: 405) agrees with Zohlnhöfer (1990: 192) that there was a 'general consensus' among West German economists in 1990 that unification would result in a second 'economic miracle'. This consensus, whether overwhelming or not, was informed above all by perceptions of the key role played by the politico-economic 'order' chosen by the first Adenauer administration under the ideological leadership of Ludwig Erhard, namely the 'social market economy' (Abelshauser 2005: 402f), and the corresponding belief that the policy formulae could be successfully applied to the transformation of the GDR. The trigger for this political transformation would be, as in 1948, the act of currency reform and the adoption by East German households and enterprises of a stable store of monetary value: the DM. Abelshauser and others, however, contest the centrality of policy in the process of postwar reconstruction and stress above all 'the exceptionally favourable constellation of factors of production and a surprisingly rich institutional legacy' (ibid.; also Abelshauser 1983: 32ff; Glastetter 1983: 108ff; Leaman 1988: 107ff). The exceptional conditions obtaining in the 1950s included the good fortune of an undervalued DM within a system of fixed exchange rates together with favourable terms of trade. This constellation meant that Germany was able to sell high-grade goods at competitive prices, but also import cheaper lower grade goods for processing or sale. A modern industrial apparatus was serviced by a highly skilled and relatively cheap, hard-working labour force, topped up at regular intervals through migration from the East and then from southern Europe. Add to this the security provided to manufacturing enterprises by universal banks as long-term stakeholders, and one has the ingredients of the remarkable success of Germany's trading economy in the postwar years. Western integration and trade liberalisation under the auspices of the United States facilitated West Germany's export-led boom. The balance sheet of domestic policy performance in the 1950s is much less impressive than the CDU's myth machine would have us believe. Clear successes in the field of transport, housing construction, regional development and health were matched by severe underinvestment in secondary and higher education, by ineffective competition policy, by the lack of cyclical coordination between the fiscal authorities at federal, regional and local level and the monetary authority of the Bundesbank. Erhard's failure as chancellor in the 1960s was a result of the marked change in Germany's domestic and international circumstances, notably by the partial evaporation of the unique set of factors that facilitated growth in the 1950s. Erhard's 'social market economy' was still in place, as was the strict monetary order overseen by the Bundesbank but, without the terms of trade, the surplus capacity, the cheap labour and with an appreciating currency, the 'economic order' was clearly not sufficient to prevent crisis.

Invoking the collective memory of the 'economic miracle' and the role of the CDU administration in the 1950s was politically astute rhetoric but it involved the repetition of a dangerous syllogism, which was likely to fail much more spectacularly in the 1990s than economic policy in Erhard's brief chancellorship (1963–66). The potency of this syllogism had nevertheless been given a fatal boost by the apparent triumph of neoliberalism over both Keynesianism and state socialism in the 1970s and 1980s. While the former bastions of state interventionism – in France, Italy and the United Kingdom – were still struggling with stagflation and worsening external balances, Germany was recovering its equilibrium, most notably in the crucial two years before the fall of the Wall (see Table 5.2).

Table 5.2 Unequal Development of Core European Economies

	Rate of Unemployment percent of total employed pop	Inflation Balances Current. Account Billion $	External against $	Exchange Rate
Germany				DM/$
1984	7.1	2.8	9.81	2.84
1985	7.1	2.0	16.42	2.94
1986	6.4	-0.5	39.50	2.17
1987	6.2	0.6	45.88	1.79
1988	6.2	1.4	50.64	1.75
1989	5.6	3.1	57.43	1.88
France				FF/$
1984	9.7	7.7	-1.16	8.7
1985	10.2	5.8	-0.22	8.9
1986	10.4	2.7	1.95	6.9
1987	10.5	3.2	-4.92	6.0
1988	10.0	2.7	-4.71	5.9
1989	9.4	3.5	-5.53	6.3
Italy				Lira//$
1984	9.4	12.0	-2.31	1757
1985	9.6	9.0	-3.58	1909
1986	10.5	6.3	2.44	1491
1987	10.9	5.3	-1.08	1297
1988	11.0	5.7	-5.78	1302
1989	10.9	6.3	-10.62	1372
Britain				£/$
1984	11.7	5.0	2.08	0.75
1985	11.2	5.4	-2.27	0.77
1986	11.2	4.4	-8.20	0.68
1987	10.3	4.3	-8.75	0.61
1988	8.6	5.0	-11.27	0.56
1989	7.1	5.8	-17.50	0.61

Source: OECD

The German rate of unemployment in 1989, while high at 5.6 per cent, was still considerably lower than in the other core economies of the EC (France: 9.4 per cent; Italy: 10.9 per cent; UK: 7.1 per cent), inflation had risen with the growth boom of 1988 (3.7 per cent) and 1989 (3.8 per cent) to 3.1 per cent, but averaged 1.6 per cent in the period 1984–89; French inflation had fallen to 3.5 per cent, Italian inflation to 6.3 per cent and UK inflation to 5.8 per cent, as a result of lower oil prices and the devaluation of the dollar, but after average annual rates of 4.6 per cent, 7.4 per cent and 5 per cent respectively in the same period. Germany's current account surplus had risen to $57.43 billion in 1989 while each of the other countries, even oil-rich Britain, had growing deficits. While all four dollar exchange rates had risen, unsurprisingly the appreciation of the DM was stronger at 33 per cent between 1984 and 1989, compared to 27.5 per cent for the Franc, 22 per cent for the Lira and 21 per cent for sterling. Thus the recovery from the turbulence of the early 1980s was interpreted not simply as the triumph of European capitalism over the bankrupted economies of COMECON but as a vindication of West Germany's hard currency monetarism and its preference for *Ordnungspolitik* (policy directed towards the framework of economic activity) in contrast to *Prozesspolitik* (policy designed to manage the economic cycle). The demonstration of West European and particularly West German superiority at the end of an otherwise problematic decade thus coincided with the challenge of unification, providing a worryingly convincing foundation for the ideological certitude with which the task of economic unification was subsequently approached.

There is no doubt that most of the Kohl cabinet would have preferred a much slower process of unification over several years. Finance Minister Waigel produced a Ten Point Programme in early January 1990 which rejected an immediate currency union and set the achievement of market-based reforms as conditions for economic unification; this was echoed by Economics Minister Haussmann, by several members of the Bundesbank directorate, including its president, Pöhl, and later president, Hans Tietmeyer, as well as by the Council of Economic Experts. The so-called Staged Plan (*Stufenplan*) was also accepted by the East German government under Hans Modrow, which envisaged a two-year programme moving towards the convertibility of the Ost-Mark by 1992. East German economists also warned against too hasty a currency union (*Neues Deutschland*, 9 February 1990).

There is also little doubt, therefore, that the decision to move rapidly to currency union was determined not by the weight of economic analysis but by a set of political considerations which together overwhelmed the logic of incremental convergence. There was a strong sense of tactical opportunism in both foreign and domestic politics: *carpe diem* (seize the day) will not have been far from the minds of the Kohl administration in relation to the chance of gaining four-power agreement to unification, while Gorbachev was still in power and while market reforms in an independent GDR had not yet been achieved; party politics within the CDU had seen Kohl's position threatened early in 1989 at the Bremen conference, such that he might have feared being outplayed in the unification stakes by other senior members of the CDU (Priewe and Hickel 1991: 81) like Geissler and Süssmuth. More telling, perhaps, was the wave of immigration from the GDR in the final quarter of 1989 (263,455) and in the first quarter of 1990 (193,634) underscoring the increasingly strident slogan of the January and February demonstrations: 'If the DM comes, we stay, if it doesn't, we go to it'. It has also been suggested that the Kohl cabinet was affronted by Modrow's demand for DM 15 billion in financial aid in February 1990. 'The view took hold: if it's going be aid, then only under a unitary currency and political unity' (Priewe and Hickel 1991: 83).

Notwithstanding the weight of these and other factors tipping the scales in favour of rapid currency union, which was probably therefore unavoidable, the subsequent political management of economic and social unification was fatally imbued with the mythology of the invincible combination of liberal markets, currency reform, Bundesbank and German *Fleiss* (industriousness), a mythology which appears to have paralysed any sense of the need for strategic long-term planning of such a unique enterprise.

Currency Union as Exogenous Shock: The Political Economy of the 'Big Bang'

Currency reform has predominantly been the product of crisis. The introduction of the Rentenmark in 1923 and the replacement of the worthless Reichsmark by the Deutsche Mark in 1948 followed periods of extreme inflation in which money essentially lost its function as a store of value and was replaced by bartering with goods; in the chaos of defeat after 1945, it was perversely the cigarette (the 'Lucky' after Lucky Strike) that proved to be a halfway reliable substitute currency (Bub 2006). There are countless other examples of European and Latin American currency reforms born of crisis. While the Ost-Mark functioned as an effective national currency within the heavily policed territory of the GDR (from which unlicensed cash exports were illegal), it remained unconvertible against the major currencies of the world. At the beginning of 1990 the GDR also had an external debt equivalent to DM 56.1 billion, 98 per cent of which was held by OECD and other countries outside COMECON (Tober 1997: 232), which was becoming increasingly difficult to service. Given the chronic waiting lists for many consumer durables, the DM already functioned as an alternative means for securing these from both inside and outside the territory, but at a black market exchange rate of between 5:1 and more than 10:1; intraGerman trade maintained an official rate of 1:1.

The collapse of the Wall and of the (economic) police state threatened to destroy the fragile foundations of the GDR currency, and with it the integrity of the productive economy. Currency reform of one variety or another was thus an essential precondition for economic survival. The decision to combine currency reform with currency union was a far greater challenge than the reform measures adopted in, say, Poland and Czechoslovakia, since the latter had the option both to devalue the złoty and the koruna against other currencies and to pursue short-term inflation as a means of devaluing domestic debt. Crucially these options were ruled out for the Ost-Mark by currency union with the Federal Republic and the hardest currency in Europe. Currency union also made the conversion rate of Ost-Mark to the new currency a critical variable in the calculations of economic and political risk. In the hectic winter of 1989–90, the SPD, through its finance policy spokesperson Ingrid Matthäus-Mayer, initially proposed a rapid currency union with a conversion rate of 5:1. On 13 February 1990, this suddenly changed to 1:1, no doubt after it had been pointed out that an 80 per cent devaluation of the Ost-Mark would have reduced wage levels in the East to a similar degree, where eastern wage rates were already approximately half the level of those in the West. Priewe and Hickel quote average monthly gross incomes for industrial workers before currency union of DM 1,322 in the East and DM 4,214 in the West. Even accounting for the much higher stoppages to gross wages in the West and price subsidies in the East, net monthly wages of DM 2,250 still represented a far higher standard of living for West German industrial workers. A conversion rate of 5:1 would have reduced monthly East German gross wages to just DM 264, way below the safety net level of social assistance of DM 400 in 1990.

In the 'brief but violent battle' over the conversion rate in April and May 1990, it was revealed in the daily press that the Bundesbank favoured a rate of 2:1 (Bundesbank 1990). This provoked widespread protests from East German citizens fearful of their standard of living and raised further fears of accelerating emigration from the East. It should be recalled also that, as a result of the liberalisation of migration from the Soviet Union, Poland and Romania in the second half of the 1980s, increasing numbers of 'ethnic Germans' were arriving in the Federal Republic: 200,000 in 1988, 380,000 in 1989 and 400,000 in 1990. If one adds to these huge numbers the 580,000 GDR citizens who migrated westwards from the beginning of 1989 up until June 1990, it is easy to understand how West German local authorities were finding it increasingly difficult to house and support them; all 1.6 million *Aussiedler* and *Übersiedler* had the right to settle in the Federal Republic and, as full citizens, to enjoy the same social benefits as all West Germans. The financial burden on state authorities was further compounded by the increased number of nonGerman migrants who, as refugees and asylum seekers were also arriving in increasing numbers. The number of foreigners on West German territory rose by 575,000 in 1990 and by a further 484,000 in 1991 to 6,066,000 (Statistisches Bundesamt); most of them were refugees from Asia, Eastern and South-East Europe (Mehrländer and Schultze 1992).

The political case for a generous conversion rate thus became as persuasive as the case for rapid currency union. The economic case against both courses of action was also persuasive but secondary and therefore, in the context of an ongoing crisis, irrelevant. The State Treaty of 18 May 1990 thus fixed the conversion rate of wages, salaries and prices at 1:1; savings were converted at a basic rate of 2:1, with fixed allowances for conversion at 1:1 which differed by age group: children up to the age of fourteen were allowed to exchange 2,000 Ost-Marks for DM 2,000; those in the age group fifteen to fifty-nine were allowed DM 4,000, and adults of sixty and above DM 6,000. As a result, the average conversion rate for savings was 1.475:1 (Priewe and Hickel 1991: 93). Debts were converted at two Ost-Marks to one DM, reducing the corporate debts of May 1990 from 231.7 billion Ost-Marks to DM 115.8 billion and those of housing corporations from 102.6 billion Ost-Marks to DM 51.3 billion.

The contrast of East Germany's currency reform to that of June 1948 in the western zones is striking. It demonstrates what Lange and Pugh rightly point out: 'in 1990 a simple principle of policy formation was ignored: namely, the outcome of reform depends not only on the prescribed measures but also on the conditions under which they are implemented' (Lange and Pugh 1998: 61). While both processes involved a devaluation of savings and debts, the 10:1 conversion of Reichsmark to DM in 1948 favoured the owners of material assets and debtors and penalised savers, i.e., it strengthened the supply-side of West Germany's productive economy by removing most of the need for balance sheet provisions for old debt, facilitating both self-financing through higher profits and external financing through reduced liabilities on company assets. The simultaneous fixing of an exchange rate of DM 3.33 to one US dollar was deemed to be less than favourable to German exports but, within fifteen months, the DM was allowed to devalue within the Bretton Woods system by 20.7 per cent to DM 4.202: $1.0, a rate which remained unchanged until 1961. The July 1990 currency 'reform'/union favoured savers and penalised debtors, since the adoption of the 'hard' DM ($1 = DM 1.99 in 1990) involved an effective revaluation of the Ost-Mark of around 300 per cent, given the vast productivity gap between East and West German industry, i.e., debts rose in real terms by around 50 per cent on 1 July 1990, while hourly wage costs were trebled. The real purchasing power of East German savers, on the other hand, rose on average by over 100 per cent. The fear of both a debt overhang and a liquidity overhang (Bundesbank 1990) was becoming a stark reality. After 1 July 1990, the debt liabilities and wage costs of East German enterprises were all the more pressing because most of them were haemorrhaging on the revenue front. With a liberalised import regime, the East German population – armed with relatively high levels of disposable savings, accumulated over years in the absence of a satisfactory consumer goods market – was now free to choose from a wide range of (Western) products, against which the products of East German factories were or appeared to be of inferior quality. 'The large increase in financial wealth … combined with the ready accessibility of Western products led to a spending spree that largely bypassed the 'inferior' East German products' (Tober 1997: 238). The Bundesbank, in its review of currency union after one year, also noted that 'the extent of the wave of spending becomes clear when one considers that in the first six months after the introduction of the D-Mark in the new Bundesländer as many road vehicles were registered as in five or six years under the old regime' (Bundesbank 1991: 22). Company revenues were also affected by the collapse of both domestic supply networks and the traditional export networks within COMECON, where consumers were likewise choosing higher grade or just more fashionable Western products and enterprises bought high-tech equipment from the West, much of it from West Germany. East German enterprises and their workforces were thus hit by both new market preferences and a massive exogenous 'revaluation shock', while their Western counterparts were barely capable of satisfying increased demand; capacity utilisation in West German manufacturing reached absolute record levels in 1990 at 89.8 per cent.

By contrast, all West German producers in 1948 were operating according to a new unitary monetary framework. As Geoff Pugh has pointed out, they were further favoured by the general devaluation of the DM exchange rate in 1949 which, in conjunction with productivity growth 'reduced relative unit labour costs…contribut(ing) to price competitiveness and growing demand' (Pugh 1998: 137). Additionally, West German industries in 1950 were shielded from foreign competition by import tariffs on industrial goods that averaged 40 per cent, which the General Agreement on Trade and Tariffs removed only gradually with a staged programme of import 'tariff disarmament'; the same industries were also favoured by the extraordinary backlog of demand that had been caused by both the destruction of war and the displacement of consumption by the arms economy. East German enterprises, on the other hand, were suddenly exposed to fiercely competitive markets within Europe and between experienced transnational corporations from both developed and emerging nations in the wider global market. Furthermore, unlike the postwar enterprises, the managements of East Germany's state-owned enterprises had, for forty years, been shielded from competitive culture per se. The meltdown of East German industry was thus in large measure preprogrammed by the speed and modality of currency reform in 1990.

This meltdown (see below) had been predictable, not simply in terms of East German products being the butt of West German sniffiness and contempt over many years, but also because of the evidence of failed currency reforms in recent European economic history. In particular, the notorious damage inflicted on the British economy by the disastrous return to the Gold Standard after the First World War should have alerted some commentators at least to the need for caution when an unconvertible currency with a black market exchange rate of 10 to 1 DM was about to be effectively revalued.

The critique of German monetary and social union is clearly easier than the prescription of alternative solutions. There is a widespread consensus among economists, political scientists and politicians that economic unification and the extension of the DM to East Germany was unavoidable under the circumstances, notably in relation to the demographic and economic perils of continental and intercontinental migration. Equally, there seems to have been no alternative to the 1:1 conversion rate for wages, salaries and prices, for similar reasons. Why should East German workers as citizens of a united country with a commitment to equality of living standards have their gross income halved, when they had the constitutional right to migrate to western regions either in search of work or in search of social benefits that exceeded their 'market' income in the East?

The treatment of the problem of a debt overhang for East German enterprises has certainly been the subject of greater debate. In particular, a debt conversion ratio which would have been high enough (4:1) to avoid a real increase in debt levels could have contributed to the improvement of the supply-side conditions of East German enterprises; this would, after all, have matched the supply-side strategy adopted in 1948 and the supply-side reform programmes of Kohl's *Wende*. It would, of course, have required either a corresponding conversion rate for bank savings or state subsidies to the East German banking system to maintain their liquidity. A better solution would have been the immediate conversion of the debt of collective enterprises into the public debt of the united country in advance of structural reforms to and/or privatisation of East Germany's state assets. The ultimate necessity for the Trustee Agency (*Treuhandanstalt*) to take on 70 per cent of the commercial debt in the East indicates the rationality of an earlier move by the federal government to remove debt burdens from enterprises that were being lined up for privatisation.

A less generous conversion ratio for savings could have reduced the problem of a liquidity overhang, even if this had been politically explosive. A more persuasive alternative, advanced by Walter Romberg, the last East German finance minister in the De Maizière cabinets, involved the staged release of East German savings, albeit converted at 1:1 (Priewe and Hickel 1991: 92). This would have gone some way to moderate the predictable spending spree that set in after July and reduced the inflationary pressures that emerged as West German manufacturers and retailers struggled to meet the surge of demand. Romberg's advice was ignored. The criticism and anxieties of some academics, notably the Alternative Economic Policy Group of left Keynesians (AAW 1990a: 14ff; AAW 1990b) were brushed aside.

The strangest position was adopted by the two major sources of advice within the neoliberal camp that had been most vociferous in their warnings about an immediate currency union. The Council of Economic Experts (the so-called 'five wise men') had on 2 February 1990 expressed the strongest warning about the fatal consequences of currency union in a letter to the federal chancellor. Four days later, on 6 February Karl-Otto Pöhl, president of the Bundesbank, described ideas of a currency union as 'premature' as a 'hair-brained idea' (*eine phantastische Idee*) after discussions with Christa Wolf, the GDR Finance Minister. This was the very day that Kohl had made his direct public offer of currency union. Despite the Bundesbank's strong opposition, Pöhl was to be seen three days later retracting his criticism at a federal press conference. After this 'piece of theatre in front of the world public' (Priewe and Hickel 1991: 82) the Bundesbank and its senior members remained oddly quiet, content to prepare and organise the extension of the DM to East Germany's 16 million citizens. The Council for Economic Experts also became eerily silent after the political decision had been taken. The temporary breach in the ranks of the *Wende* consensus group (CDU/CSU, FDP, Bundesbank and SVR) had seemingly been repaired. Stranger still was the subsequent analysis of both the SVR and the Bundesbank.

Firstly, the Bundesbank was quite unwilling to see East Germany's problems – deindustrialisation, unemployment and a huge demand–output gap – as the result of currency union, even though it had earlier expressed very strong warnings about its inherent dangers. One year on, the process of unemployment:

> is not somehow the 'price' for introducing the DM, it is rather the mistakes of the old system that have to bear the blame: because of the state fixing of prices, the price relationship on goods and factor markets did not correspond to the conditions of scarcity. This distortion, which was further reinforced by the state's job guarantee, led to a lack of incentives to work and as a result to over-staffing in many areas of the East German economy and in public administration. (Bundesbank 1991: 23)

The Bundesbank's amnesia was mirrored in the Special Report of the Council for Economic Experts, presented to the federal government in April 1991 under the heading: 'Maintain the Market Economic Course: Concerning Economic Policy in the Five New Federal States' (SVR 1991). It is worth citing at length because it reflects the colossal intellectual dilemma of neoliberal economists confronted by a politicoeconomic crisis which was even less amenable to neoliberal recipes than 'ordinary' economies.

The SVR bemoans the fact that:

the political environment for an economic policy, which accords market forces the key role in economic renewal, has deteriorated decisively, in part also as a result of political pressure in the west of the Federal Republic. In both East and West the unreasonable suggestion is being made that the state itself should take on a leading role in the new Länder with the necessary rehabilitation of enterprises and with structural adjustment. Only if the state were to intervene in the rehabilitation of east German enterprises and only if it were to ensure that the traditional regional structures did not collapse, would it be possible to prevent the total collapse of the east German economy...

The immediate reason for this special report is the concern that the growing unrest might cause economic policy makers to take over-hasty actions and thus lead to mistakes. This path has already been taken with the ever wider expansion of state measures to promote economic development. The impatience over the slowness of any employment success could further accelerate the tempo of actionism in economic policy.

The Special Report is opposed to the continuation of this course of economic policy' (SVR 1991: paras 2 and 3)

The complacency of the introduction and further parts of this Special Report is staggering. Why was it so unreasonable to suggest that the state should take an active part in the transition of the GDR to market capitalism, when the same state took the series of political decisions to merge two very

Table 5.3 Decline in Employment in East Germany by Sector 1989–1991

Economic Sectors	Working Population in '000s						
	1989		1990				1991
	Q I&II	QIII&IV	QI	QII	QIII	QIV	QI
Agriculture/Forestry	961	959	885	840	790	720	640
Industry	4 269	4 237	4 106	3 872	3 555	3 195	2 717
Of which: Mining &							
Manufacturing	3 670	3 641	3 536	3 391	3 090	2 760	2 360
Construction	600	596	569	481	464	435	357
Transport & Commerce	1 409	1 407	1 399	1 365	1 283	1 178	1 120
Commerce	732	732	728	708	646	575	550
Transport	678	676	671	657	636	602	570
Services & State	3 025	3 014	2 976	2 969	2 942	2 869	2 860
Services	1 088	1 085	1 074	1 082	1 094	1 114	1 115
State	1 750	1 743	1 720	1 710	1 680	1 600	1 600
Private non-commercial							
organisations	187	187	182	177	168	155	145
Total	**9 664**	**9 616**	**9 366**	**9 045**	**8 569**	**7 962**	**7 337**

Source: Priewe & Hickel 1991: 34

different economies in the first place, decisions criticised by the same authors of the report? Even if the GDR state can be blamed for the desperate state of the country's enterprises, its infrastructure, its housing stock and its environment, the need for remedial state action is not somehow eliminated by this example of state failure. Furthermore, every capitalist state of whatever hue intervenes in times of crisis in one way or another. Additionally, the West German state – like many other European states – had for decades provided massive structural subsidies to shipbuilding, mining, transport and agriculture, as a means of maintaining employment and preventing the economic collapse of specific regions and specific communities. It was not as if the scale of East Germany's transition crisis were not apparent by April 1991 (See Table 5.3).

By the end of the first quarter of 1991 the working population in East Germany had fallen by 2.3 million to 7.3 million or by 24 per cent from 1989 levels. Agricultural employment had fallen by 33 per cent, industrial employment by 36 per cent, but transport and commerce (retail and wholesale trade) by 'only' 20.5 per cent. The official number of total unemployed in the second quarter of 1991 of 843,000 would have looked far worse, had not 755,000 people moved to West Germany in the same period, had there not been 335,000 commuters from East to West, had there not been 400,000 West Germans on short-term job-creation schemes and retraining programmes. Of those still with jobs, 1,965,000 (27 per cent of the working population) were working short-time. In this calamitous situation, the SVR deemed it unreasonable to require the state to do more to help and warned of 'over-hasty actions'.

Not one single OECD country would have tolerated the haemorrhaging of employment that was afflicting East Germany in the first year of German economic union; the state authorities of Belgium, the Netherlands, Austria, Portugal – countries with a smaller population than East Germany – would have instituted drastic measures of crisis management in situations that were a fraction as critical as that in the East, where GDP had declined by 22 per cent in 1990 and was set to decline by even more in 1991 (-28 per cent). It is inconceivable that any of the larger West German Länder (North-Rhine Westfalia, Bavaria, Baden-Württemberg) would have refrained from taking 'over-hasty actions' if their regional economies had suffered the implosion of economic life that was befalling the East.

The SVR nevertheless counselled caution and urged the maintenance of the primacy of the market in resolving the woes of the East, expressing a surprising optimism about the region's prospects: 'The Council of Economic Experts does not share the view that the collapse of the east German economy (sic) will develop into a long-term structural crisis. It judges the medium-term growth prospects in the new Länder to be good. There is no reason for actionism in economic policy' (SVR 1991: para 3). It would be illuminating to know what would constitute a good reason for state intervention in the eyes of the 'five wise men' if not the virtual halving of GDP in two years. What the SVR's Special Report of April 1991 does reveal is the extraordinary mindset of the *Wende* consensus, which continued to cling religiously to the belief in the 'healing' properties of the market *in all circumstances*, even in the unprecedented debacle of East Germany's economy: 'The critical economic situation in the new federal Länder requires not the retreat from an economic policy based on market forces, but its consistent application. This includes above all removing the obstacles for economic activities that still exist; for it is because of these that market forces have been unable hitherto to develop fully in the East' (SVR 1991: para 3). The SVR's conclusion is strongly worded: 'If the framework conditions are set properly, market forces can be trusted. It would be a mistake to conduct the reform of a formally centrally organised economy by means of structural policy or industrial policy. The Council of Economic Experts emphatically warns against the adoption of this path.' (SVR 1991: para 49). This statement begs the question what the correct 'framework conditions' are and why market forces could be expected to achieve the transformation of an economy where '(t)o a large extent, goods were produced of such low quality that, in a free market, they were unsaleable at virtually any price' (Lange and Pugh 1998: 41).

The Framework Conditions for the 'Aufbau Ost'

The SVR had a relatively narrow conception of the appropriate framework conditions for the transformation of the economy in the East: the improvement of the capital stock, the integration of East Germany into the international trading system and the development of trust in the market economy on the part of the population. (SVR 1991: para 10).

The improvement of the industrial and commercial *capital stock* would be primarily the responsibility of existing (but) privatised enterprises in the East and by inward investment by other private enterprises; privatisation was therefore an absolute priority (ibid. paras 26–30). The improvement of the economic infrastructure would be the responsibility of the state utilities – the federal railways and the now separate Deutsche Telekom – as well as East German local authorities; the financing of infrastructural investments by local and regional authorities was deemed to be adequately covered by changes made to the distribution of VAT and by federal grants. Beyond this the SVR saw considerable potential for the privatisation of infrastructural responsibilities (ibid. para 32). The state also had a responsibility to encourage such private investments through fiscal measures, but financed only through the reduction in other state expenditures, not through increased taxation or increased borrowing (ibid. para 35).

The SVR was confident about the 'exploitation of the foreign trade and location advantages of the new federal states which had hitherto not been fully utilised ... The east German economy will for example in the long term be both an exporter and importer of engineering products' (para 13). The most important factor for maximising the location potential of the new states were 'the abilities of the people' (ibid. para 14). The latter could not be helped by the state subsidising employment in unviable enterprises. A 'further reduction in unprofitable jobs was required' (ibid. para 16); the application of shock therapy to the labour market would provide more rapid help to the economy than short-term 'fire-brigade' measures: 'What may provide relief in the short term, is a considerable disadvantage in the long term' (ibid. para 17).

The SVR's diagnosis and forecast was thus a sanguine one, albeit predicated on a radical programme of rapid privatisation and a reduction in employment levels – 'in the long term fewer people will be in work in the new federal states than in the old GDR' (ibid. para 45). 'Policy cannot make the mistake of increasing the impatience of the people and operating *ad hoc* on an individual problem, like the fire brigade so to speak. The task of policy is not to treat symptoms, but in the sense of a causal therapy (*sic*) to grasp the problems by the roots' (ibid. para 49). This blithely confident view was entirely misplaced and ignored/reinforced the shambolic approach to economic policy in the crucial early years of the unification process. The key authorities at the level of fiscal and monetary policy – supported by academic opinion – manifested an extraordinary indifference to the magnitude of the greatest exogenous shock since the Second World War when it came to the formulation of an adequate state response. Historical comparisons are illuminating here. The Great Depression and the Second World War produced significant changes in both the whole architecture of national and international economic policy, in a conscious effort to prevent future shocks to global development, including far-reaching elements of international policy cooperation and coordination (ERP, OEEC, OECD, GATT, World Bank, IMF, UN, EEC etc.). In Germany, in late 1966 a modest recession (-0.1 per cent) and a small rise in unemployment was considered serious enough to form a Grand Coalition of both major parties (CDU/CSU and SPD), committed to immediate crisis management and to policy coordination on both a fiscal level (Bund, Länder and local authorities) and with the Federal Bank, together with the corporatist institution of Concerted Action (state, employers and trade unions). In contrast, East Germany's transformation crisis, which saw a virtual halving of the region's GDP in just two years (1990–91), elicited no coordination between fiscal and monetary policy, little coordination between central, regional and local authorities in the initial stages and very little coherent policymaking at a supranational level.

How does one explain this indifference? The simple explanation would probably be that the economic, political and academic elites of the major

OECD countries shared a common (if relatively recent) scepticism of the potential of the state and/or supranational bodies to manage either the cyclical or the structural crises of national or regional economies in the late twentieth century and a common faith in the superior ability of markets to allocate social resources optimally. The states of these major countries had spent the last decade liberalising their internal markets, privatising their utilities and removing exchange controls and other external barriers to trade. The OECD (1983 and 1989), the World Bank and the IMF (2006: 44ff) were (and still are) agreed upon the essential virtue of liberalisation, privatisation and deregulation both for developed and developing countries. Finally, within the European Community the twelve member states had embarked on a key reform process aimed at the liberalisation of all factor markets within the Community, with the Single European Act of 1986, due for implementation in 1992 and representing a fundamental act of faith in the superiority of integrated markets over mercantilist strategies of economic management. The Cecchini Report (1988) identified major advantages accruing from the opening up of fragmented markets to competition and from the restructuring of industrial and commercial sectors resulting from increased cross border competition. The great ship of neoliberalism was thus in full sail. The collapse of the Soviet Union and most of the socialist regimes in the Soviet bloc provided an even fairer wind, both in terms of the 'proven' superiority of the market over the state and in terms of the radical recipes recommended for the transition from socialism to capitalism. In this heady intellectual atmosphere, it is possibly understandable why East Germany's uniqueness was overlooked (see above).

The complacency of both the German authorities and those of the EC was nevertheless culpable. Kohl's assurance that the cost of unification would be borne by simply deploying 'some of our future additional wealth' for the benefit of 'our compatriots in the GDR – as help towards self-help' (Kohl in a television broadcast, 1 July 1990) was deeply dishonest; Theo Waigel's dismissal of talk of unity costing hundreds of billions as 'an illusion' (*Financial Times*, 30 November 1989; quoted in Lange and Pugh 1998: 21) likewise. When in March 1991 – just before the publication of the SVR Special Report – Economics Minister Jürgen Möllemann suggested that the economic convergence of East and West would take a mere five years, Department VI-IIb of the Bonn Finance Ministry was producing an internal paper warning of the 'threat of de-industrialisation' in the East, where only 20 per cent of manufacturing jobs would survive (Vilmar and Dümcke 1996: 36). Wolfgang Schäuble, who helped negotiate the Unification Treaty and one of Kohl's closest confidants, had been under no illusion that unification would have very negative effects on the economy of the East (Schäuble 1991: 99).

The framework of currency reform, private property, commercial law, competition policy and an independent central bank was largely in place, but the notion that after completion of the privatisation process and the flexibilisation of the East German labour market the medium-term prospects for the East were favourable was entirely unconvincing in 1991 and since. If one takes a slightly broader view of the 'framework' of the '*Aufbau-Ost*' programme, the reasons for pessimism become clearer.

As noted above, the collapse of production and employment in the East, worse in scale than between 1929 and 1932, illicited no serious programme of coordinated crisis management on the part of the German state. The exact opposite seemed to apply: policy in the East operated rather on the basis of a number of disparate (and frequently colliding) imperatives.

- *Privatisation imperative*. The transformation of the East German economy was made the responsibility of an independent 'Trustee Agency' (*Treuhandanstalt*), tasked under a revised law of 17 June 1990, 'to reduce the entrepreneurial activity of the state as quickly as possible' through privatisation. After political union on 3 October 1990 the THA became an institution of public law, was supervised by the Federal Finance Ministry, but retained operational autonomy. The fact that it was not answerable to the Federal Economics Ministry underscored its narrow brief, as a temporary holding company, to place the 8,000 or so enterprises under its control into private hands and not to conduct anything resembling structural policy. The preamble to the June Law (still the law of the GDR) also includes the task to 'render as many enterprises as possible competitive and thus secure jobs and create new ones'. The THA conducted its business exclusively in relation to the five new Länder. It operated according to a limited brief and an urgent timetable, not to ensure the viability of the economy of the East, but to dispose of its economic assets before 31 December 1994. It fulfilled that brief successfully under extremely difficult circumstances and cannot be blamed for the fact that its brief was so limited.
- *Neoliberal roll-back imperative*. The new regional governments in the East – in Brandenburg, Mecklenburg-Western Pomerania, Saxony, Saxony-Anhalt and Thuringia – were created as vehicles for the imposition of the institutional structures and norms of the old Federal Republic, with its highly decentralised culture of subsidiarity. They were thus designed to fit in with an existing polity, not as instruments for the specific management of a unique problem. This existing polity was also committed to reducing its share of national income and to limiting the role of the state in allocating social resources. Accordingly, the five new Länder did not constitute a unique group with their own cooperative institutions directed towards the specific problems of the East as a region. Rather they were largely excluded from strategic macroeconomic decision making in the crucial early stages of unification. Only in March 1991 was agreement reached to improve coordination, with the

publication of the 'principles of cooperation between Bund, new Länder and the Trustee Agency for Recovery East (*Aufschwung Ost*)'. Even in this situation, the new Länder were preoccupied with the (re)establishment of regional political and administrative structures, with staffing and managing the ministerial departments for internal affairs, education, finance, justice, science and social affairs within a strongly decentralised system of federalism. The Länder and their respective local authorities often lacked the political, legal and administrative expertise to operate the highly complex systems of budgetary, planning, social and civil law which characterised the political system in the Federal Republic (Eisen and Wollmann 1996; Seibel, Benz and Mäding 1993). The resourcing of the East German Länder up until 1994 was also provisional and organised both through the standard formulae for distributing federal taxes, through the newly imposed regional and local taxes and, in lieu of the normal financial equalisation process, through the German Unity Fund (*Fonds Deutsche Einheit*) which up until 1994 provided an additional DM155 billion for the East. Regional and local policy nevertheless remained the responsibility of these subnational units, unaided by a well-considered centrally coordinated set of structural / regional policies. The new Länder were thus primarily part of the continuum representing the roll-back imperative.

- *Deflationary imperative.* Monetary policy, in contrast to Länder politics, was conducted in relation to the whole of the united German economy by the independent Bundesbank, and as such looked very much like 'business as usual'. It is a central conclusion of this book that the Bundesbank's behaviour in the crucial first years of unification played a crucial role in preventing the development of an appropriate strategy for resolving the East's transformation crisis. 'Business as usual' was culpably inappropriate to the needs of the crumbling East German economy. In particular, the imposition of a deflationary credit squeeze from 1989 to 1994 depressed growth and investments in an entirely dysfunctional manner at a crucial stage of the East's transformation (see below).

- *Containment imperative.* The framework for policymaking in the East's transformation crisis was also strongly influenced by the external commitments of the Federal Republic to a number of multilateral institutions, in particular to the EC. Even before unification, German legislation was obliged to incorporate an increasing number of European directives into German law: 2,413 alone in the legislative period 1987–1990. More importantly, the function of the EC as a vehicle for containing and neutralising unilateral action on the part of member states (most notably of Germany) became more starkly relevant for the bargaining process which accompanied and followed the 4+2 Agreement in September 1990. Fears of 'German dominance' expressed by the French and British governments (Thatcher 1993: 796–99; Larres 2002; *Economist*,

17 May 2001) and by Shevardnadse – '90 per cent of the Russian people would vote against the reunification of Germany' (cited in: Albrecht 1997: 1) – informed the diplomacy of three of the four powers involved in the restoration of German national sovereignty; the United States was generally sanguine about the issue. Not just the fear of German dominance, but also of a shifting of Germany's geoeconomic axis away from Western Europe towards central and Eastern Europe exercised the minds of European leaders, most notably Francois Mitterand. There is strong support for the view that the bargain struck in particular between France and Germany in 1990 involved 'French support for German unification in return for German support for a decisive push towards European monetary union' (Garton Ash 1996). EMU, according to Marsh (1993: 235) and others was the price Germany paid for unification (see below). In this context it illustrates the operation of a strong containment imperative in relation to Germany's future development, anchoring the country more tellingly in the institutional architecture of the EU, as it was to become, and reducing its room for manoeuvre as it sought to resolve East Germany's transformation crisis.

- *The blossoming landscapes imperative.* In his television broadcast on 1 July 1990, Chancellor Kohl uttered the famous and fatal words, 'through a joint effort we will soon succeed in transforming Mecklenburg-Western Pomerania and Saxony-Anhalt, Brandenburg, Saxony and Thuringia into blossoming landscapes once more', signalling the intention of achieving the rapid convergence of East Germany's economy with that of the West, even if he was very vague about the strategy and means by which that would be achieved. Such convergence could only be achieved by real economic growth in the East being consistently stronger than in the West, so that per capita GDP roughly matched that of western levels. This growth imperative was informed firstly by the constitutional obligation to ensure equal living conditions for all citizens of the Federal Republic (§106 Basic Law), secondly by the urgency of reducing the fiscal burden of the East on state budgets – securing a sustainable regional economy in the East – and thirdly, not least, by the need to secure the reelection of the governing coalition and avoid the electoral punishment that accompanies economic failure. In retrospect, it is clear that Kohl's electoral defeat in 1998 was in large measure the result of the failure to deliver the promised 'blossoming landscapes'. The very concept has become an ironic cliché in German political culture, the title of a regular column by the Dresden born journalist Peter Richter in the *Frankfurter Allgemeine Sonntagszeitung* and a book by the same author (Richter 2004).

The framework for the realisation of the '*Aufbau Ost*' or '*Aufschwung Ost*' was thus by no stretch of the imagination benign. The five imperatives above (to which one can add more; see Leaman 2005) provided, together with the structural economic disadvantages outlined above, an altogether dismal foundation for rebuilding anything. Like five cats in a bag, the chances of a unitary policy mix were minimal; the likelihood above all of the deflationary imperative colliding head-on with the growth imperative, and the growth imperative being further thwarted by the roll-back imperative, the privatisation imperative and the containment imperative was very considerable. Above all, the auspices for exploiting the narrow time window for ensuring the speediest convergence of East and West were not good.

Within the overall framework of noncoordination, a key role in preventing a dynamic of economic recovery in the East was played by the Bundesbank. After presiding over the organisational triumph of actual currency union, of producing and distributing notes and coins for 1 July 1990, of establishing a network of regional central banks to service the clearing and refinancing needs of the five new Länder, Germany's central bank set about managing the money supply, as if unification had not happened, interpreting macroeconomic developments – notably of consumer prices and the demand for credit – as processes within a normal political economy. The political economy of Germany postunification, however, was and has remained *distinctively abnormal*, requiring a correspondingly appropriate policy mix, in particular a high degree of collaboration between all state actors and key nonstate actors as well as a very strong degree of urgency. Time was an absolutely key factor in maximising the potential of economic unification and minimising the damage. The shorter the period of convergence between West and East, the lower the material cost to the German state – i.e., to the German people as taxpayers – and the lower the political and social cost of divergence and disparity.

The deflationary imperative, espoused by the parties to the neoliberal *Wende* consensus of 1982 – CDU/CSU, FDP, Bundesbank and the Council of Economic Experts – continued to dominate macroeconomic policy from 1989 onwards, ostensibly without open contradiction from the Kohl administration. Increases in the Bundesbank's key interest rates – discount rate and Lombard rate – had already been triggered by increases in the rate of consumer price inflation and the money supply (M3) in 1988 and 1989 as a result of two good years of economic growth (see Figure 5.1). By the end of 1989 the discount rate stood at 6 per cent; the Lombard rate at 8 per cent. In November 1990, a month after unification, the Lombard rate was raised to 8.5 per cent and in the course of 1991 both rates were raised in three steps to 8 per cent and 9.75 per cent respectively. The discount rate peaked in July 1992 when it rose to an historic record of 8.75 per cent (Lombard rate stayed on 9.75 per cent). As Figure 5.1 shows, consumer price inflation rose to a peak of 4.5 per cent in 1993 but then fell back to below 2 per cent, the Bundesbank's 'normative' definition of price stability

(Bofinger 1999) for the rest of the period before the launch of EMU in 1999. The graph also shows an increasing disparity between discount rate and rate of inflation but a roughly parallel relationship between the development of M3 and the bank's basic rate for refinancing bank borrowing, though only up until 1994. Despite renewed increases in the money stock after 1995, the Bundesbank continued to lower the discount rate up until the end of 1998, i.e., the 1995 rise in M3 does not trigger the same response as the rises in 1988 and 1989. The discount rate can nevertheless be seen to remain at or above 4.5 per cent until 31 March 1995, almost six years (seventy-one months) after the 21 April 1989 increase to 4.5 per cent. It was the longest and most intense credit squeeze in the history of the Federal Republic and as such raises a set of worrying questions.

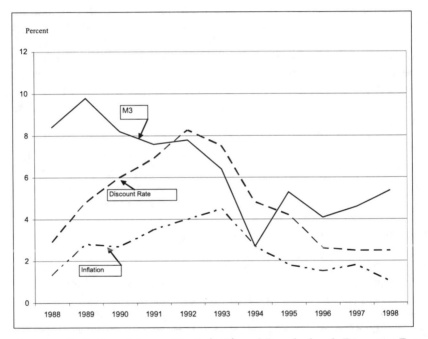

Figure 5.1 Inflation, Money Stock (M3) and Bundesbank Discount Rate 1988–1998
Source: Bundesbank Monthly Reports (various)

- Firstly, in this context, why did Germany's central bank and the dominant central bank in Europe impose a squeeze on corporate and private credit beyond 1990 at a time when East German enterprises, under the weight of increased debt burdens, high costs, collapsing demand and environmental damage, had either already gone bankrupt or had been forced to shed hundreds of thousands of jobs, and when East German GDP had been virtually halved?

- Secondly, why did the Bundesbank persist with a policy of high interest rates, when Germany's fiscal authorities at central, regional and local level, as well as the Trustee Agency as a para-public institution, were obliged to increase their borrowing to cope with both the unavoidable cost of unification and the cost of integrating and supporting hundreds of thousands of ethnic Germans and refugees, thus forcing up the proportion of state expenditure devoted to debt servicing to unprecedented levels?
- Why, thirdly, did the Bundesbank maintain high interest rates pro-cyclically through a period in which thirteen European economies went into recession (See Table 5.4)?

Table 5.4 European Economies in Recession 1990–1993

	European OECD Countries in Recession	Real GDP in percent	Central Bank Discount Rate (end of year)
1990	Greece	-0.1	20.5
1991	United Kingdom	-2.2	10.375
	Finland	-6.1	8.5
1992	Finland	-4.2	9.5
	Iceland	-3.1	
	Sweden	-1.2	10
1993	Belgium	-1.0	5.25
	Denmark	-0.1	6.25
	Finland	-1.2	5.5
	France	-0.8	6.2
	Germany	-0.8	5.75
	Greece	-1.6	21.5
	Italy	-0.9	8
	Portugal	-2.0	13
	Spain	-1.0	9
	Sweden	-2.0	5
	Switzerland	-0.2	4

Source: OECD Economic Outlook Nos 51 & 79; Bank of Finland

There is no simple answer to the conundrum. Its own self-defence that, 'by maintaining a stable environment and trust in the currency, monetary policy serves economic growth and employment' (cf. Deutsche Bundesbank 1994: 63) does not bear close examination. The 'environment' was marked not just by sharp increases in bankruptcies and unemployment across the EC, but by exchange rate mayhem and two significant crises of the EMS. What seems nevertheless to be clear is that Bundesbank policy was, even by its own historically severe standards, out-of-the-ordinary, conforming neither to previous patterns of restrictive behaviour nor to monetarist logic, and certainly not any wise pragmatism ascribed to it by its more ardent admirers (Balkhausen 1992). Arguments identifying a strong political dimension to Bundesbank policy are much more persuasive (Schulmeister 1997; Marsh 1993: 228–55; Leaman 2001: 229–45).

If one looks at the issue of consistency, it becomes clear from Table 5.5 that the deflationary squeeze from 1989 to 1995 was abnormally long and abnormally intense. In the four cases, the highest rate of inflation – in terms of both peak (7 per cent) and average (6.3 per cent) – was in the thirty-one-month squeeze between 1972 and 1975, coinciding with the first oil price shock. The discount rate rose to a peak of 7 per cent in June 1973 and stayed at that level for sixteen months until October 1974, falling in seven stages to 4 per cent by August 1975, the year of severe recession. The intensity of the squeeze, which can be measured by real interest rates or by comparing the average rate of inflation with the average discount rate, was relatively benign (cf. Column 4 Table 5.5). The discount rate was lowered rapidly during 1975 when inflation still averaged 6 per cent, falling to 4.3 per cent in 1976 and 3.3 per cent in 1977. While it can be argued that the Bundesbank took the brakes off too late, it still accepted a relatively high if declining level of inflation. The 1979–83 squeeze was longer (forty-four months) and more intense, with a peak discount rate of 7.5 per cent, which was maintained for twenty-eight months, while inflation levels were lower than 1972–75. The 1989–95 squeeze was almost twice as long as its predecessor and saw the discount rate rise inexorably to its record 8.75 per cent in July 1992, while the maximum rate of inflation was only 4.5 per cent and the average for the whole deflationary period only 2.6 per cent, indicating an intensity which far exceeded anything that had gone before. The global environment of inflation was also much less worrying in 1989 – when consumer prices rises averaged 4.5 per cent across all OECD countries – compared to 1973 (OECD average: 8.1 per cent) and 1979 (8.6 per cent). The Bundesbank itself recorded the continued decline in

Table 5.5 Comparison of Periods of Restrictive Monetary Policy in Germany

Deflationary Period	1 Discount Rate Annual Average (percent)	2 Inflation Rate maximum (year on year in percent)	3 Inflation Rate (RPI) Annual Average (percent)	4 Ratio of 1 to 3
1969-1971: 30 Months	5.85	5.2	3.5	1.69
1972-1975: 31 Months	5.0	7.0	6.3	0.79
1979-1983: 44 Months	6.85	6.3	4.76	1.43
1989-1995: 71 Months	6.34	4.5	2.6	2.43

Source: Deutsche Bundesbank. Monthly Report December 1989 & December 1998, own calculations

import prices in 1990 (-2.3 per cent), 1991 (+0.4 per cent), 1992 (-3.3 per cent) and 1993 (-2 per cent), when they reached a level 21 percentage points below 1985 levels (Bundesbank 1994: 27f), just as it recorded the 20 per cent rise in import prices from 1980 to the beginning of 1984 (Bundesbank 1984: 15).

Price developments within the newly unified Germany were also distinctly different from those of early phases of inflation. Annual real growth in the West in 1990 accelerated to 5.7 per cent, driven by a strong rise in order books for (West) German manufactured goods in 1989 (+11.1 per cent) from both domestic customers (+10.8 per cent) and export markets (+11.5 per cent). Industrial production rose by 5.5 per cent in the West in 1990, notably for consumer goods (+6.3 per cent), fed by the release of East German savings, and domestic order books continued to grow (+5.7 per cent). Foreign orders for German manufactured products, however, began to decline in 1990 and continued to fall for the next three years; by 1993 they were 11.3 per cent below 1989 levels. The decline is explicable both in terms of the 12.8 per cent appreciation of the DM against other EU currencies between 1989 and 1993 and in terms of the growth weaknesses of these countries that by 1994 accounted for 57.8 per cent of all German exports. Upward price pressures after 1989 thus derived from domestic demand, but with marked differences between product and service categories. Building costs soared between 1990 and 1993, reflecting high construction orders, abnormally high growth in bank lending for housing construction (averaging 27 per cent per annum between 1991 and 1993) and a degree of profiteering. The cost of services and repairs, many linked to the construction boom, also grew strongly up to 1994. Foodstuffs and other consumer goods showed fewer inflationary tendencies.

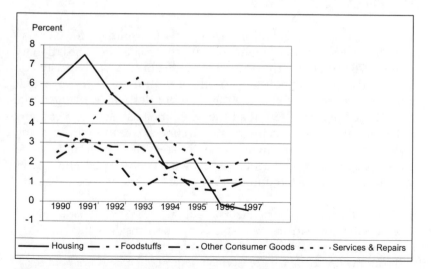

Figure 5.2 Price Developments in Germany 1990–1997
Source: Bundesbank Monthly Reports (various)

A key indicator of underlying inflationary tendencies is the development of factory gate prices which, as Table 5.6 shows, were very modest in the period under discussion, averaging 1.3 per cent in the West in the six years up to 1995 and 1.7 per cent in the East. Inflation in the East was evidently higher in the early stages of unification but this was in large measure the result of the suspension of price controls on rents, power, transport and staple foods, as well as rises in indirect taxes. The cost of living rose by a full 21 per cent in 1991 and a further 11.2 per cent in 1992. However, *price liberalisation in the East was a unique adjustment*; it would not be repeated. Furthermore its effects and those of sharp rises in fuel duty could be expected to be short-lived, given in particular the benign development of import prices and factory gate prices.

Table 5.6 Factory Gate and Consumer Price Trends in Germany 1990–1995

(Figures in percent)							
	Factory	Gate	Prices	Cost	of	Living	Index
Year	FRG	West	East	FRG	West	East	East*
1990		1.7			2.7		
1991		2.5	1.6		3.6	21.3	8.7
1992	1.4	1.4	2.3	5.1	4.0	11.2	4.4
1993	0.2	±0.0	1.9	4.5	3.6	8.8	4.0
1994	0.6	0.6	1.2	2.7	2.7	3.4	2.6
1995	1.8	1.7	1.4	1.8	1.7	2.1	n.a.

* without rent or energy
Source: Leaman, *The Bundesbank Myth*

The medium-term domestic and international environment for German inflation in the 1990s was thus benign, in stark contrast to the stagflationary crises of the 1970s and the early 1980s, and yet the Bundesbank insisted on the appropriateness of its counter-inflationary strategy with particular reference to wages and state borrowing. The Bundesbank's 1990 Annual Report, published in April 1991 at a time when the East German economy was in melt-down, notes correctly the rise in state expenditure in 1990 and the corresponding rise in borrowing by all three levels of government and the prospect of a PSBR of 5 per cent in 1991, against just 0.5 per cent in 1989. It concedes no more than a temporary unavoidable necessity for such action:

At first glance, this kind of deficit might not appear to be extraordinarily high by international comparison, particularly if one considers the current exceptional burden of German unification. As persuasive as this argument might be for the first two years of German unification, it does not hold for future years, when the Federal Republic should not get used to 'standards' of public deficits which will dangerously limit the future latitude of fiscal policy and put excessive burdens on the stabilisation task of monetary policy. (Deutsche Bundesbank 1991a: 31–32)

This warning is repeated several times in the same report (ibid. 26–28) and regularly in subsequent reports (Deutsche Bundesbank 1992: 31–32; Deutsche Bundesbank 1993: 38; Deutsche Bundesbank 1994: 42f). Similar warnings are sounded about the 'high wage increases' in the five new Länder, agreed as part of national bargaining between German employers and trade unions to achieve the speedy convergence of wage levels in East and West. The complex reasoning behind this convergence programme, in particular the desire to prevent further East–West migration and to avoid employer exploitation of low East German wages to reduce West German wage costs, is overlooked. Rather, convergence is seen by the Bundesbank as 'unhelpful' (*wenig förderlich*) to economic improvements in the East (1991a: 23) as a 'key obstacle' to growth (1995: 34). Additionally, however, the Bundesbank urges not narrower but wider wage differentials and flexibilisation of employment throughout the macroeconomy (ibid: 44ff). The Bundesbank's primary time consideration involved the most rapid consolidation of the state's fiscal balances rather than the most rapid macroeconomic convergence of East and West. This constituted a direct and destructive contradiction of the growth imperative, urged by the minority of German Keynesian economists and pursued in a piecemeal fashion by various agencies of government, including central, regional and local authorities, the Unity Fund and the *Kreditanstalt für Wiederaufbau*. The imposition of six years of high real interest rates was fundamentally unconducive to both the growth of economic activity in the East and the convergence of East and West.

The logic of the growth imperative is implicitly rejected by the Bundesbank, but its core arguments were, notwithstanding the unfavourable conditions for economic recovery in the East, arguably more persuasive than the faith in stable money as a vehicle for East Germany's economic transformation. The Keynesian logic, in its pure form, involves the absolute prioritising of growth and the strategic deployment of fiscal resources on a large scale, raising significant volumes of capital through state borrowing. The objective of deficit-financed state intervention is to generate investment, employment, increased productivity and higher state revenue, thereby closing the dangerous demand–output gap in the East and eliminating the fiscal dependency of the East on the West in the medium term. The short-term cost – and the strategic risk – of high state borrowing is, according to this view, neutralised by the consolidation of revenue in the medium term. The strategy obviously assumes a benign monetary policy which both facilitates investment and relieves the cost of debt servicing by both state and private sector through the maintenance of low real interest rates. It constitutes an ambitious programme that is essentially structural economic in nature, i.e., one that targets the fundamental structural deficiencies of the both the regional and sectoral landscape of the eastern region. It was, however, rejected by key institutions of the state, including the federal government and the Bundesbank.

In summary, the central bank's defence of its strategy was highly flawed and in large measure disingenuous in three key respects:

- The national and international environment for medium-term price stability was very favourable; the key determinants of earlier outbreaks of inflation were not present; price rises associated with the end of GDR state controls were predictable and predictably unique.

Table 5.7 Comparison of Money Supply Targets (Percentage Growth) in 1979–1985 and 1989–1995

1979	1980	1981	1982	1983	1984	1985
6-9	5-8	4-7	4-7	4-7	4-6	3-5
1989	1990	1991	1992	1993	1994	1995
5	4-6	3-5	3.5-5.5	4.5-6.5	4-6	4-6

Source: Deutsche Bundesbank. Zeitreihen-Datenbank

- Money supply growth in the period 1989–93 was strong, indeed far stronger in every year except 1993 than the Bundesbank had assumed with its targets (see Table 5.8); special factors – above all the adoption of the DM as alternative currency in several CEECs – help to explain the anomaly. What is noteworthy, however, is that the Bundesbank *made money supply targets for the 1989–95 deflationary period significantly less generous than those of the 1979–83 period;* this would make the likelihood of failure (of perilous looking overshoots) that much greater and therefore the need for Bundesbank toughness ostensibly more urgent (c.f. Bofinger 1997: 220). Given both the particular circumstances and the unrealistic targets, it is arguably no surprise that every M3 growth target was met between 1979 and 1985, but was missed in five out of the seven years between 1989 and 1995 (See Table 5.8).
- Thirdly, in contrast to 1979–83, there was no need to defend Germany's exchange rate against an appreciating dollar or any European currency with interest rate competition in the period 1989–95, nor any urgency to make capital imports more attractive through increases in real interest rates. If anything, the Bundesbank rates promoted excessive imports of liquidity from abroad, putting upward pressure on M3.

Table 5.8 Bundesbank Money Stock Targeting 1988–1998

	88	89	90	91	92	93	94	95	96	97	98
M3 Target (A)	3–6	5	4–6	3–5	3.5–5.5	4.5–6.5	4–6	4–6	4–7	3.5–6.5	3–6
M3 Outcome (B)	8.4	9.8	8.2	7.6	7.8	6.4	2.7	5.3	4.1	4.6	5.4
Target achieved?	N	N	N	N	N	Y	N	Y	Y	Y	Y

Source: Deutsche Bundesbank, Zeitreihen-Datenbank

Returning to Table 5.4, it would be nonsense to suggest that high real interest rates, driven by the Bundesbank, were the dominant factor in causing recessions in all the countries listed, but *there can be little doubt that they compounded existing cyclical weaknesses*; Helmut Schmidt contends that it 'contributed in considerable measure' to Germany's own recession in 1993 and others in the EC (1993: 90). More importantly, Bundesbank rate increases caused serious disruption within the EMS, a fact which brings us closer to an understanding of the bank's otherwise anomalous action during East Germany's transformation crisis.

The Deflationary Politics of Resistance

While Lange and Pugh (1998: 168) judge Bundesbank policy to have enhanced its credibility and its 'reputation for monetary stability', they also concede that 'exceptionally tight monetary policy was in part a "punishment strategy" to offset the potentially inflationary effects of exceptionally loose fiscal policy and exceptional wage pressure' (ibid. 169; cf. also Bofinger 1997: 219). Helmut Schmidt identifies a 'war on two fronts' (1994: 90) against fiscal policy and high wages, but stops short of suggesting punishment or revenge as motive. Schulmeister, in a much less benign account of Bundesbank behaviour than Lange and Pugh, underscores the 'great bitterness' within the Bundesbank over government 'disregard' of its views prior to GEMSU as a reason for its excessively tough monetary policy (1997: 299–300); Marsh talks of serious 'discontent' within the bank over both GEMSU and EMU (1993: 214). The evidence supporting the notion of a 'punishment strategy' informing Bundesbank policy is certainly circumstantial. While there were significant tensions between Kohl and Pöhl over the latter's criticism of federal government policy (Marsh 1983: 217–25) there are no indicators that Kohl sought significantly to modify the Bundesbank's tight monetary policy (as Schmidt had done) or achieve closer coordination between fiscal and monetary authorities; Bickerich (1999: 299) cites a 'personal intervention' by Kohl in the summer of 1992, ignored by the then temporary Bundesbank president Schlesinger, but little else. There is, however, much stronger evidence for a campaign on the part of the Bundesbank to prevent or delay the process of EMU. Indeed, given the entirely anomalous length and intensity of the 1989–95 squeeze, this would seem to be the only satisfactory explanation.

Firstly, there is a clear view, expressed both before and after 1999, that 'the Bundesbank would be the principal loser' in EMU (Marsh 1983: 235; Risse et al. 1999), sacrificed 'on the "altars" of German and European unification' (Schulmeister 1997: 299). Conservative critics of EMU have spoken of the 'disempowerment of the Bundesbank' (Balkhausen 1998; Hamer 2005); one talks bluntly about 'vulgar French national interests: disempowering the Bundesbank and abolishing the D-Mark' (Bayer 1997). Several French commentaries confirm the existence of a Franco-German rivalry – a 'seven years war' (Aeschimann and Riché 1996) – which dominated monetary policy in the 1980s and 1990s and which ended in a French victory and the elimination of German 'monetary semi-hegemony' (Le Gloannec 2001: 126ff).

The perception of a loss of power and of French designs on the DM was certainly strong within the Bundesbank itself. Pöhl is quoted by Marsh, complaining about 'France trying to "get a grip on the D-Mark"' (Marsh 1993: 236); Wilhelm Nölling (1992: 19), the president of the Hamburg Land Central Bank was strongly opposed; he later joined forces with opponents of EMU in an official appeal to the Constitutional Court to prevent ratification of the Maastricht Treaty. Hans Tietmeyer, later president of the Bundesbank, stressed in June 1991 – i.e., before the conclusion of the Maastricht Treaty – that a 'United Germany has much to lose in the forthcoming reordering of European currencies, namely one of the most successful and best monetary constitutions in the world' (quoted in: Marsh 1993: 236).

The prehistory of Bundesbank opposition to supranational controls of national monetary policy is well documented. Given its particular history of success within the post-Bretton Woods world, it is small wonder that it was hostile to initiatives to reregulate currency fluctuations. In its March 1979 Monthly Report, coinciding with the launch of Schmidt's and Giscard d'Estaing's EMS, the Bundesbank poured cold water on the EMS' chances of success. It nevertheless proceeded to adapt to the EMS and 'turn the original concept on its head by making the strongest currency the yardstick of the system' (Pöhl in a speech in Frankfurt, 27 August 1991). After the Delors Report on monetary integration was published in 1988, the Bundesbank warned of 'hasty steps' and asserted that the EMS 'in its current shape offered good framework conditions for the functioning of the internal market' (Bundesbank 1989: 79–80). It repeated its caution and scepticism after the official start of Stage One of the Community's Economic and Currency Union on 1 July 1990, both in an official statement (cf. Bundesbank 1990b) and in its Annual Report for 1990 (Bundesbank 1991: 6–11), setting out a strict set of preconditions for the concrete shape of the policy architecture of any future monetary union.

Open opposition to the EMU project was out of the question, as was any idea that the most powerful central bank in the EMS system might boycott the preparatory work for the Maastricht Treaty. The Bundesbank was in a strategic dilemma having thought that 'nothing will come of EMU' (Otmar Issing, quoted in Marsh 1993: 245). When German unification galvanised decisive support for the scheme from major players like Mitterand and Andreotti, it was 'decided to advance to the head of the movement with the aim of making the Bundesbank's position clear at a European level' (ibid.). The Bank's 'position', however, was disingenuous according to both Schulmeister (1997: 299) and Marsh: 'The Bundesbank's chosen method was to give ostensible backing to the aim of EMU, but to seek to obstruct it by posing conditions which would simply not be acceptable to the other countries' (Marsh 1993: 245). A 'memorable piece of German political theatre' ensued (ibid. 241), 'a struggle over currency union' organised, according to Schulmeister, into five 'acts' (Schulmeister 1997: 299–304). After the initiation of the project (Act One), 'attempts to satisfy the Bundesbank' produced a treaty which reflected precisely the preferences of the German central bank (Act Two): a European Central Bank 'cloned' from the Bundesbank, autonomous, committed only to monetary stability (in contrast to the US Federal Reserve), with free choice of policy instruments. Additionally, membership of EMU would be subject to very strict 'convergence criteria'. Act Three was occupied with the 'monetary division of Europe 1992/93', Act Four by the consequences of tight monetary policy for Germany itself and Act Five, by dint of the article's publication date (1997) an ominous period of austerity combined with high real interest rates, leaving the audience in suspense over the 'ultimate' results of the play's action. Notwithstanding the dramatisation of this crucial period of German and European history, Schulmeister presents a convincing picture of an institution not in sovereign control of macroeconomic affairs, but determined to preserve its dominant position in German and European economic policy, driven by a naked 'instinct of self-preservation'.

The decisive 'act' was the third, the act that would help to explain the anomalous intensity of the Bundesbank's disastrous politics of tight money. It began on 16 August 1991, during the negotiation phase for the Maastricht Treaty, when the German central bank raised its discount rate by a full percentage point from 6.5 per cent to 7.5 per cent with a further hike in the Lombard rate from 9 per cent to 9.25 per cent. This obliged the vast majority of other European central banks to follow suit (see Table 5.8), despite the clear evidence of a continuing cyclical downturn; ignoring the German central bank's move would have put further downward pressure on their exchange rates and endangered both current account balances (higher real import bills, lower real export revenue) and their capital balances, as investors sought higher real earnings in securities denominated in an appreciating DM. When the provisions of the Maastricht Treaty were agreed upon on 17 December the same year, it took the Bundesbank only three days to raise its two key rates by a further 0.5

per cent to 8 per cent and 9.75 per cent respectively, triggering further rises in EMS member states. The combination of weakening real economic activity in Europe and higher real interest rates produced an intensified period of currency speculation, as 'hot money' avoided less promising investments in production and service provision and sought higher gains from exploiting exchange rate disparities and the commitment of European central banks to defend currencies under attack within the narrow bands allowed by the ERM. For example, George Soros used a £10 billion loan to buy DM; after Sterling had fallen against the Mark, he repurchased cheaper pounds and paid back the debt with a net gain of around £1 billion. The exchange rate 'mayhem' (Eichengreen) in the first half of 1992 was compounded by a further raising of the German discount rate to 8.75 per cent on 17 July. Speculation against Sterling, the French Franc and the Italian Lira increased, against the background of bitter wrangles between French and German economic authorities, leading firstly to the devaluation of the Italian Lira within the EMS. After pointed remarks by Helmut Schlesinger about the likelihood that 'one or two other currencies might come under pressure', the pressure on Sterling and the Lira proved too great, despite or because of the half-point reduction in the German discount rate to 8.25 per cent and a quarter point reduction of the Lombard rate to 9.5 per cent on 15 Sept, and both withdrew from the EMS entirely on 16 September. The Spanish Peseta was devalued by 5 per cent the same day and by a further 6 per cent, along with the Escudo, on 22 November. Despite strong economic fundamentals, the Irish Punt was forced to devalue by 10 per cent at the end of January 1993. Peseta and Escudo were devalued again in May 1993. Pressure was then directed on the French Franc, which had been doggedly pegged to the Mark for several years in the name of the *franc fort*. Bundesbank rates were reduced during the course of 1993 but in seven very small steps of no more than half a point each time, despite overwhelming evidence of recessions throughout Europe (see Table 5.4) (rate rises were generally bolder). The effect was to increase speculation against the Franc such that in the first weeks of July DM 107 billion (*sic*) were deployed by EMS states to support the Franc within the EMS. French demands that the Bundesbank should lower the discount rate to take pressure off the Franc were studiously ignored at the Central Bank Council's meeting on 29 July, with the result that the following day the French central bank was obliged to spend FF 150 billion and the Bundesbank DM 30 billion to support the Franc, a record in the history of the EMS. The viability of the system, designed to create exchange rate stability and facilitate convergence à la EMU, was cast into further doubt by the decision on 2 August 1993 to widen the fluctuation bands from +/- 2.25 per cent to +/- 15 per cent. Serious doubts were expressed about an early realisation of monetary union, doubts which were arguably a key objective of Bundesbank policy in this extraordinary period.

The 30 per cent fluctuation band of the recast ERM represented the effective return to floating exchange rates; the exception that proved this rule was the continuing bilateral commitment by Germany and the Netherlands to maintain the narrow bands of fluctuation. Germany's central bank was clearly satisfied with the result: 'The Bundesbank has regained room for manoeuvre in monetary policy through the recent decisions on currency policy' (Bundesbank 1993, August Monthly Report: 25). Ironically, the move to wide bands ended much of the currency speculation that depended so heavily on the commitments of EMS members to support narrow ceilings and floors with reciprocal purchasing of weaker and selling of stronger currencies.

Bundesbank resistance to EMU can certainly be seen in terms of a persuasive logic (Cobham 1997: 36ff); the EU's acceleration of monetary integration was arguably premature, given the very particular circumstances of German unification, whichever policy mix was adopted to resolve the transformation crisis of the former GDR; there were strong doubts about the ability of divergent political economies – notably those of Southern Europe – to achieve a real and sustainable macroeconomic convergence with their northern partners, involving their borrowing cultures, their toleration of inflation and high nominal interest rates; there were further doubts from the monetarist perspective about moving to supranational monetary policy while maintaining national fiscal regimes, i.e., not complementing monetary with political union and common approaches to taxation, borrowing and state investment as in Germany. However, while such arguments are persuasive, the mode of resistance was firstly disingenuous; it masked its motives of self-preservation with specious monetarist logic (Leaman 2001: 238). Secondly, it was economically dysfunctional, inflicting long-term damage on both the German and other European economies. Thirdly, it underscored the democratic deficit of a system, beholden to an unanswerable central bank, be it within the EMS or within EMU at a time when electorates were being asked (or not) to legitimate the move to radical European monetary integration.

The macroeconomic effects of the Bundesbank's dogged deflationary policy on European economies were divisive. Firstly, it ushered in a period of suboptimal annual growth in GDP which has persisted up until today (2009). While inflation has been held at or around target levels, growth has been insufficient to prevent the worsening of structural unemployment: 'Obviously a policy of continuous interest rate increases can slow down inflation, albeit at the price of a recession: this kind of strategy therefore does not specifically attack inflation, but to a certain extent the whole economy' (Schulmeister 1997: 302). Where the primary engines of inflation are seen to be wage costs and deficit spending by state authorities, and high real interest rates over an extended period both reduce incentives to invest in productive capacity and jobs and force states to spend more on debt servicing and less on investment, Bundesbank policy can also be seen as coresponsible for the now chronic asymmetries of demand, where domestic demand factors (enterprises, households, state) are unable to grow as strongly as external demand and economies become increasingly dependent on exports as vehicles of growth (see Chapter Eight).

The policy options chosen by Germany's and the EC's authorities after 1990 were in large measure counter-productive and represent an important stage in the slow unravelling of neoliberalism. The decision to 'complete the Single Market' by moving to monetary integration was predicated on the assumption of the higher growth benefits of 'Europe' and the higher growth costs of 'non-Europe' (Cecchini Report); in fact, aggregate real growth in the economies that stayed out of EMU (Britain, Sweden, Denmark) has been more favourable than growth within the Eurozone. It was also predicated on the assumption that German unification did not constitute a crisis which would affect Germany's ability to function as a locomotive of growth and as dominant net contributor to the Commission's budget. This has been a lamentable example of political blindness. In quantitative terms, German unification costs (at 4–5 per cent of GDP per annum) dwarf anything that the EU (or any of its member states) has ever committed to the long-term development of problem regions. The diversion of financial resources to sustain both consumption and investment in the East represents their nonallocation to investment programmes and consumption in the rest of Germany and/or the rest of Europe; the multiplicator effects of this diversion are at best neutral and at worst seriously negative. Most indicators suggest that the effects have been negative.

Helmut Kohl's own retrospective assessment of the problems of unification acknowledged his misplaced optimism but disingenuously laid the blame on the GDR: 'We didn't know in truth how bankrupt GDR industry really was. Many were entrapped by the legend of the GDR as the "tenth industrial nation of the world"' (Kohl 1998). Wolfgang Schäuble, Kohl's Interior Minister in the transition administration after 21 April 1989 and key negotiator with the de Maiziere administration in the East, is much more honest in his judgement of the situation: 'It was as clear to Lothar de Maiziere as to Tietmeyer and me that, with the introduction of the western currency, east German enterprises would at a stroke no longer be competititive. We were able to imagine the dramatic way in which this "intervention" would become visible' (Schäuble 1991: 99). It is inconceivable that Kohl was immune to the forebodings of meltdown proffered him by senior party members, cabinet colleagues, the Council of Economic Experts, the Academic Subcommittees of both Economics and Finance Ministries and the Bundesbank. It is far more plausible that a politically and electorally astute Chancellor persuaded his own party and his FDP coalition partners that telling the truth about the inevitable high cost of a now unavoidable unification would not enhance their electoral chances. 'Looking on the bright side' was thus shrewd opportunism and excusable as such. What was inexcusable was the failure to manage Germany's unification crisis, to recognise it for what it was: the greatest exogenous shock to Germany's political economy since the Second World War.

Table 5.9 Discount Rates (Central Bank Refinancing Rates) in Europe 1991–1993

	Ger	Aust	B/Lux	Den	Fra	Gre	GB	Ire	It	Neth	Port	Spa	Swe
1991	6.5 (1.2); 7.5 (16.8); 8.5 (20.12)	7 (1.2); 7.5 (16.8); 8 (20.12)	10.5; 7.5 (17.6); 8 (16.8); 8.5 (20.12)	9.5; 9 (22.5); 9.5 (16.8); 9 (21.10); 9.5 (20.12)	9.25; 9 (18.3); 8.75 (17.10); 9.25 (18.11); 9.6 (23.12)	19	12.825; 11.825 (12.4); 11.325 (24.5); 10.825 (12.7); 10.325 (4.9)	11.25; 11 (28.3); 10.75 (9.4); 10.25 (23.7); 10.75 (20.12)	12.5; 11.5 (22.5); 12 (23.12)	7.75 (1.2); 8 (16.8); 8.5 (20.12)	14.5	14.5 (14.2); 13.5 (15.3); 12.75 (16.5); 12.6 (23.8); 12.5 (13.11); 12.75 (23.12)	10 (9.3); 9 (31.5); 8 (3.10)
1992	8.75 (17.7); 8.25 (15.9)	8.5 (17.7); 8.25 (15.9); 8 (22.10)	8.25 (15.9); 8 (16.9); 7.75 (22.10)	11.5 (4.2); 10.5 (22.2)	9.35 (2.11); 9.1 (13.11)		9.825 (5.5); 8.825 (22.9); 7.75 (16.10); 6.78 (13.11)	10.5 (8.5); 10.75 (21.8); 13.75 (28.9); 13 (22.2); 12 (3.3); ??????	13 (6.7); 13.75 (17.7); 13.25 (4.8); 15 (4.9); 14 (26.10); 13 (13.11); 12 (23.12)	8.25 (15.9); 8 (16.9); 7.75 (22.10)		12.65 (14.1); 8.5 (17.1); 12.4 (25.2); 13 (23.7); 13.75 (23.11)	
1993	8 (5.2); 7.5 (19.3); 7.25 (23.4); 6.75 (2.7)	7.5 (5.2); 7 (19.3); 6.75 (30.4); 6.5 (13.5); 6.25 (28.5); 6 (2.7)	7.5 (8.1); 7 (19.3); 6.75 (29.4); 6.25 (28.5); 6 (2.7)	10 (19.3); 9.5 (29.3); 9.25 (23.4); 8.25 (19.5); 8.25 (19.5); 7.75 (8.6); 7.25 (2.7); 9.25 (19.7)	8.25 (29.4); 8 (7.5); 7.75 (13.5); 7.5 (24.5); 7 (21.6); 6.75 (5.7)	20.5 (16.6)	5.825 (26.1)	10.25 (29.3); ??????; 9.5 (5.4); 9 (16.4); 8.75 (26.4); 8.25 (21.5); 8 (31.5); 7.75 (23.6); 7.5 (2.7)	11.5 (4.2); 11 (23.4); 10.5 (19.5); 10 (14.6); 9 (6.7)	7.5 (8.1); 7 (19.3); 6.75 (29.4); 6.5 (13.5); 6.25 (28.5); 6 (2.7)	13.5 (21.5)	13.5 (22.1); 13 (12.2); ???????; 11.5 (14.5); 11.25 (24.5); 11 (2.7)	10 (1.10); 9 (5.1); 7 (2.4); 6 (2.7)

Continued

Table 5.9 *Continued*

Ger	Aust	B/Lux	Den	Fra	Gre	GB	Ire	It	Neth	Port	Spa	Swe
LR: 7.75 (30.7)					21 (13.8)				5.75 (30.7)			
DR (6.75)												
LR: 6.25		10.5 (2.8)									10 (3.9)	
		7 (2.9)										
6.25 (10.9)	5.75 (10.9)	6.5 (10.9)	8.75 (16.9)		22 (4.10)			8.5 (10.9)	5.5 (10.9)		9.5 (14.10)	
			8.25 (27.9)									
			7.75 (12.10)									
5.75 (22.10)	5.25 (22.10)	6 (22.10)	7.25 (22.10)	6.45 (22.10)	21.5 (26.10)			7 (26.10)	8 (22.10)	5.25 (22.10)	13 (2.11)	9.25 (22.10)
		5.5 (18.11)	7 (4.11)	6.2 (3.12)		5.325 (23.11)			5 (3.12)		9 (3.12)	
			6.75 (16.11)									
			6.5 (6.5)									
			6.25 (22.1)									

THE TRANSFORMATION CRISIS IN THE EAST IN AN INTERNATIONAL CONTEXT: 1995–2006

By the end of 1994, as envisaged, the *Treuhandanstalt* had virtually completed its task of disposing of the economic assets of the former East German state. Of the 8,500 enterprises which had passed into the hands of this state holding company on 1 July 1990 – multiplied to 13,781 through separation of parts from whole enterprises – only 140 remained in December 1994 (with some 40,000 employees) to be passed on to its successor institution, the Federal Agency for Special Tasks relating to Unification (*Bundesanstalt für vereinigungsbedingte Sonderaufgaben*); land suitable for commercial development came under the control of the Land Trust Company (*Treuhandliegengesellschaft*) while the remaining holdings of agricultural and forestry land passed to the Company for Land Use and Administration (*Bodenverwertungs- und Verwaltungsgesellschaft*). Birgit Breuel, who had succeeded the assassinated Detlev Rohwedder as president of the *Treuhandanstalt* in April 1991, painted the achievements of the agency and the prospects for the East in glowing terms: 'The catching-up process in East Germany is gaining in tempo and breadth: East Germany as a location for investment is becoming more attractive. Thus the economics research institutes expect growth this year of over 8 per cent' (Breuel 1994: 19). This optimism was echoed by other agencies of the state. However, other observers were less sanguine, the more extreme expressing grim irony of a 'successful operation; patient dead' (poster wording by anti-*Treuhand* protesters). The Bundesbank saw its policies vindicated by low inflation and strong growth in both parts of Germany, but perceived continuing dangers of excessive wage settlements and excessive state expenditure (Bundesbank 1995: 32ff).

With the benefit of hindsight, a truer picture would have to emphasise the continuing wide disparities between East and West and suggest that the foundations for the modernisation of the economy of the eastern regions and their convergence with the West were extremely shaky, however promising three years of strong eastern growth might have led people to believe. In their book published in 1998, Lange and Pugh extrapolated a 'best case scenario' for convergence between East and West, suggesting that 'if we exclude lower growth rates from 1995, complete convergence of per capita GDP with western Germany is projected for the year 2003 and with the three poorest western states by about 2000' (Lange and Pugh 1998: 142). Of course, the joint authors hedged this scenario with serious doubts; a 'lower boundary for plausible estimates' suggested ten to fifteen years, i.e., 2005 to 2010, convergence being conditional on the progress of investment and profitability (ibid. 142f). They nevertheless dissented from the pessimistic view of Barro and Sala-i-Martin (1995), who in 1995 suggested an eighty-four-year long catch-up period, and fixed on twenty to thirty years (2015/2025) as more 'plausible, conditional upon prolonged wage restraint allowing sustained profitability in the eastern enterprise sector'.

If nothing else, Table 6.1 demonstrates the futility of forecasts based on assumptions from short-term trends that Lange and Pugh, with many others, had produced. The heartening levels of real GDP growth in the East in 1992 (7.8 per cent), 1993 (5.8 per cent) and 1994 (9.2 per cent) were firstly from a very low base; GDP per employee in 1991 was just 42 per cent of West German levels, with strong growth and a further decline in employment of 1,018,000 up to 1994, labour productivity increased to 54.3 per cent of Western levels. And secondly, the growth acceleration achieved between 1992 and 1994 was simply not sustained in subsequent years; 1995 produced 5.3 per cent, still 3.5 percentage points above Western growth levels. However, between 1997 and 2005 there has not been a single year in which growth in the East has exceeded 2 per cent and, in five out of the eight years, growth in the West has in fact been higher than in the East. There can never be any convergence without significantly higher growth in the East: it is a mathematical impossibility. The growth is best measured in relation to the overall population of the region, as opposed to labour force, since a calculation that only considered the 80 per cent of the working population in employment would ignore the dependent nonworking population (unemployed, young people, dependent adults and pensioners) and hence the critical disparity between consumption and production (the demand–output gap) which determines the level of fiscal transfers from West to East. On the other hand per capita GDP in the East could be exaggerated by the gradual depletion of the population in the region as a result of East–West migration. Currently, however, labour productivity remains higher than per capita GDP relative to Western levels.

Table 6.1 Development of Main Convergence Indicators in East Germany

(West Germany = 100)	1991	2002
Real Gross Domestic Product per capita of population	33	63
Household Income (net)	54	81
Labour Costs Wage/Salary per worker	49	77
Working Time (annual)	99	110
Productivity (real GDP per member of workforce)	42	72
Unit labour costs	119	108
Investments per capita	66	93
Equipment investments per capita	62	81
Building investments per capita	70	102
Capital stock per capita	38	68
Export ratio	52	61
Research intensity (personnel in R & D)	49	44
Patents per capita	23	25
Scientific expenditure per capita	82	103
Labour participation ratio	96	87
Self-employed ratio	50	88
Unemployment ratio	216	254
Social budget	184	164
Average pension (men)	56	97
Average pension (women)	94	134
Public infrastructure per capita	50	75
Primary tax yield	15	34
Expenditure of Länder per capita	120	139
Indebtedness of Länder per capita	0	114

Source: 'Der Aufbau Ostdeutschlands — struktureller Fortschritt bei wirtschaftlicher Stagnation', *iw-trends 4/2003*, Cologne

Table 6.2 Growth of Real GDP in East*and West Germany 1992–2005

	1992	1993	1994	1995	1996	1997	1998	1999	2000	2001	2002	2003	2004	2005
East	7.8	8.9	9.9	5.3	2.0	1.7	1.0	1.4	1.5	0.0	1.1	1.0	1.9	-0.1
West	1.8	-1.9	2.2	1.6	1.3	2.3	2.2	1.6	3.0	0.6	-0.1	-0.3	1.6	1.0

* Including Berlin; Source: Statistisches Bundesamt

Table 6.1 provides a useful picture of the scale of the 'failure' to achieve economic convergence – as promised by the optimistic forecasts of 1990 and later studies which deemed it at least feasible in the medium term. Per capita GDP grew from 33 per cent of Western levels in 1991 to 63 per cent in 2002; it has continued to rise but at a reduced pace, reaching just 64.3 per cent in 2004. With labour productivity now stagnating at around 72 per cent of Western levels, it has even been calculated that the East–West ratio of per capita GDP will worsen in the medium term, falling to 60 per cent by 2020 (Deutsche Bank Research 2004: 44) or even 57.1 per cent (Mai 2006: 5). It is not difficult to account for the persistence of this key and politically most pressing disparity. When, in 1990, East German wages were firstly converted at 1:1 in the currency union agreement and secondly were set on a convergence path by a series of national branch-based wage agreements between employers and (West German) trade unions, Germany's political economy implicitly committed itself to a high-wage strategy. This kind of strategy was only ever going to be viable if it were accompanied by a corresponding commitment to high levels of investment in high technology and human capital (Lange and Pugh 1997: 120ff). Figure 6.1 indicates that the only area of investment in which the East has exceeded Western levels is in fixed assets, i.e., construction of industrial, commercial and residential property. The construction boom of the early 1990s in the East produced feverish activity peaking at a level of 178 per cent of Western values in 1997, encouraged by direct and indirect fiscal inducements. The result has been a chronic surplus of commercial and residential property, falling prices, bankruptcies among construction companies and briefly (2006) very high vacancy rates of 16 per cent in residential housing. There were in 2006, for example, 1.4 square metres of commercial space per head of population in Germany, compared to 0.8 square metres in Britain (*Die Welt am Sonntag*, 26 March 2006). Leipzig, a city experiencing strong dynamic growth, had a surplus of commercial space of 22 per cent.

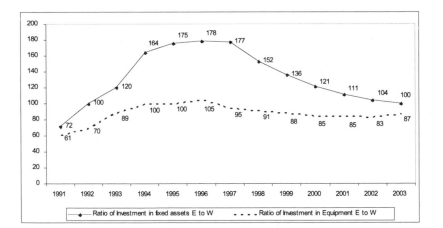

Figure 6.1 Ratio of East German Investments to West German Levels 1991–2003*

* Annual average per capita. Source: Satistisches Bundesamt

Equipment purchases – the key investment factor in any high-tech programme – still lag behind West German levels at 87 per cent (2003) after a brief period of convergence with the West from 1994 to 1996. Overall capital stock per capita has risen, but again only from 38 per cent to 68 per cent of Western levels. The research intensity of German enterprises has even declined from 49 per cent to 44 per cent compared to the West (Table 6.1); industrial and commercial patent registrations are a mere quarter of the West's (albeit very high) output of innovations. Unit wage costs have improved but still exceed West German levels by 8 per cent. There have been prodigious programmes of state infrastructural investments in the East, many of which have resulted in world-class transport and telecommunications in the region, but the total stock of public infrastructural assets per capita in the East is still only three quarters of the West's. Figures like these confirm the deep-seated persistence of East Germany's productivity gap. They also arguably confirm the greater delusions of neoliberal theorists who asserted that sound money and market exposure would be sufficient to effect the required modernisation of the East's productive and commercial apparatus (Kowalski 2004). Figure 6.2 indicates that mining and agriculture are the exceptions that prove the rule, with labour productivity above Western levels in 2003. Manufacturing (72 per cent), construction (61 per cent), transport and commerce (74 per cent), industrial services (73 per cent) and public services (88 per cent) all fall well short of their counterparts in the West.

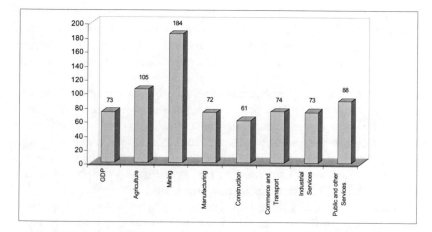

Figure 6.2 Productivity in Individual Branches of the East German Economy 2003 (West Germany = 100)
Source: Ragnitz, Joachim (2005) 'Zur Diskussion um den Produktivitätsrückst and Ostdeutschlands', IWH-Internetpublikation, March 2005

The persistence of low aggregate labour productivity can only be satisfactorily explained with reference to structural economic deficiencies, as well as the absence of coherent structural economic policies in the key initial phase of transformation. Most critical studies of the productivity gap stress key *differences in the scale economies* of the East compared with the West (Ragnitz 2005; Hickel 2001; Mai 2006; Kowalski 2004).

- East German enterprises are smaller on average than their Western counterparts: 63.7 per cent of the East German workforce are employed in enterprises with less than 200 employees (Table 6.3), compared to just 38 per cent in the West, but only 16.8 per cent are employed in companies with a workforce of over 500 (West: 42 per cent). The turnover comparison is even more striking with large companies (500+) in the West accounting for 54.7 per cent of all turnover, compared to just 27 per cent for companies of the same size in the East. Ragnitz (2005: 16) notes that East German companies employing between 300 and 499 achieve higher labour productivity than their Western counterparts. As noted above, productivity in both agriculture and mining – both characterised by high levels of concentration in East Germany – also exceed Western levels.
- Size is a critical advantage in allowing not simply the scale economies of lower overheads per factor of production, but also of allowing both higher levels of self-financing through accumulated reserves and more favourable access to credit and equity financing. Greater size also allows companies to exploit the market power of the supplier (as oligopoly) or of demand (as oligopsony).
- The smaller size of East German enterprises is a function firstly of the privatisation strategy of the *Treuhandanstalt* which, in its efforts to find buyers for state assets, separated the more viable elements of larger enterprises from the less viable elements, sold the former and liquidated the latter. In the process of this 'policy of restructuring and filleting' (Hickel 2001: 7) the East lost the advantages of 'industrial cores' around which component suppliers and industrial services could have been located. The second reason for the smaller scale of economic activity is the simple fact of the numerous new (small) company registrations in the wake of factory closures and workforce shakeouts in the early years of economic transformation. Two out of every three companies in the East were established after unification (ibid. 10).
- The sectoral structure of the East German economy has seen a marked weakening of manufacturing, which in 2003 contributed only 16.1 per cent of GDP (West: 23 per cent) and employed only 15.4 per cent of the workforce: 633,000 workers against 3.34 million in 1989 (Busch 2005: 144). Rudolf Hickel's assessment is entirely appropriate when he says that '(i)n comparison to West Germany an economic structure has emerged which puts downward pressure on productivity. The share of economic branches which are orientated towards the future is too low. Those branches which bring higher productivity are less strongly

represented, while there are more with weak levels of productivity. In the manufacturing sector furthermore R and D-intensity is lower and therefore labour productivity is lower' (Hickel 2001: 10).

- Enterprises in the manufacturing sector with majority West German and foreign parent companies manifest both a higher level of concentration than those under East German ownership and significantly higher levels of productivity than their counterparts in either East or West Germany. The Economics Research Institute in Halle has calculated average productivity levels of 112.7 per cent for companies with majority West German owners and 140 per cent for companies with majority foreign owners compared to the West German average. By contrast the (on average smaller) companies in majority East German ownership achieve only 61.1 per cent of West German levels (figures for 2003 cited in Ragnitz 2005: 14).
- The proportion of parent companies in the East is far lower than in the West. It is in the headquarters in West Germany that 'the functions which enhance productivity are concentrated (marketing, research and development), while the workbenches in East Germany are assigned subordinate, less productive assembly activities' (Hickel 2001: 11). 'The subsidiary neither organizes the control of its commercial activity nor the marketing and distribution of its products. The parent company decides' (Reissig 2000: 56). There is also the danger with arbitrary transfer pricing arrangements that East German subsidiaries lose out to parent companies in revenue distribution. (See also Monopolkommission 2006: 148) Rolf Reissig uses the English term 'branch plant economy' to describe the subordinate character of the region's economy, in which the exceptions like Jenoptik prove the rule (Reissig 2000: 56)
- Disparities in the branch and ownership structures produce in turn disparities in the distribution of the workforce according to skill requirements. While East German enterprises contain employees with executive functions at just over 60 per cent and professionally trained employers at 80 per cent of West German levels, semi-skilled employees are overrepresented at 145 per cent (Ragnitz 2005: 13). Within manufacturing the proportion of staff engaged in research and development constitutes 4 per cent of the total workforce, in the East it is only 3 per cent (Hickel 2001: 11). Ragnitz sees a clear failure to exploit the available (high) level of skills within the East German labour force (Ragnitz 2005: 13). Priewe and Hickel cite the 'widespread loss of the R and D potential of East German enterprises' whereby 80 to 85 per cent of industrial research capacity in the East was liquidated 'with the approval of the Treuhand' – as one of the major deficiencies of the privatisation process (Priewe and Hickel 1994: 74–76).
- A general and now chronic determinant of low productivity in the East is the simple fact that the owners of capital have had a wide range of choices for investing their capital, both in terms of modes of

accumulation (financial or productive) and in terms of where they invest. Potential investors are driven fundamentally by expectations of the optimal valorisation of capital, by the best rate of return on invested capital. For branches which rely on market proximity (retail trade, high street banking, household services) there is a stronger need to locate investments within the five new Länder than, for example, transnational manufacturing companies that use multiple locations according to a variety of supply conditions. For the high-wage strategy implicitly adopted in 1990, the locational attractiveness of East Germany for (inward) investors needed to be outstanding, as did the rate of return; it manifestly is not. With a lower capital stock per head of population, both in terms of public infrastructure and private enterprises, it is inconceivable that the aggregate rate of return on capital could be anything but suboptimal. Unsurprisingly, Karl Mai cites figures for the profit ratio (share of national income from entrepreneurial activity and wealth) in East German Länder, which are not much more than half West German levels. East Germany – without Berlin – had an average profit ratio of 16 per cent in 2003; West Germany, including Berlin, achieved a profit ratio of 29.4 per cent (Mai 2006: 9). At this very basic level, there is a *clear mismatch of the political aspiration to encourage inward investment and the economic logic of capital productivity*, particularly in an era of 'shareholder value' demanding short-term high returns on investments.

Table 6.3 Size of Companies in East and West Germany 2002

Size	Companies		Workforce		Turnover	
Total employees	East	West	East	West	East	West
1-19	60.3	58.9	9.4	5.4	6.2	3.1
20-49	20.3	18.3	16.7	8.9	10.5	5.2
50-99	10.6	10.1	18.6	10.5	14.8	7.0
100-199	5.4	6.4	19.0	13.3	17.7	10.8
200-299	1.8	2.4	11.0	8.7	12.0	8.2
300-499	0.9	2.0	8.5	11.2	11.8	11.0
500 +	0.7	2.0	16.8	42.0	27.0	54.7
Total	100	100	100	100	100	100

Source: Ragnitz 2005

While labour costs are not the exclusive determinants of the preparedness/reluctance of corporations to invest in a particular location, the fact that average East German unit labour costs continue to exceed those of the West by some 8 percentage points (Table 6.1) and that there is a considerable difference between direct and indirect labour costs in the rest of central and Eastern Europe and in both parts of Germany, make the failure to attract inward investment quite understandable (see Table 6.4). The highest level of labour costs in CEECs was found in Slovenia in 2002 with €9.01 per hour or just 45 per cent of East German levels, while the major locations for German foreign direct investment (FDI) in the region – the Czech Republic, Hungary, Poland and Slovakia – had total hourly wage costs of between one-quarter and one-fifth of those in east Germany.

Table 6.4 Total Hourly Labour Costs in Central and Eastern European Countries (2002)

Country	Total €	Direct €	Indirect €	As percent of East G
Slovenia	9.01	5.38	3.63	45
Czech Republic	5.03	2.75	2.28	26
Hungary	5.03	2.82	2.21	26
Poland	4.49	2.82	1.67	23.5
Slovakia	3.46	2.02	1.44	18.1
Estonia	3.19	2.09	1.11	16.7
Lithuania	2.83	1.86	0.96	14.8
Latvia	2.29	1.59	0.69	12.0
Romania	1.46	0.86	0.6	7.6
Bulgaria	1.23	0.73	0.5	6.4
West Germany	31.67	17.84	13.83	
East Germany	19.09	11.65	7.44	

Source: 'Der Aufbau Ostdeutschlands — struktureller Fortschritt bei wirtschaftlicher Stagnation," *iw-trends 4/2003*, Cologne

Table 6.5 The Share of German Companies in Total Foreign Direct Investment in Central and East European Countries

Country	German Share of Total FDI in percent 2000*
Bulgaria (1999 figures)	19.3
Croatia	23.3
Czech Republic	25.5
Hungary	25.8
Latvia	11.1
Lithuania	7.4
Poland	19.0
Russian Federation	7.8
Slovakia	28.7
Slovenia	12.5

* Unless otherwise stated; Source: UNCTAD, *World Investment Directory 2003*

It can therefore come as no surprise that 'efficiency seeking' FDI (UNCTAD 1998: 91) has tended to bypass the five new Länder – with their disadvantages of both high total labour costs and a chronic productivity gap – and head for lower cost locations in Eastern and central Europe, where lower productivity (compared to West Germany) is compensated by labour costs one quarter or less of Western levels (see Table 6.4). The extent of the involvement of (West) German companies in such investment is revealed in Table 6.5, which shows the German share of inward investment in the major CEECs. The overwhelming proportion of all FDI in these countries derives from Western Europe, and within the group German companies stand out as the dominant actors, commanding between around one-fifth and one-quarter of all foreign owned assets in the 2004 EU accession countries. The Netherlands is the only other EU country which comes close to Germany's level of FDI penetration (UNCTAD 2003: 6).

The position of German companies in the CEECs is even more markedly demonstrated by their control of twelve out of the forty (30 per cent) largest foreign affiliates of industrial and tertiary corporations in the region, representing 35 per cent of the turnover of this elite group in 2000, compared to the next largest, the United States with a mere 16 per cent of turnover (UNCTAD 2003: 15).

German FDI penetration mirrors the export penetration of German industrial goods within the transition countries of central and Eastern Europe, where again German presence dwarfs that of any other OECD country. Figure 6.3 shows the high dependency of CEECs on German imports.

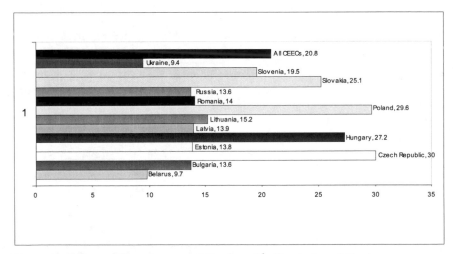

Figure 6.3 German Dominance of Trade with Central and Eastern European Countries Share of Total Imports in 2005
Source: IMF *Direction of Trade Statistics*

More significantly, in this context, is the interaction between the FDI and export strategies of German corporations in the region, as this reflects not just the reluctance to invest heavily in East Germany, but also a partial shift of focus towards increasing FDI in central European locations and exporting from these locations. This is particularly striking in the case of vehicle manufacturing. This is a branch which is not simply central to the economic success of Germany as an industrial trading country but also illustrates key developments in the global political economy. By 2004 Germany's automobile industry with its upstream parts suppliers accounted for 18.1 per cent of all industrial turnover, over 50 per cent of the country's trade surplus and 25 per cent of total manufacturing investment. The automotive branch was responsible for 34 per cent of all industrial research and development. Together with upstream and downstream operations, the vehicles industry employs some 5.3 million workers in Germany, or one in seven of the labour force. In the post-Cold War period, Germany's main vehicle corporations – Volkswagen, Audi, BMW and Daimler-Benz (now Daimler-Chrysler) – have responded aggressively to increased global competition, predominantly through merger and acquisition activity, but also through strategic alliances and the development of extensive supplier networks. This was driven in part by the fear of severe overcapacity in the automotive industry (Sturgeon 1997: 9) and the perceived need to consolidate market positions and restore oligopolistic advantages (ibid. 5). Whereas at the beginning of the 1990s there was limited overseas production by German car companies (the exception being Latin America), major FDI programmes in the Czech Republic, Hungary, Poland and Slovakia produced a situation where, in 2003, German subsidiaries in central and Eastern Europe were producing almost three quarters of a million vehicles a year, of which over a third were imported back into Germany and exports to central Europe stagnated (see Table 6.6).

Table 6.6 Passenger Car Production by German Subsidiaries in Central Europe, China and Latin America 1990–2003 (1000 Units)

	Central Europe			China			Brazil & Mexico		
	Total Prod	Imports from	Exports to	Total Prod	Imports from	Exports to	Total Prod	Imports from	Exports to
1990	0.0	11.0	6.6	0.0	0.0	2.8	425.8	1.3	1.1
1996	240.1	68.9	126.2	226.4	0.0	4.0	735.0	6.9	11.9
2002	782.4	261.6	100.7	437.6	0.3	22.9	799.8	24.0	33.9
2003	733.9	270.6	115.8	624.8	3.5	44.2	716.4	45.5	28.4

Source: Nunnenkamp (2005): 8

The role of German car production units in central and Eastern Europe clearly differs from that in overseas locations, firstly in terms of their integration into a production and trading network; production in China (at 140 plants), Latin America and North America (over 300 plants) supplies predominantly local markets. Secondly, German automotive companies have been engaged in the development of integrated components networks across the whole of Europe, either through direct ownership of preproduct plants, like Audi and Opel in Hungary, or by promoting local supply networks for German subsidiaries, like Volkswagen in the Czech Republic in relation to Skoda. In addition, German car components suppliers have established their own subsidiaries in CECs, employing over 100,000 workers in the region (Nunnenkamp 2005: 14). Within this new integrated European automotive sector, controlled largely by German but also other West European corporations, there has been a marked shift in production patterns away from Western towards CEC locations. According to the Association of German Automotive Producers (VDA), a key factor is the weakness of domestic demand in Germany and the rest of Western Europe:

> (T)he continuing market weakness in Germany has other, further-reaching implications, including economic ones. Over the past decade [since 1994] the relative importance of Germany to the German automotive industry has been continually falling. While production abroad went up by 119 per cent, exports of passenger cars rose by 62 per cent and those of commercial vehicles by 83 per cent, passenger car production in Germany only rose by 27 per cent. Since 1994 foreign turnover has gone up by 168 per cent, i.e. more than twice as much as domestic turnover, which rose by 68 per cent. This means that Germany as an automotive location is coming under pressure in the long term just as much as the whole European industry in relation to the whole EU. (VDA 2005: 4)

Thus, while a number of German car manufacturers have established production units in East Germany – Volkswagen in Chemnitz, Mosel and Dresden; BMW in Leipzig; Opel in Eisenach – these subsidiaries are dwarfed by the companies' presence in CECs. For example, Volkswagen employs some 8,100 workers in its East German plants but over 20,000 in Poland, Slovakia and Hungary and 23,400 in the Czech Republic. BMW's decision to open a plant in Leipzig employing up to 5,500 workers was not unconnected with the offer of a €360 million grant from the Land of Saxony, approved by the EU, just as Volkswagen's decision to open a factory in Slovakia was sweetened by ten years exemption from taxation.

The tension (or indeed contradiction) between the political imperative of attracting inward investment and the microeconomic imperative of maximising returns on invested capital could not be better illustrated than by the bargaining between fiscally hard-pressed territorial authorities and cash-rich car corporations. The extreme supply-side subsidies offered by the Republic of Slovakia have succeeded in attracting firstly Volkswagen and subsequently Hyundai, Kia and Peugeot with both tax breaks and direct grants, primarily as a means of reducing unemployment levels in this 'transition country' which averaged 18.5 per cent between 2000 and 2004. The car lightbulb producer, Osram Slovakia, part of the Siemens group, was provided with a direct grant of €153.2 million towards a €380 million production facility (*Sita Special* 17–23 August 2004), i.e., a full 40 per cent of the total cost. In 2004, the general government debt in Slovakia was 3.8 per cent of GDP. By March 2006, the Volkswagen corporation had net financial reserves of €4.4 billion. Siemens, in its 2005 annual report, noted total financial reserves, including equities, of €9.91 billion; its Osram division recorded an annual profit of €465 million the same year (Siemens 2005). BMW recorded profits of €3.383 billion in 2004 and by 2005 could boast net financial assets of €4.877 billion, while the Land of Saxony had a per capita debt of €2,849 in 2004 and a rate of unemployment of around 20 per cent.

An interesting development within the Volkswagen Group came in 2002 when it shifted 10 per cent of the production of the SEAT *Ibiza* model from its plant in Martorell, Catalonia, to its Bratislava factory, stating the failure of negotiations with Martorell Workers' Committee over flexible working as the reason for the relocation and emphasising that, 'if demand falls it will be the Martorell plant that reduces production' (EIRO Online, 25 October 2002).

A Promising Location in an Even More Promising Global Environment

In a study of East Germany's potential locational advantages, commissioned by major cities in the five new Länder, KPMG examined the relative attractions of the region with those of East European cities, including Bratislava, Košice, Warsaw, Riga and Tallinn. The study's conclusions are positive but still little comfort to the commissioning parties as it acknowledges the attractiveness of East Germany, above all for enterprises interested in higher technology operations that are less sensitive to wage costs, but it also acknowledges that 'location competition remains fierce and the analyses of this study show that East European cities are also endeavouring to improve the framework conditions and thus to increase their attractiveness for investors' (KPMG 2006: 23). In order to achieve sustained successes, both political and private agents 'must cooperate intensively and concertedly'. What the KPMG study does not point out, however, is that *the cooperation of private economic and public political agencies is fundamentally asymmetrical.* There is an unequal interdependence between the territorially bound (political) locations and the territorially and strategically mobile transnational corporations, which can and does allow public money to boost the profitability of corporations, either by foregoing taxation revenues or by relieving companies of investment costs or recurrent costs (through wage subsidies etc.). BMW is reported to have had seven options in the programme that eventually led to the Leipzig deal. In all seven cases there was evidence of taxpayers' money being offered to induce a favourable decision. The vaunted claim that BMW was manifesting some kind of German patriotism (Fischer 2004) is dented not just by the hard bargain struck with Saxony and Leipzig but also by the fact that as a corporation it has done its best not to pay taxes in Germany (Eissel 1997: 138f). Eissel quotes the BMW finance director, Volker Doppelfeld, who openly admitted that, 'we try to generate costs in places where the taxes are highest, and that is in the domestic market' (ibid. 139).

Internal transfer pricing has been one of the main tricks in this 'patriot's' toolkit. This involves adjusting the price of goods and services that are traded between subsidiaries of the same company that are based in different national locations, allowing a higher loading of costs in those locations with less generous tax regimes and a lower cost-loading in lower tax regimes. Reducing tax liabilities within high tax territories increases the aggregate profit across the whole corporation. In the 1990s, transfer pricing was arguably one of four key commercial features of nonfinancial FDIs, the other three being market proximity, maximisation of cost advantages at specific locations (above wages and preproducts) and the avoidance of import duties. Arguably the 'reform' of tax regimes within the OECD – above all the reduction of corporation tax and other taxes on business income – has been a direct consequence of the tax avoidance strategies of TNCs embodied in transfer pricing. For example, the average level of corporation tax within the EU-15 fell from 44.8 per cent in 1980 to 28.5 per cent in 2005 (Schratzenstaller 2004). Between 1985 and 2004 the average level for the top rates of income tax, paid by non-incorporated (smaller) businesses, fell in the EU-15 from 62.3 per cent to 46.2 per cent (Giegold 2005: 1). German taxation policy has, if anything, been even more generous in relation to the tax burdens of corporations and non-incorporated businesses. From the heady days of the 1960s when corporation tax and assessed income tax accounted for 24.5 per cent of all tax revenues, or 1980 when they still represented 17.2 per cent, the reforms of the 1980s and 1990s have reduced revenues from these sources dramatically *and deliberately*, to 13.1 per cent in 1990, 8.2 per cent in 2000 and 6.2 per cent in 2005; as noted in Chapter Three it is part of an overall programme of supply-side relief for 'wealth creators' and employers. The fact that national tax authorities, with the help of the OECD (2005), have more recently introduced stricter policing of tax avoidance through transfer pricing, is arguably a glaring case of closing the stable door after it has been left open for a considerable time. There is nevertheless still enough latitude within the system to warrant the use by corporations of the extensive and expensive services of big global accountancy firms, as advertised by KPMG on its website:

> The Global Transfer Pricing Services Team develops concepts for the implementation of tax-optimized intra-group transfer pricing systems. Then precisely with the formation of foreign subsidiaries and permanent establishments the question arises of how to properly structure and account for the intra-group flow of products and services. For this purpose, we conduct margin analyses, royalty computations, and provide particular assistance in the creation of transfer pricing documentation systems. (http://kpmg.de/lib/search.asp)

Even in the context of Germany's ongoing taxation reform, the ability of East German locations to attract investment has remained highly problematic, particularly given the increasing popularity among CEECs of 'flat tax' regimes with lower rates of both corporation tax and personal income tax than anywhere in Western Europe. Pioneered by Estonia and Lithuania in 1994, there are flat tax regimes in nine countries of central and Eastern Europe. So extraordinary has been the spread of nonprogressive schemes of income taxation that their attractions have been debated in several West European states, including Germany during the 2005 national elections. While the idea was rapidly abandoned by the opposition CDU in its electoral campaign, the very fact that it should have been discussed at all in a country with an historically steep curve of progression is astonishing. It clearly betokens the anxiety of German politicians over the increasing pace of tax competition in Europe.

Foreign perceptions of the rival attractions of Europe's locations for FDI are therefore unsurprising and explain the predicament of the five new Länder: 'Eastern Europe's cheaper labor market and growing reliance on flat taxes leave Western European economies struggling to compete' (*Christian Science Monitor*, 8 March 2005). The International Labour Organisation notes that 'the new EU Member States show a significant advantage in terms of international competitiveness with unit labour costs 70 per cent of the US level' (ILO 2005). The *Financial Times* FDI Report is unequivocal: 'The hit parade of foreign investment in Europe shows that FDI flows are moving east. The combination of cheap and often highly skilled labour, low taxation and attractive incentives is changing perceptions of the newly developing economies of central and eastern Europe' (www.fdimagazine.com, 3 October 2005). The Ernst and Young 'European Attractiveness Survey' from 2005 found that '52 per cent of international business executives survey regard this 'new Europe' as the top destination for expected investments over the next three years' (cited in www.fdimagazine.com, 3 October 2005).

Table 6.7 'Flat Taxes' in Central and Eastern Europe

Country	Corporation Tax	Value Added Tax	Personal Income Tax
Estonia	0 *	18	23**
Lithuania	15	18	27
Latvia	15	18	25
Russia	24	18	13
Serbia	10	20	14
Slovakia	19	19	19
Ukraine	25	20	15
Georgia	20	18	12
Romania	16	19	16

* For retained earnings only; ** set to decrease to 20 percent by 2009
Source: IMF

Such perceptions are qualified by the more hard-nosed entrepreneurial spirits, like those in the German Textile and Fashion Confederation which, while conceding that labour costs in CEECs are still a fraction of Western levels, suggest that they, 'have forfeited a part of their competitive advantage' (www.textil-online.net/englisch/Press/E1429.htm). This perception cannot be unconnected with the fact that the main FDI destination for the German Textiles Industry since 2000 has been China (ibid.); by 2004 Chinese textiles exports dwarfed those of every other country in the world. It comes as no surprise that East Germany which, before the division of Germany in 1949, had a thriving textiles sector employing hundreds of thousands of skilled workers, only employed 16,298 people in the whole branch in 2004 (GDTM 2005: Statistical Appendix: 10).

The persistence of high unemployment, sluggish high technology investment and the demand–output gap in the five new Länder can be seen as the consequence of an unfortunate set of coincidences. Political failure – the choice of an entirely inappropriate policy mix – was probably the most avoidable of the misfortunes that have been visited on the economy and working population of the East. As the above analysis demonstrates, East Germany has been bypassed in large measure by 'efficiency seeking' or 'rent seeking' capital because capital is mobile and has a wide choice of investment locations and investment modes.

The most mobile of Germany's companies tend to be the biggest, which tend also to be the most dependent on exports. Their behaviour is indicative of the general trends of employment and investment, arguably prefiguring the future behaviour of other, smaller enterprises. Thus between 2002 and 2004 there was a 4.17 per cent decline in jobs in Germany that were covered by standard social insurance arrangements; the decline within the top 100 enterprises in Germany was 8.28 per cent, ascribed

Table 6.8 The Fifty Largest German Industrial Companies 2004 by Domestic and Global Turnover (€ Million)

	Company		Domestic Turnover €Millions	Global Turnover €Millions		Company		Domestic Turnover €Millions	Global Turnover €Millions
1	Volkswagen	A	67 220	88 963	26	Porsche	A	5 774	6 359
2	Daimler-Chrysler	A	61 548	142 059	27	Heraeus Holding	Im	5 623	8 338
3	BMW	A	41 508	44 335	28	EADS (D)	Ae	4 322	31 761
4	Siemens	E	41 000	75 167	29	Boehringer KG	Ph	4 314	8 157
5	E.ON	P	31 388	49 103	30	Philips (D)	E	4 268	30 319
6	BP (D)	O	29 276	216 645	31	Motorola (D)	El	4 235	23 805
7	RWE	P	28 178	40 996	32	Tchibo Holding	Cg	4 235	8 330
8	Robert Bosch	E	27 622	40 007	33	St Gobain (D)	Im	4 093	32 025
9	Shell (D)	O	26 093	201 544	34	Linde AG	En	4 074	9 421
10	ThyssenKrupp	St	22 081	39 342	35	BSH (Bosch-Siemens)	E	3 629	6 884
11	BASF	C	15 216	37 537	36	Nokia (D)	El	3 581	29 267
12	General Motors (D)	A	14 341	147 073	37	Nestlé (D)	F	3 555	56 200
13	RAG	P	14 285	18 697	38	Unilever (D)	F	3 199	40 169
14	Ford (D)	A	13 800	111 822	39	Dow (D)	C	3 137	30 522
15	Bayer	C	13 670	29 758	40	Sanofi Aventis	Ph	3 100	15 043
16	Vattenfall	P	10 706	10 706	41	Henkel	C	3 097	10 592
17	Exxon (D)	O	9 142	221 352	42	Stadtwerke Köln	P	3 026	3 026
18	Energie Bad-Württ	P	8 720	11 177	43	Roche (D)	Ph	3 005	20 256
19	Total (D)	O	8 500	122 700	44	Stadtwerke München	P	2 949	2 949
20	Altria (D)	To	8 434	68 104	45	EWE AG	P	2 876	5 955
21	MAN	En	8 060	14 947	46	Bilfinger Berger	B	2 864	5 438
22	ZF Friedrichshafen	Ap	7 359	9 899	47	Arcelor (D)	St	2 842	30 176
23	Continental AG	Ap	6 734	12 597	48	Benteler	En	2 785	4 450
24	IBM (D)	It	6 541	73 183	49	Oetker KG	F	2 729	6 434
25	Hewlett-Packard (D)	It	5 905	60 728	50	ABB (D)	En	2 687	15 748

A: Automotive; Ae: Aerospace; Ap: Automotive Parts; B: Construction; C: Chemicals; Cg: Consumer Goods; E: Electro-technical; El: Consumer Electronics; En: Engineering; F: Food Manufacturing; Im: Industrial Materials; It: Information Technology; P: Power generation; Ph: Pharmaceuticals; St: Steel; To: Tobacco
Source: Monopolkommission 2006

correctly by Germany's Monopoly Commission to increased foreign outsourcing (Monopolkommission 2006: 187f). In the same period the top ten German corporations raised the proportion of their net foreign earnings from 43.3 per cent to 69.8 per cent of domestic earnings. Individual companies, most notably in the chemical sector, generate more than half of their turnover abroad: for example, BASF (59.5 per cent), Bayer (54.1 per cent) or Henkel (70.8 per cent) with production locations in dozens of foreign countries. Yet others are part of giant global corporations whose investment decisions are even less driven by any sense of national identity (see Table 6.8). The traditional view of *Deutschland AG*, of a national political economy which operated as a 'joint stock company' (AG) promoting the interests of its 'shareholders' – the citizens – was never a particularly appropriate metaphor to describe the oligarchic character of corporate ownership, control and strategy in the Federal Republic. But it is arguably even less appropriate today in the era of shareholder value, where the ownership structures of German and 'foreign' corporations show an increasing degree of both internationalisation and 'rent seeking'.

Anke Hassel et al. (2000: 98ff) have produced figures for the degree of international penetration into German large companies, which mirrors the penetration of German capital into foreign corporations. While the hostile takeover of Mannesmann by Vodafone AirTouch in February 2000 was widely interpreted as the breaching of the hitherto impenetrable walls of a German corporate fortress, the reality of extensive foreign holdings in Germany's top companies told a different story.

The majority of Mannesmann shares (62 per cent) were already in foreign hands before the takeover. Table 6.9 indicates the extent of foreign penetration in 1998, before the acceleration of reciprocal FDI activity (Bundesbank 2006). Brakman et al. (2005: 6), in their study of cross-border mergers, note that in the merger waves between 1981 and 1998, a good third were cross-border takeovers. Between 1987 and 1997, MandA deals averaged 57 per cent of global FDI. In the big merger wave from 1998-2001, this rose to 76.23 per cent for global FDI and a full 88.96 per cent for FDI in developed countries.

The stock of German FDI more than doubled from around €300 billion in 1998 to a peak of €700 in 2001 and stood at €677 billion in 2004 (1990: €116 billion), compared to foreign FDI holdings in Germany of 'only' €345 billion (1990: €85 billion) (Bundesbank 2006: 46ff). The ratio of German FDI to inward investment into Germany thus shifted from 136 per cent in 1990 to 196 per cent in 2004. This is clear evidence of the effect of internationalisation on the strategic behaviour of both 'German' and 'foreign' transnational corporations. Germany remains a significant location for foreign companies, but the trend indicates a widening gap between FDI inflows and FDI outflows (higher net outflows). The branch distribution of German FDI stocks is illuminating. On the one hand they are dominated by the service sector in value terms (71 per cent of total), compared to only 25 per cent for the manufacturing sector. On the other hand, manufacturing accounts for 57 per cent of all employment in German FDI, with 17 per cent alone in vehicle manufacturing (Bundesbank 2006: 49). The key independent variables for explaining this anomaly have got to be the high labour intensity of the manufacturing operations and the lower cost of labour in the host countries, a fact conceded by the Bundesbank in an otherwise benign commentary on the 'macro-economic effects' of recent German FDI activity (ibid. 49). It is certainly no coincidence that the workforce of German manufacturing companies' is equivalent to one-third of the respective workforce in Germany; in the chemical and automotive industries the ratio is around three-quarters (ibid. 51).

Table 6.9 Foreign Holdings in Major German Companies (1998)

Company	Foreign Holding in percent	Company	Foreign Holding in percent
Allianz	19.6	Mannesmann (now part of Vodafone)	62.0
BASF	30.4	Metallgesellschaft (now mg-technologies)	65.0
Bayer	46.6	Metro	24.0
Bilfinger & Berger	25.0	Munich-Reinsurance	23.0
BMW	32.7	Preussag (now TUI)	24.3
Commerzbank	38.0	Rheinmetall (Röchling Group)	22.0
Daimler-Benz (now Daimler-Chrysler)	36.0	RWE	22.8
Degussa (now part of E.ON)	18.0	SAP	36.6
Deutsche Babcock (Babcock-Borsig)	45.0	Schering	41.0
Deutsche Bank	41.0	Siemens	38.0
Deutsche Lufthansa	29.4	Spar	25.0
Dresdner Bank (now part of Allianz)	25.0	Telekom AG	45.0
Hoechst (now part of Aventis)	48.0	Thyssen (now ThyseenKrupp)	18.0
Linde	31.0	VEBA (merged with VIAG to form E.ON)	44.0
MAN	15.0	VIAG (merged with VEBA to form E.ON)	23.9

Source: Hassel, A. et al. 2000; Liedtke 2001

In summary, the structural problems of Germany's political economy, but notably of the five new Länder, have not been helped by globalisation, by the internationalisation of capital, by the competition of other national locations for inward investment, nor by the policy architecture maintained by the German state and subsequently mimicked within the eurozone. In the absence of a coordinated and, yes, mercantilist strategy aimed at neutralising the asymmetries of productivity, investment, scale economies, regional and sectoral distribution, the working population of both East and West Germany will remain caught in a now endemic contradiction between the territorial logic of politics – which seeks to promote growth and employment within Germany – and the economic logic of capital, which is targeted at the maximisation of returns on investments for its limited group of shareholders. The internationalisation of capital through mergers and acquisitions, through intensified trade, through multi-locational production and distribution and through global financial markets, compounds this endemic contradiction.

The next chapter seeks to outline the way in which the German state, along with other states, has responded to the effects of this contradiction, notably through the modernisation of its 'social democratic' agenda.

SQUARING THE CIRCLE: POLITICO-ECONOMIC TRENDS IN THE SCHRÖDER ERA

The federal election results of September 1998 arguably represented a defeat for Kohl's second postunification administration, as it did a victory for the resurgent SPD. The CDU/CSU achieved their worst result since 1953 with just 35.2 per cent of the vote. The SPD, with an additional forty-six seats in the Bundestag and 40.9 per cent of the vote, and the PDS with six more seats were the clear beneficiaries of the CDU/CSU's failure to deliver the promised 'blossoming landscapes' in the East and the removal of unification burdens on Western taxpayers. The CDU/CSU retained its strongholds in Bavaria, Baden-Württemberg and the Rhineland-Palatinate but lost the bulk of its constituencies in the East and key seats in Schleswig-Holstein, the Saarland, Hessen, Northrhine-Westfalia and Saxony. The formation of the first Red–Green coalition (SPD/Alliance '90/The Greens) was also favoured by the existence of an SPD majority in the Federal Council (Bundesrat), which promised, theoretically at least, an easier passage for its legislative reforms. The coalition programme was focused on ambitious, incremental tax reforms, pensions, family policy and employment policy; at a meeting of the federal government with employers' organisations and trade unions on 7 December 1998, an 'Alliance for Work, Training and Competitiveness' was established, with special working groups concerned with marginal wage costs, the flexibilisation of working lives and business taxation. The coalition was also favoured by a slight improvement in the rate of real GDP growth in 1998 (to 2 per cent) and a slight fall in aggregate unemployment (down from 12.7 per cent in 1997 to 12.3 per cent in 1998). This 'fair wind' for the new coalition was, however, not helped by arguments within the cabinet, firstly over nuclear energy and then over Europe; Oskar Lafontaine's demonstrative resignation as Federal Finance Minister in March 1999 dealt a severe blow to hopes of a combative fiscal policy at national and

European level. The surprise victory of the CDU in the Hessen Land elections in February 1999 – after a decline in the Green vote – also removed the SPD majority in the Bundesrat. The scene was set for seven strange years of social democratic 'modernisation'.

In fact, the party-political impasse of a federal government 'checked' by an opposition majority in the Bundesrat – a fate endured by Schmidt before 1982 and latterly by Kohl as well – merely reinforced the extremely limited room for manoeuvre allowed by Germany's extreme federalism, by the erosion of the nation-state as a result of globalisation, by the macropolitical primacy of 'stable money' and the transfer of monetary sovereignty from the Bundesbank to the European Central Bank on 1 January 1999, just three months after the formation of a 'Red–Green ' administration. Lafontaine's withdrawal was arguably driven as much by the realisation of his political powerlessness in this unfriendliest of contexts (and the likelihood of being associated with failure) as with any issues of political principle. Suffice it to say, his successor Hans Eichel was a more willing accepter of the politico-economic straitjacket that 1999 offered the Schröder administration. The rhetorical centrepiece – 'the central commitment of government policy' (Eichel cited in Müller 2006: 107) – of the coalition agreement was the reduction of mass unemployment; Schröder even set the halving of unemployment within the first legislative period as the yardstick by which he wished to be judged at the next elections in September 2002 (Butterwegge 2005: 160ff). The objective was understandably 'central': an average of 4,279,288 citizens without jobs in 1998, 992,522 in job-creation schemes and 115,205 on short-time represented a massive waste of human skills and a cultural catastrophe in an affluent society. The means to fulfilling the objective remained the traditional vehicle of macroeconomic growth, which needed to be sustained at a minimum of 2 per cent per annum over the medium term in order to be successful. More significantly, the policy mix adopted by the Red–Green coalition manifested strong elements of continuity from the Kohl administration that it had just replaced. Even more significantly, the reform programmes instituted between 1999 and 2005 by the Red–Green coalition were more radical, more thoroughgoing, more extensive and more ruthless than anything that the four Kohl administrations had managed in their sixteen years of power.

The new administration did manage to revoke some of the social policy measures of the previous Kohl government, including restrictions on sick pay entitlement, reductions in employment protection, reductions in free entitlements in dental treatment and increases in prescription charges. Recent reductions in pension entitlements were also reversed, as were the measures setting severance pay against unemployment benefit entitlement (ibid. 159). Nevertheless, the key thrust of the macroeconomic policy mix of 'Red–Green ' corresponded to the logic of 'location competition' which had dominated federal policy since the early 1980s: private enterprises must be induced to invest in new capacity and new jobs by rendering the 'supply-side' conditions optimal, i.e., by contributing to the reduction in employers' costs. The logic of this position was supported by the explicit espousal of a 'new supply-side agenda for the Left', as laid out in the so-called Schröder–Blair Paper, published in the summer of 1999 after the supposedly epochal meeting of the two modernisers of social democracy (Blair and Schröder 1999). The new supply-sidism of Germany's Left – which, *nota bene*, was actively shared by the modernising 'Realos' within Alliance '90/The Greens – was most clearly evident in the reform measures covering taxation (1999–2005), pensions (2000–2001) and the labour market (2002–2005). Each set of measures reflects not simply the surprising degree of continuity in policy preferences from 1982 to the present day, but the implicit redefinition of the concept of social justice traditionally associated with 'social democracy'.

Taxation Policy

As noted above, the Red–Green coalition was operating within the parameters of a supranational monetary policy which gave absolute primacy to price stability – in the institutional form of an independent European Central Bank – and which was supported both by the strict convergence criteria of the 1991 Maastricht Treaty (notably national commitments to a PSBR ceiling of 3 per cent of GDP and an overall state debt ratio of 60 per cent of GDP) and by the more recent commitment to budgetary consolidation and balanced budgets in the medium term, set out in the 1997 Stability and Growth Pact (SGP). On 4 January 1999, parallel to the start of EMU, Schröder's federal cabinet, still including Oskar Lafontaine as Finance Minister, underscored its commitment to the SGP in a public statement of intent to reduce government spending increases to 2 per cent per annum, to reduce the PSBR to 1 per cent of GDP by 2002 and to reduce the overall state debt ratio to 59.5 per cent by the same date (Bundesbank 2000: 96). This commitment to 'consolidation' (qua austerity) is the point of departure for the subsequent wave of tax reforms. Only two months later, on 3 and 4 March, the Bundestag allowed the passage of two key tax reform laws:

- The Law governing the Implementation of Ecological Tax Reform, which imposes a new levy on electricity generation with the explicit objective of reducing pension contributions by 0.8 percentage points to 19.5 per cent of gross wages and salaries. This hypothecation of an environmental tax as an additional federal subsidy for the statutory pensions insurance system was applauded by employers as a first step towards reducing the burden of indirect labour costs, where they had hitherto been obliged to fund 50 per cent of employees' pensions contributions, but was criticised by environmentalists as an inappropriate use of a tax that could/should have been deployed to promote environmental policies. The 'Ecological Tax Reform' is extended in August 1999 by fixing tax increases for oil and related fuels of six pfennigs a litre for the four years 2000–2003 and of five pfennigs per KwH per annum for electricity over the same period.

- The Law governing Tax Relief 1999/2000/2002 which envisages incremental reductions in the marginal rates of income tax at both the top and the bottom end of the line of progression, accompanied by the abolition/reduction in business related tax allowances. Basic allowances, however, are to be raised, as are children's tax allowances/child allowance. The cumulative net relief effect of this three-stage reform is set at around DM 20 billion (c. €10 billion). In December 1999 the federal cabinet agrees to bring forward the third stage of income tax relief from 2002 to 2001 and sets a longer term target for the reduction of marginal rates from 53 per cent to 45 per cent at the top of the line of progression and from 25.9 per cent to 15 per cent at the bottom by 2005. The additional measures would produce total net relief of DM 42.5 billion. In the succeeding months the opposition Union parties (CDU/CSU), by dint of their majority in the Bundesrat, invoke the Mediation Committee and negotiate above all a further flattening of the curve of progression – with a top rate of income tax of 42 per cent by 2005 – and particular relief measures for the self-employed.

These two key elements of taxation reform were supplemented by a radical modification of corporation tax in proposals published in December 1999, following the so-called Brühl Recommendations of the Working Party on Business Taxation. The reform would introduce a unitary rate of corporation tax of 25 per cent for both retained profits (previously 30 per cent) and distributed profits (hitherto 45 per cent); additionally, it proposed the removal of capital gains tax liability for profits deriving from the disposal by German enterprises of parcel holdings in other domestic enterprises. The introduction of this flat rate, which brought German capital tax levels towards the bottom of the EU league, was flanked by reductions in offset allowances. Nevertheless, the two central measures produced reactions of amazement on the side of Left-leaning critics of the government (Schratzenstaller 2000; Hickel 2000; Eissel 2004) and an almost equally astonished euphoria on the part of corporations and their shareholders; after the publication of the proposals, share prices on Germany's stock markets rose markedly before and after Christmas 1999 (Butterwegge 2005: 173). The corporation tax and capital tax changes came into force on 1 January 2001; there was a partial modification of corporation tax in January 2003, when a temporary supplementary levy of 1.5 per cent was introduced to provide relief for the August 2002 floods in East Germany, but the overall effect of the reduction in corporation tax and of top-rate income tax has been a marked reduction in revenues from business taxation. Figure 7.1 indicates the gradual shift of burdens from direct to indirect taxes, with VAT accounting for over a quarter of all revenues (26.1 per cent) in 2005 after 15.4 per cent in 1990; secondly it shows the marked downward trend of revenues from both assessed income tax and corporation tax from a combined 17.2 per cent of all revenue in 1980 (1966 24.4 percent) to 7.9 per cent in 1999 to just 6.3 per cent in 2005. In the first year of tax reform 2000, the state even paid back corporation tax to companies, producing a combined net share of just 2 per cent of total tax revenue for corporation tax and assessed income tax. The share of income tax from wages and salaries (equivalent to PAYE)[1] peaked as a proportion of total tax revenue in 1990 at 35.1 per cent and, as a result of the Red–Green reform measures, fell to 28.6 per cent in 2005. The share of mass taxes (wages tax, VAT, import turnover tax, oil and tobacco duties) increased to 74 per cent in 2003, while the share of corporation tax, assessed income tax and capital gains tax was just 6.7 per cent (1991: 12.9 per cent).

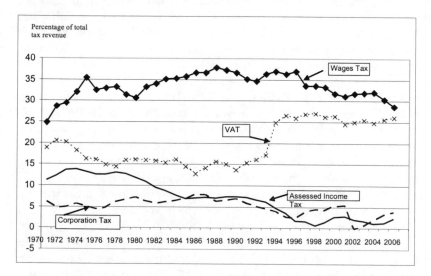

Figure 7.1 Proportion of Individual Taxes in Total Tax Revenue 1970–2005
Source: Statistisches Bundesamt; own calculations

---

1. PAYE (pay as you earn) is the main form of wage and salary taxation in the United Kingdom and is levied at source by employers for the state's Customs and Revenue service.

While the share of business income taxes (corporation tax and assessed income tax) has fallen significantly, the share of local business tax (*Gewerbesteuer*) remained relatively constant in the period of the Red–Green coalition, averaging around 5.5 per cent of total revenue, albeit down from 7.4 per cent in 1980. More significant from the point of view of the functioning of Germany's political economy is the decline of taxation revenues as a percentage of GDP, evident in Table 7.1. Despite the colossal fiscal burden of unification, the taxation reforms of the Kohl period, but in particular of the Schröder era reduced the ratio of tax revenue to GDP from 24.6 per cent in 1980 to 22 per cent in 1991 to just 20 per cent in 2005. While the public expenditure systems of Germany and its European partners differ significantly, it is illuminating that Germany has the lowest taxation ratio of all. OECD figures for 2004 give a German tax ratio of 20.4 per cent (20.3 per cent according to AAW calculations in Table 7.1), compared to Denmark with 48.4 per cent, Sweden with 36.2 per cent, Belgium 31.5 per cent, Finland 32.4 per cent, Britain 29.4 per cent, Italy 29.5 per cent and Austria 28.3 per cent. Of the major OECD countries, only Japan (15.8 per cent) and the United States (18.7 per cent) have lower tax ratios than Germany. Dieter Vesper (2006: 471ff) sees Germany's low tax ratio as a critical functional impediment to the resolution of both the transformation crisis of the East and the overall stagnation of German growth and employment (see also Kühn 2003: 735). Above all he stresses the critical flaws in the economic assumptions behind the supply-side tax reforms of Schröder, Kohl and now Merkel eras. A key assumption was, as noted above, that cost relief for businesses would not merely generate higher profits but also the preparedness to reinvest those higher profits in new capacity and new jobs. This assumption was proven demonstrably wrong in the early years of the Kohl *Wende* in the 1980s, it was even more emphatically disproved by the resistance of German and other enterprises to invest their, in many cases, vast financial reserves in either East or West Germany after unification. It would seem to have been proven wrong once more in the wake of the tax reform measures outlined above. Table 7.2 demonstrates no obvious correlation between the fiscal relief measures and investments. In 2001, when corporation tax was lowered to 25 per cent, gross profits rose by 5.4 per cent – considerably faster than real GDP (+1.2 per cent) after 5.6 per cent in 2000, business tax liabilities fell by almost two-thirds, but investment in both machinery (–3.7 per cent) and fixed assets (–4.6 per cent) fell sharply. In the whole tax reform period (2000–2005), gross profits rose by an average of 6.6 per cent per annum, while GDP grew at less than 1 per cent (0.98 per cent), machinery investments by 1.2 per cent and building investments fell every year at an annual average of 3.4 per cent.

The observable correlation in Table 7.2 is unsurprisingly between, firstly, investment and capacity utilisation and secondly between investments and GDP. Even though exports continued to boom during this period (annual average growth +6.5 per cent), businesses could not be expected to invest in new plant and machinery if existing capacity was not fully utilised and domestic growth

Table 7.1 Tax Revenues in Germany 1991–2005

Year	Total of Revenue from Taxation	Mass Taxes	of which		Taxes on Profits and Wealth	of which			Tax Ratio as percentage of GDP	Total State Debt
		Total	Wages Tax	Turnover Taxes*	Total	Assessed Income Tax	Corporation Tax	Capital Gains Tax		
					Billion Euro				percent	€ Billion
1991	338.4	235.6	109.5	91.9	69.2	21.2	16.2	6.0	22.0	599
1995	416.3	308.2	144.5	120.0	59.0	7.2	9.3	15.2	21.9	1 019
2000	467.3	325.9	135.7	140.9	87.1	12.2	23.6	20.8	24.2	1 198
2001	443.2	324.3	132.6	138.9	66.1	8.8	0.4	29.8	21.5	1 204
2002	441.7	326.4	132.2	138.2	59.7	7.5	2.9	22.5	22.3	1 253
2003	442.2	327.4	133.1	137.0	56.1	4.6	8.3	16.6	22.3	1 326
2004	442.8	316.7	123.9	137.4	67.9	5.4	13.1	16.8	20.3	1 395
2005	447.9	313.0	118.9	139.7	77.7	9.8	16.3	16.9	20.0	1 447
	Share of Individual Taxes in Total Tax Revenue in Percent									1991 = 100
1991	100	69.6	32.4	27.2	20.4	6.3	4.8	1.8		100
1995	100	74.0	34.7	28.8	14.2	1.7	2.2	3.7		170.1
2000	100	69.7	29.0	30.2	18.6	2.6	5.0	4.5		200.0
2001	100	72.7	29.7	31.1	14.8	2.0	-0.1	6.7		202.1
2002	100	73.9	29.9	31.3	13.5	1.7	0.7	5.1		209.2
2003	100	74.0	30.1	31.0	12.7	1.0	1.9	3.8		221.4
2004	100	71.5	28.0	31.0	15.3	1.2	3.0	3.8		232.9
2005	100	69.9	26.5	31.2	17.3	2.2	3.6	3.8		241.6
	Position in 2005 compared to 1991 in percent (1991 = 100)									
	132.4	132.9	108.6	152.0	112.3	46.2	100.5	282.4		

Source: AAW, Memorandum 2004 and 2006; * Turnover Taxes include VAT, Import Turnover Tax, Oil and Tobacco duties

was virtually nonexistent; orders could be easily supplied out of existing capacities. The neoliberal supply-side transmission mechanism broke down after the first link: net profits rose as a result of both higher gross returns on turnover and lower stoppages through tax relief (and pension cost relief) but then the machine slipped out of gear. The stimulus did not work. It was never likely to.

Table 7.2 Taxation of Businesses, Profits and Investment 1999–2005

Year	GDP	Gross Profits		Investments		Taxes on Capital	Capacity Utilisation Manufacturing %	
		€ Billion	Change %	Machinery	Construction	€ Billion	West G	East G
1999	2.0	288.46	-4.1	8.7	1.5	30.22	85.4	82.1
2000	3.2	304.64	+5.6	10.7	-2.4	34.59	87.1	83.6
2001	1.2	320.98	+5.4	-3.7	-4.6	12.25	84.6	81.3
2002	0.1	326.16	+1.6	-7.5	-5.8	12.46	83.4	79.8
2003	-0.2	327.39	+0.4	-0.2	-1.6	16.19	82.7	81.4
2004	1.6	376.76	+15.1	2.6	-2.3	20.80	84.0	81.6
2005	0.9	419.96	+11.5	4.0	-3.6	24.67	83.3	82.0

Sources: Schäfer (2006); AAW (2006)

Table 7.3 Growth of Unemployment in Germany 2000–2005 (Thousands)

	2000	2001	2002	2003	2004	2005
Unemployed	3,889	3,852	4,060	4,377	4,381	4,861
Vacancies	514	406	451	355	286	413
Hidden Unemployed*	1,810	1,761	1,773	1,524	1,405	1,291
Unemployed Reserve**	1,528	1,660	1,604	1,781	1,809	1,500

Sources: Bundesbank, Bundesagentur für Arbeit; * Includes those on short-time working week, job-creation schemes, retraining schemes; ** Includes those not working but not registered as unemployed, who would take work if it were available.

However, Hans Eichel's taxation reforms and his Finance Ministry's budget programmes assumed that it would. Success was predicated on the assumption of an average annual rate of real GDP growth of 2.5 per cent (Vesper 2006: 471 fn.1). With the exception of the year 2000, when the ECB allowed the exchange rate of the euro to slip against the dollar and German exports as a result grew by 13.5 per cent, not a single year has approached 2 per cent, let alone 2.5 per cent; as noted above, it averaged 0.98 per cent; there was a mild recession in 2003. Germany limped behind its eurozone partners with the worst growth record. The negative multiplier effects of virtual growth stagnation are evident from Table 7.1: lower rates of GDP growth produce lower rates of revenue growth; where marginal tax rates are lowered and basic allowances are raised without a sufficient broadening of the tax base, nominal tax revenue actually falls – from a peak of €467 billion in 2000 to levels consistently below €450 billion in all subsequent years. The tax relief measures cannot thus be financed out of increased revenue and have therefore to be covered by a mixture of expenditure cuts and – because of rising unemployment (Table 7.3) – by increased state borrowing. Eissel estimates the total fiscal cost of unemployment at around € 100 billion per year (Eissel 2006: 256).

Germany's public sector borrowing requirement consequently rose from 1.1 per cent of GDP in 2000 to 2.8 per cent in 2001 and remained well above the SGP ceiling of 3 per cent for the next four years. The overall state debt rose from just under € 1.2 trillion in 2000 (59.7 per cent of GDP) to € 1.44 trillion in 2005 (67.9 per cent); see Table 7.1. This was the opposite of the intended outcome; in December 2001, Schröder's government presented a revised Stability Programme, as required by the Stability and Growth Pact, in which it acknowledged the likely failure to meet the December 2000 targets for 2001 and 2002 but renewed its commitment to achieve a balanced budget for all state authorities by 2004. This target was to be reached by a consistent reduction in the state ratio (state expenditure as a proportion of GDP) from 48 per cent in 2002 to 44.5 in 2005. The Stability Programme included a worst case scenario, where lower GDP growth would delay the achievement of balanced budgets until 2006.

Dieter Vesper (2006: 472) and many others (Eissel 2006; Hein and Truger 2004; Hickel 2004; Truger 2004) lay the blame for the evident failure to achieve even the worst case outcome on government finance policy itself: 'Aside from the stubborn stagnation, the high deficits were caused by a failed taxation policy' (Vesper 2006: 473). The persistent stress on the need for budgetary consolidation had generated an utterly dysfunctional deflationary process where any possible benefits of fiscal relief measures were more than neutralised by increasingly destructive cutbacks in important areas of state expenditure (ibid. 474). The greatest, and in the long term potentially most dangerous, reductions in expenditure are in the area of state investments and in education. State investments are the most convenient target for expenditure cutbacks, as they are to a greater degree sporadic and strategic in nature and not part of recurrent budgets; central, regional and local government has to be financed on an ongoing basis; schools, universities, hospitals, the police, the army, social workers cannot be so readily starved of funds as roads, bridges, coastal defences, state buildings, social housing. The decline of state investments has been inexorable, most notably since the beginning of the 1980s; in 1974 state investment still constituted 15 per cent of overall state expenditure or 4.8 per cent of GDP; in 1982 it was still 11 per cent (3.6 per cent of GDP) and in 1990, 9.5 per cent (2.7 per cent of GDP). In the period since unification, which has arguably demanded the most extensive programme of reconstruction and infrastructural modernisation in Germany since the 1950s, state expenditure on investments in 2005 had shrunk to just 2.8 per cent of overall expenditure or a mere 1.3 per cent of GDP. This constitutes the lowest level of all industrialised countries (Kühn 2003: 734). The European average is 2.5 per cent of GDP, but no other country in Europe has been confronted with the colossal challenge of transforming a region of currently 15 million inhabitants into a competitive economic entity. Expenditure in the East has thus undeniably been at the expense of state investment projects in the West.

Of equal significance for the future of Germany's high-skill economy is the contribution of education and training. The Programme for International Student Assessment (PISA) Study, however inexact its procedures were, revealed significant weaknesses in German education. Against the background of perceived innovation weaknesses in German research and development, Vesper sees a clear correlation between Germany's (and Japan's) growth weaknesses and low levels of expenditure on education; the European average for educational expenditure is 5.3 per cent of GDP, considerably above Germany with just 3.5 per cent.

The dominant critique of German economic policy is that it ignores the demand side. Vesper's study constructs a line of development which sets actual state expenditure against a 'line of neutrality' above which state demand impulses are positive and below which they are negative. The result of charting state investment, state consumption, state transfers and supply-side fiscal relief measures indicates a negative and thus counter-productive trend of macroeconomic stimuli (see Table 7.4). Even in a state with 'normal' expenditure responsibilities, the maintenance of austerity over successive business cycles, i.e., regardless of cyclical conditions, the fiscal stance of the Schröder–Eichel era would have been highly questionable, but where the abnormality of the country's unification cum transformation crisis demands the long-term deployment of 4 per cent of GDP per annum, it verges on the nonsensical.

Table 7.4 Counterproductive State Fiscal Policy 2001–2007

	2001	2002	2003	2004	2005	2006*	2007*
Expenditure (actual volume)							
€ Bill	997.1	1023.7	1038.8	1031.2	1042.1	1046.7	1056.7
Line of neutral effect	1002.8	1024.4	1047.1	1062.3	1049.2	1060.9	1067.7
Difference = +/- Stimuli	-5.7	-0.7	-8.3	-31.1	-7.1	-14.2	-11.0
Net Fiscal Relief +/- Stimuli	22.6	20.3	12.6	25.1	-0.7	1.0	-9.9
Overall Demand Stimuli +/-	16.9	19.6	4.2	-6.0	-7.8	-13.2	-20.9

Source: Vesper 2006; * estimates

Pension Reform

On 11 May 2001, the federal government's highly contested Pensions Reform Plan was finally passed by both houses of the German Federal Parliament. Germany's new Law governing Security in Old Age represented the most thorough attempt at resolving the looming crisis in the pensions system. By reducing benefits in the statutory insurance-based pensions system and by subsidising the creation of private top-up pensions, the new Law sought firstly to alleviate the effects of severe demographic imbalance – increasing numbers of pensioners dependent on a diminishing number of working contributors to pension funds – and to reduce the associated pressure on employers' nonwage costs. It also opened the field for the creation of a large new field of activity for private pension fund management. Germany's Federal Minister of Labour and former leading trade unionist Walter Riester accordingly described the 2001 pensions law as the 'greatest programme of wealth creation in the history of the Federal Republic'. It was calculated that, if there were a mere 50 per cent take-up of state grants and tax-relief incentives covering top-up pensions up to 2010, private pension fund assets would grow to some €350 billion, or 20 per cent of German GDP. The new law, like the tax reform legislation, was very much the child of compromise. Earlier draft laws had been consistently rejected by the Bundesrat, and the Mediation Committee of the Federal Parliament, chaired by a Christian Democrat, had to be invoked four times before compromise was reached.

Some elements of pensions reform had already been put in place by the Schröder administration, including the deployment of revenues from the new tax on energy ('Eco-Tax') to subsidise contributions by employers and employees to the statutory pension funds, reducing the growing pressure on marginal wage costs. Other issues remained unresolved until the fourth round of mediation talks between Bundestag and Bundesrat. These included, above all, the intention of earlier drafts to exclude domestic property from eligibility for state pensions subsidies and the planned reduction of widows' benefits. The 2001 Law contained the following core provisions:

- In order to keep pension contributions below 20 per cent of gross incomes by 2020 and below 22 per cent by 2030, a staged reduction of benefits was to be instituted from 70 per cent of final average individual income (after a full forty-five years of contributions) to 67 per cent by 2020 and to 65 per cent by 2030.
- From 2002 employees with incomes up to a maximum of DM 8,600 (c. €4,400) per month would be allowed to divert 1 per cent of their gross incomes into an individual private pension scheme or a company pension scheme, reducing their taxable income accordingly; this would rise every two years until 2008 when a maximum of 4 per cent of gross income would be eligible for tax exemption. Low- and middle-income families, with individual incomes up to DM 35,000 (c. €17,500) per annum, would in addition receive annual individual pension grants of DM 37.50 (€19.2) rising to DM 300 (€153) by 2008 and a further grant of DM 45 (€23) for every child, rising to DM 360 (€184) in the same period. The total annual cost to the state of high tax allowances and direct pension grants would amount to around 21 billion DM (€10.7 billion) by 2008.

- Whereas Riester's earlier programme offered tax incentives and grants to pension schemes based on insurance and investment funds only, the incentive system was extended to domestic property investment; this represented a significant concession to both major opposition parties (Christian Democrats and Free Democrats). From 2002 money from private pension accounts could be deployed to help finance home ownership up to a maximum of 100,000 DM (€51,150). The diverted proportion would have to be repaid into the pension account in full in monthly instalments before the end of the individual's sixty-fifth year.
- Child rearing became pensionable, such that the first child represented two years of average pensionable income and every subsequent child one year.
- Widows' pensions were reduced from 60 per cent of the deceased partner's pension to 55 per cent; however, if one of the partners were over forty at the time of bereavement, no such cut would occur. Tax allowances for widows' additional earnings would not, as originally planned, be frozen, but income from capital would be included fully in calculating tax liabilities.

If one sets aside the controversy about whether demographic changes actually posed a threat to a pension system in an affluent and highly productive economy, the main criticisms of the reform were directed at the perceived departure from the principles of equity and social justice supposedly embedded in Germany's system of insurance-based social security. With the exception of accident insurance, which is borne entirely by employers, the three pillars of health, pensions and unemployment insurance had always operated on the basis of equally shared funding between employers and employees. The fifth pillar of long-term care insurance, introduced in 1995 to take pressure off both pensions and health insurance systems, maintained parity financing, but employers were compensated by the removal of one day from the list of obligatory state holidays (the day of 'prayer and repentance'). The top-up pension – now dubbed the 'Riester-Rente' – is funded by the employee alone with tax-funded support from the state. The fact that state support increases proportionately to the top-up premiums (with generous upper limits) is furthermore seen as favouring the better-off and thus promoting income inequality in old age (Butterwegge 2005: 178). The complexity of the application procedure is also seen as a disincentive for less educated workers to pursue the optional top-up schemes, a tendency arguably reinforced by the sudden weakness of global financial markets at the end of 2001; suffice it to say that the uptake of top-up pensions to date (second quarter of 2006) has not lived up to the initial expectations. While 6.2 million top-up contracts have been concluded since 2001, this is nowhere near the predicted 50 per cent of Germany's employed labour force (currently totalling some 34.4 million). The staged reduction of pension benefits is seen to go further than the reform proposals of Norbert Blüm, Kohl's Minister of Labour (Kreutz 2002: 467).

Within a very short time, however, the 2001 pension reform laws were judged to be inadequate for ensuring the viability of the statutory pensions insurance system. As a result, the second Schröder administration appointed a commission of experts concerned with 'the sustainability of financing the social insurance systems' in November 2002, which came to be known as the Rürup Commission after its chairman, the economist Bernd Rürup. In its August 2003 Report, the Rürup Commission recommended firstly a staged increase in the retirement age from sixty-five to sixty-seven and, secondly, the introduction of a 'sustainability factor' in calculating pension levels. While there was no immediate legislation governing retirement age, government policy focused more strongly on the objective of raising the actual average age of retirement from currently fifty-nine to closer to sixty-five. The Grand Coalition has subsequently formally proposed that the retirement age should rise incrementally to sixty-seven from 2012 to 2029. The sustainability factor, on the other hand, was introduced almost immediately into federal legislation with the Law on Sustainability of Pensions Insurance of 21 July 2004. The central element of the 'sustainability factor' is the ratio of pension insurance contributors to pensioners. After a pensions freeze in 2004, as a result of gross wages and salaries stagnating, the sustainability factor contributed to a further zero round for pensions in the summer of 2005; the decline of gross wages in 2005 would have produced a fall in nominal pensions and the new Merkel administration was obliged to legislate for 'stable pensions' (i.e. a zero nominal rise) in May 2006; with the VAT increases set for January 2007 and predicted consumer price inflation of 2.3 per cent, the effect will not be 'stability' but a real erosion of the purchasing power of pensions.

Statutory pension levels in Germany – assuming a full lifetime of contributions – have been and will remain generous by international comparison; real pension benefits vary considerably, however, largely as a result of varying levels of accredited contributions, but also in terms of the relatively low participation ratio of (West German) women and their subsequent dependency on either the better pensions of husbands or on state welfare. Figure 7.2 shows the relatively favourable position of East German men and, in particular, East German women, compared to their Western counterparts. The unification treaty brought all citizens of the GDR under the umbrella of the Federal Republic's social insurance schemes, even though in actuarial terms the new members – contributors and beneficiaries – brought no accumulated funds into any of these schemes, most notably pensions. By dint of longer working lives, the pension entitlements of East German retirees is thus paradoxically greater. What Figure 7.2 also reveals, however, is the gradual decline in the nominal (*sic*) value of German pensions which, in the case of West German men, peaked in 2000 with an average of €883 per month and have subsequently declined to €793 in 2005. This common trend is a clear indication of the radical character of pension reform under the Red–Green coalition, with its stronger welfarist associations, compared to the minor adjustments under the ostensibly pioneering neoliberal administration of Helmut Kohl. The evidence is supported by data on the reversal of the retirement age trend in Figure 7.3. While the sporadic government campaigns to reduce mass unemployment are revealed by the sudden falls in retirement ages – in the late 1970s and, in particular in the early stages of unification in the East – the more gradual downward trend continues roughly until the transition from Kohl to Schröder in 1998 when the effect of earlier retirement on the finances of the statutory pensions insurance system is put into sharp focus by the new demographic mindset. Since 1998 average retirement ages for men have risen by 1.2 percentage points in the West to 60.9 years and by 1.9 percentage points in the East to 59.7 years (Figure 7.3).

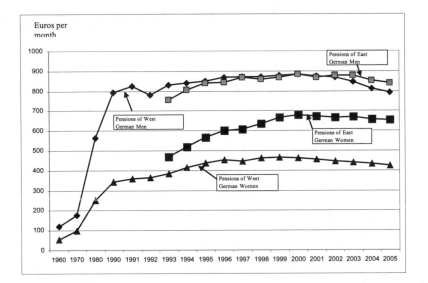

Figure 7.2 Nominal Pensions in Germany 1960–2005 in €
Source: Rentenversicherung in Zeitreihen 2006: 127–8

Regardless of the general, the intergenerational or the gender specific fairness of the 2001–2004 reforms, the importance of pensions in the refined political economy of a country like Germany cannot be reduced to the level of (marginal labour) costs. Pensions represent household income and purchasing power in increasingly differentiated spheres of market demand. Reducing the 'cost' of pensions does not – as in the case of tax relief – ensure that the cost-saving as employer/employee benefit is deployed as demand to the same degree as the spending of pensioner households.

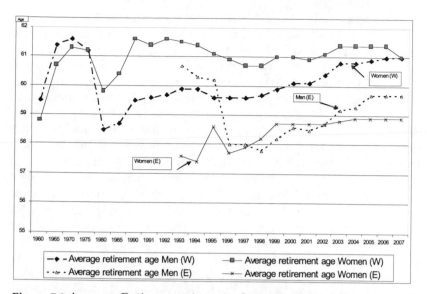

Figure 7.3 Average Retirement Ages in Germany 1960–2005
Source: Rentenversicherung in Zeitreihen 2008

As the demographic distribution of consumers and of paid employment changes, so the allocation of social resources becomes a politically far more acute problem than can be solved by the application of the scarcity principle and the efficiency of market mechanisms, as the next section on labour market reforms also suggests.

Red–Green Employment Law Reforms

The employment law reforms of the Kohl era were roundly criticised by the SPD and the Greens in opposition. A cursory glance at the election programmes of both parties between 1987 and 1998 reveals policy standpoints which seek above all to stress the responsibility of the state to help create employment and guarantee social justice in contrast to the toleration of unemployment and the redistribution of wealth and income under Kohl (SPD 1987: 10). 'Create Work' is the very first section of the 1994 manifesto 'Work, Innovation and Justice', the title of the 1998 electoral programme. Schröder placed the halving of unemployment at the heart of his government programme for the 1998–2002 electoral period. The subsequent route chosen, however, marked a clear break with the policies of his social democratic predecessors and reflected a strong preference for the 'Third Way' employment policies of the first Blair administration in Britain, established in 1997, a year before the Red–Green coalition.

In their joint programme – published in 1999 under the title *The Way Forward for Europe's Social Democrats* – Gerhard Schröder and Tony Blair make an immediate distinction between the (old) politics of redistribution and the (new) politics of enablement. In old-style social democracy 'the promotion of social justice was sometimes confused with the imposition of equality of outcome. The result was neglect of the importance of rewarding effort and responsibility, and the association of social democracy with conformity and mediocrity, rather than the celebration of creativity, diversity and excellence' (Blair and Schröder 1999: Ch.1). The rest of the document, mirrored in the work of Giddens (2000) and Hombach (2000) represents an explicit rejection of welfarist Keynesianism and demand-side state interventionism and the explicit espousal of a 'new supply-side agenda for the Left' as well as 'an active labour market policy for the Left' (ibid: Ch. 1). The shift from a demand-side to a supply-side focus also represented a shift from a macroeconomic to a microeconomic focus (cf. Knuth et al. 2004). The direct or indirect fiscal stimulation of demand (for labour/consumption) and thus growth at the level of the macroeconomy is to be supplanted by the improvement of the individual attributes of the jobseeker as commodity on the labour market (qua human capital), which in accordance with a kind of Say's Law of the Labour Market is supposed to generate demand (employer interest) in that commodity.

Germany's performance in terms of macroeconomic growth and labour market reform has in recent years frequently been the object of criticism, in particular from the OECD (OECD 2002, OECD 2003, OECD 2005). Germany 'bringing up the rear', the *Schlußlicht* in GDP growth and in structural reform of labour markets has been meat and drink to headline writers for some time (Bertelsmann-Stiftung 2003).[2] The absence/lateness above all of appropriate 'activation' measures of labour market policy are identified as critical deficiencies of Germany's political economy (OECD 2003, OECD 2005; Sinn 2005); reform was urged upon Germany and other European countries by the European Commission following the launching of the European Employment Strategy (Büchs 2004).

However, as the urgency of introducing 'activation' measures increased, so the concept itself drew some critical attention as 'fuzzy and ambivalent' (Siegel 2004: 23) or 'controversial' (Bothfeld 2005: 420). Taylor-Gooby (2004) actually distinguishes between negative and positive activation which corresponds in part to Bothfeld's distinction between a 'liberal' activation concept which motivates jobseekers through the reduction in job and social security along 'workfare' lines and a 'universalistic' concept of activation which addresses the needs of the unemployed/underemployed through high benefits and reintegration assistance through personal advice and

---

2. A trawl on the internet on the subject 'Schlußlicht Deutschland' produces thousands upon thousands of references, most recently supplemented by opposition politicians in the federal election campaign: e.g. <www.bernd-schmidbauer.de/>; <www.ilse-aigner.de>.

subsidised placements (Bothfeld 2005: 420). There is therefore little difficulty in establishing a consensus about the desirability of 'activation' strategies within current German discussions, encompassing both the neoliberal camp (Bundesbank 2004) and the more worker-centred, universalistic camp (Bothfeld 2005; Trube 2005 etc.). The Bundesbank's espousal of activation is typically linked to a catalogue of demands for the flexibilisation of labour markets and the reduction of state expenditure on 'active' labour market measures (Bundesbank 2004).

The history of recent 'activation' policies shows a preponderance of negative measures that have reduced job security for full-time employees and increased the scope of part-time, fixed-term and casual subcontracted labour. It is noteworthy that the bulk of the measures have been introduced since 1998. The OECD has indeed noted the particular intensity of labour market reform in recent years (Brandt et al. 2005).

- Employment Protection. The Employment Protection Act was modified in 1996, raising the threshold for the applicability of the Act from six to eleven employees. This modification was reversed by the incoming Red–Green coalition in 1999 but restored in 2004. Germany, along with most European states – with the exception of Ireland and the UK – is considered to have a strong employment protection culture (See Table 7.5).
- Part-time employment. In 2001 the Act concerning Part-Time and Fixed-Term Employment established a statutory right to part-time employment and the right to return to full-time employment. In 1999, the exemption from paying taxes and social security contributions for workers in low-paid part-time work (mini-jobs) was abolished but partly restored in 2003 for employees with a maximum of one additional low-paid part-time job; reduced social security contributions for midi-jobs were introduced.
- Fixed-term employment. Up until 1985 limited-term employment contracts were only permissible for 'justified reason' through application. The Employment Protection Act of 1985 removed this restriction and introduced an eighteen-month maximum term. A revision of the Act in 1996 raised the maximum to twenty-four months and removed all restrictions for workers over sixty. The Act concerning Part-Time and Fixed-Term Employment of 2001 reintroduced justified reason for the bulk of adult workers but allowed limited-term employment for new recruits and for all employees over fifty-eight; in the Hartz 1 and 2 Reforms of 2003, freedom from all restrictions was extended to all workers over fifty-two. In 2004 the maximum period for standard limited-term contracts was raised to four years.
- Subcontracted labour. Until 1985, subcontracting was heavily restricted (maximum of three months), which produced significant problems in the shape of a black economy, in particular within the building trades. Under the Kohl administrations (1982–98) the maximum period was raised in stages

to twelve months. In 2002 the Red–Green coalition raised the maximum period to twenty-four months but introduced the principle of equal pay for equal work for casual employees. In 2004 most restrictions on casual labour were removed, but provision of employment advice for affected workers was established with the creation of personnel service agencies.

• Self-employment. In 1999 the Act promoting Self-Employment outlawed pseudo-self-employment, rife in the construction industry (partly reversed in 2003). Start-up grants for unemployed persons who become self-employed were introduced in 2003, with maximum duration of three years. In 2004, amendments to craft trade legislation removed the requirement of a Master Craftsman qualification from fifty-three out of ninety-four craft trades, allowing the possibility of qualified journeymen becoming self-employed artisans.

Table 7.5 Employment Protection Legislation in Europe 1990–1998*

	Overall Measure		Regular Employment		Temporary Employment	
	1990	1998	1990	1998	1990	1998
Austria	2.4	2.4	2.8	2.8	2.0	2.0
Belgium	3.0	2.1	1.6	1.6	4.4	2.6
Denmark	2.4	1.5	1.8	1.7	3.1	1.2
Finland	2.2	2.1	2.5	2.3	1.9	1.9
France	2.7	3.1	2.4	2.5	3.0	3.7
Germany	3.6	2.8	2.9	3.0	4.2	2.5
Greece	3.6	3.5	2.8	2.6	4.5	4.5
Ireland	1.0	1.0	1.7	1.7	0.3	0.3
Italy	4.2	3.3	3.0	3.0	5.3	3.6
Netherlands	3.1	2.4	3.1	3.2	3.0	1.5
Norway	3.1	2.9	2.9	2.9	3.2	2.8
Portugal	4.2	3.7	5.0	4.3	3.5	3.2
Spain	3.7	3.2	3.8	2.8	3.5	3.7
Sweden	3.4	2.4	3.1	3.0	3.8	1.8
Switzerland	1.3	1.3	1.3	1.3	1.2	1.2
UK	0.5	0.5	0.7	0.7	0.3	0.3
For comparison						
Japan	2.6	2.6	2.5	3.0	2.7	2.3
US	0.2	0.2	0.1	0.1	0.3	0.3

* Higher scores indicate a higher level of employment protection
Source: Nicoletti, G. & Scarpetti, Stefano 2003

These alterations to Federal Employment and Contract Law form the backdrop to the most radical of employment law reforms, associated with the Hartz Commission, which were introduced between 2002 and 2005, but must be seen as having an activating function in the sense of permitting the expansion of employment opportunities that provide, by definition, less security – in terms of material gain, social security entitlements and length of job tenure. Notwithstanding the particular circumstances of German unification, there has been a marked increase in the incidence of part-time employment in Germany from 2.3 per cent of total employment in 1990 to 6.3 per cent in 2004; part-time work already accounted for 29.8 per cent of all female employment in 1990 and rose to 37 per cent in 2004, not far behind the United Kingdom, with just over 40 per cent, barely altered since 1990 (OECD 2005).

Activation, in terms of the targeted measures of advice, training, placements and employment subsidies, was promoted intensively in the first three phases of the Hartz reforms, which also saw significant changes to the institutional arrangements for the delivery of employment policy measures and the provision of benefits.

The First and Second Law on Modern Services in the Labour Market (1 January 2003 and 1 April 2003 respectively) brought about:

- Reductions in benefits for earnings-related unemployment benefit (*Arbeitslosen-geld*) and unemployment assistance (*Arbeitslosenhilfe*) and *Unterhaltsgeld*, as well as stricter monitoring of need in the case of unemployment assistance.
- Stricter rules governing the degree to which job offers can be rejected on the grounds of quality (*Zumutbarkeit*) and periods when benefit is not paid (*Sperrzeiten*).
- The reorganisation of continuing education, notably with the introduction of training vouchers.
- Establishment of *PersonalServiceAgenturen* (*sic*) as public, private or public–private agencies, operating as job agencies and advice centres; extension of temping agencies.
- Introduction of the so-called *Ich-AG* (individual joint stock company!) with grants and tax concessions for individual unemployed persons wishing to become self-employed.

The Third Law on Modern Services in the Labour Market (2004) involved above all:

- The restructuring of the Federal Institute for Labour in Nuremberg (renamed Federal Agency for Labour), extending its administrative role for delivering unemployment benefit to encompass social assistance, hitherto delivered by local authorities and allowing for the subcontracting of labour agency functions to the PSAs.
- Cuts in active job creation schemes and reductions in benefits (to be implemented between 2004 and 2006).

The Fourth Law on Modern Services in the Labour Market came into force on 1 January 2005 and involved arguably the most significant change in (negative) activation, namely the conflation of the hitherto earnings-related unemployment assistance, paid to long-term unemployed persons after the initial period of the more generous unemployment benefit (*Arbeitslosengeld* now re-termed *Arbeitslosengeld I*), with the flat-rate social assistance (*Sozialhilfe*) to produce the so-called unemployment benefit II, which is paid at a flat rate, generally at much lower levels than the discarded unemployment assistance. The Federal Agency for Labour is solely responsible for the delivery of both *Arbeitslosengeld I* and *Arbeitslosengeld II*, with the help of increased federal government grants to supplement its revenue from unemployment insurance. The passage of this Hartz-IV Law was accompanied by largescale protests on behalf of the long-term unemployed, and the first eight months of its implementation have brought further opposition and considerable hardship for the benefit recipients. The sheer magnitude of this break with the tradition of generous long-term social security for the unemployed – in terms of both the microeconomic fate of individual households and the macroeconomic decline in effective demand – has arguably deflected attention away from the activation effects of the Hartz I–III reforms and partly neutralised the positive features of individual activation. Apart from its key objective of reducing Germany's comparatively high indirect labour costs, it is also clearly intended to alter the fundamental conditions of unemployment and the fundamental perceptions and expectations of the unemployed as the prerequisite to accepting job offers of a lower quality, of limited extent (part-time or fixed-term) and by definition with lower levels of job security.

A detailed assessment of the effects of the Hartz reforms and other labour market measures under the Red–Green Coalition is not feasible, given their relative newness as well as the overall difficulty in making reliable cause–effect correlations. Some preliminary observations are necessary, particularly in view of the most recent claims by Frank-Jürgen Wiese, the director of the Federal Agency for Labour, that the Hartz IV reforms – reducing benefits for the long-term unemployed – were having a definite effect, contributing to the marked improvement in unemployment in late 2006 (quoted in *Die Neue Epoche*, 26 December 2006). The evidence of a cyclical improvement is undeniable: average levels of unemployment were down by 374,000 to 4, 487,000; the total labour force had grown to 39.7 million by the end of November 2006, with 26.9 million in jobs covered by social insurance, up 392,000 year-on-year. Whether the improvement can be ascribed further to labour market deregulation is less certain. What is certain is that the security of employment has been significantly reduced, the power of employers to hire and fire labour and to deploy labour flexibly within employment contracts has been enhanced and the material rewards of labour – in the form of real wages – have stagnated.

National collective wage bargaining – traditionally a perceived strength of corporate governance in Germany – has declined in popularity among German employers' associations, with only 59 per cent of West German employees covered by such agreements in 2005 (1996: 69 per cent) and only 42 per cent of East German workers (1996: 56 per cent). The average duration of wage agreements has risen from 12.7 months in 1998 to 25.2 months in 2005 in the West and 28.4 months in East Germany. Furthermore, most national wage agreements now contain partial get-out clauses that allow the variation of wages and of working times, according to the required volume of work. These get-out clauses now apply to at least three-quarters of all firms with a Works Council – i.e., with five or more employees) – and are used predominantly to alter contractual working hours (Bispinck 2005: 303). The get-out clauses are frequently negotiated within the framework of an enterprise-based 'alliance for work' (*Bündnis für Arbeit*) where companies commit themselves to limit redundancies in exchange for flexible working arrangements (Seifert 2006: 603). These alliances, together with the increasing decentralisation of wage negotiations, have reinforced the flexibility allowed by the 1994 Law on Working Time; the proportion of workers working Sunday shifts rose from 17.1 per cent to 24.5 per cent in 2005 (ibid. 603). A significant shift in working-time arrangements in Germany is the increasing use of 'working-time accounts' which are deployed predominantly to ensure optimal use of machinery, to minimise down-times and storage costs, but which can and have been deployed to match the individual needs of workers. According to Seifert (ibid.), around two-thirds of all companies use working-time accounts. The discourse around such accounts has also spilt over into discussions of life-course working-time accounts which promote both the notion of 'sabbatical' interruptions and extended/tapered working lives (see Chapter Eight).

The deregulation of temporary contract labour has already increased the proportion of 'temping' workers from almost zero to 1.3 per cent of all employees (i.e., some 448,000 individuals) in 2006. Short-term contracts – now permissible up to twenty-four months – affected some 8 per cent of all employees in 2005 or some 2.75 million, while small-scale employment (limited hours per week) has grown in popularity among employers since the liberalisation measures of Hartz II in 2003, rising from 4.1 million employees to 6.8 million in 2006 (Bundesagentur für Arbeit 2006). This statistic is arguably the strongest for demonstrating the degree to which employers are benefiting from labour market deregulation, allowing above all temping agencies and mini-jobs to absorb the cyclical effects of fluctuating order books and allowing employers to avoid costly and divisive dismissals of core staff.

The cost-savings for employers have been arguably most significant in the development of wage rates in Germany; not only do most wage contracts run for at least two years, but settlements have been very modest (1.6 per cent in 2005); with inflation at 2 per cent in 2005, real contractual rates fell by 0.4 per cent. Effective wages – which are adjusted for fluctuations in the volume of labour and actual total gross wages – fell by 0.5 per cent. On the basis of effective average wage rates, Reinhard Bispinck demonstrates the consistent 'wage drift' over the thirteen years from 1993 to 2005 (see Table 7.6). It is little wonder therefore that the share of wages and salaries in national income continued to decline in the period of the Red–Green coalition; the unadjusted gross wages ratio fell from 70.4 per cent in 1998 to 67.4 per cent in 2005 (with a further deterioration likely in 2006); the adjusted gross wages ratio (which takes account of the proportion of waged and salaried employees to the total workforce) fell from 72 per cent to 69 per cent in the same period. Within this overall deterioration of the position of wage-earners in both absolute and relative terms, there has been a more clearly marked widening of wage differentials, in part as a result of labour market deregulation but also in the absence of a minimum wage in Germany; as a result the proportion of full-time employees on low incomes increased from 15.9 per cent to 18.6 per cent between 1997 and 2004 (Seifert 2006: 604). The corollary of Germany (and Austria) having the weakest record of wage developments over the last ten years (Schulten 2006: 369) is the very favourable development of German employers' wage costs, which rose the least among all EU countries between 2000 and 2005 (Seifert 2006: 605). Unit wage costs – an even clearer indicator of entrepreneurial advantage – rose by only 0.2 per cent per annum. between 1995 and 2005, bettered only by Latvia (–0.1 per cent) but exceeded by all other EU member states by a significant margin (France, Belgium: 0.8 per cent; Italy: 1.2 per cent; Denmark, Sweden: 1.6 per cent; Netherlands, Poland, United Kingdom: 1.9 per cent) (Eissel 2006: 264).

Table 7.6 Percentage Annual Wage Drift in Germany 1993–2005*

1993	1994	1995	1996	1997	1998	1999	2000	2001	2002	2003	2004	2005
-2.0	-0.0	-1.3	-0.9	-1.2	-0.8	-1.2	-0.3	-0.1	-1.2	-0.9	-1.2	-0.9

* Wage drift denotes the deviation of wages and salaries per employee from contractual monthly earnings
Source: Reinhard Bispinck 2006: 67

All three areas discussed in this chapter – taxation, pensions and employment law – saw an intensification of the emphasis on cost-relief compared even to the Kohl administrations (Lahusen and Stark 2003: 364f). Chancellor Schröder, Finance Minister Eichel, Labour Minister Riester and Economics Ministers Müller and Clement instituted incisive and radical changes to the statutory framework of these key areas of economic policy – albeit with the 'assistance' of an obstructive opposition in the Bundesrat.

They were instituted in the spirit of supply-side convictions, which assumed that reduced entrepreneurial costs and increased flexibility in economic governance would trigger a virtuous circle of dynamic investment, growth and employment. The radicality of the reforms, however, was until the cyclical recovery of 2006, in inverse proportion to the results; Germany has been the weakest performer in the eurozone since its inception in 1999 and, barring extreme surprises (or a radical shift in economic orthodoxy), would seem set to underperform for the rest of the current cycle. The preconditions for a domestic recovery are simply not present in the shape of sustainable demand from all three major elements of demand: households, enterprises and state. Hartmut Seifert is correct to point out that success on the growth and employment front can be achieved by quite different types of welfare 'polities', when he cites Scandinavian and Anglo-Saxon examples to contrast with Germany's weak record in boosting growth and combating mass unemployment (2006: 606). But he, and others, could still stress the overwhelming contrast between current German dilemmas and the 'normality' of differing societal systems that have evolved organically and adapted to global conditions without the colossal structural challenge of unification. Germany's failures over the last two decades can only be explained adequately if its abnormality is kept in full view, and one of those failures has been to ignore the implications of that abnormality for the conduct of policy reform and the policy architecture that is put in place to address both the macroabnormality and the sectoral policy problems. All too often, the policy approach has been that of 'business as usual', pretending that Germany's problems are no different from those of its eurozone/ EU partners, that it can behave normally within the orthodoxy of Brussels, the OECD or the Washington Consensus (after all, it coauthored the rules). The evidence of the last sixteen years indicates that a neoliberal 'business as usual' approach is entirely inappropriate to Germany; by reducing the state ratio to below the levels of many other European countries it reduces the state's manoeuvrability in an historical period where it is most needed (see Table 7.7). As the table shows, all of the OECD countries with higher state ratios than Germany have superior records of economic growth between 1995 and 2002. Japan, with the lowest state ratio, is the only country with a worse growth record than Germany. The strong showing of Spain, Greece, Poland, Slovakia and Ireland – countries that combine high growth with a relatively low deployment of national income by the state – neither proves the case for the transportability of their policy preferences to other political economies, nor the appropriateness of roll-back politics in this critical period of German history. The German state cannot be expected to fund 21 per cent of the EU budget, provide 6.2 per cent of the IMF's quotas and 9.2 per cent of UN funding, devote 4 per cent of its own GDP to sustaining the five new Länder *and* reduce its expenditure commitments as a proportion of GDP.

Table 7.7 State Ratios and Rates of GDP Growth in Selected OECD Countries

Country	State Ratio*	Average Rate of Growth 1995-2002 % p.a.
Sweden	50.6	2.8
Denmark	49.4	2.3
Belgium	46.2	2.1
Finland	45.9	3.9
France	44.2	2.4
Austria	44.1	2.2
Norway	43.1	3.2
Luxembourg	42.3	5.5
Italy	41.1	1.7
Czech Rep	39.2	1.6
Hungary	37.7	3.8
Germany	36.2	1.4
Britain	35.9	2.8
Spain	35.6	3.4
Greece	34.8	3.6
Poland	34.3	4
Portugal	34	3.1
Slovakia	33.8	3.8
USA	28.9	3.3
Ireland	28	8.9
Japan	27.3	1

Source: OECD * State ratio here denotes the sum of both taxation and statutory social insurance levies as a proportion of GDP

This chapter has sought in particular to demonstrate both the continuity of policy priorities between the Kohl administrations of the pre- and post-unification periods and between the Kohl era and the Red–Green administrations of 1998 to 2005. In the view of this author it is a continuity which is ominous because, put quite simply, it represents a policy mix which failed in the 1980s, failed even more lamentably in the 1990s and is now set to fail beyond the first decade of the twenty-first century. However, in contrast to the protestations of post-experience *Besserwessis* who, like Kohl, blame their failure on the ostensibly unknown frailties of the East German economy, it is the political persistence with an inappropriate policy mix in combination with the structural economic weaknesses of both East and West that represents the failure. The primary failure was the inability to translate supply-side cost relief and increased business profits into higher investments and fuller employment from the beginning of the post-1982 era. It could have been expected that, with the persistence of structural unemployment, a modification of macroeconomic policies would have been considered even without the challenge of unification. What ensued was quite the opposite, namely the persistence with a policy mix that failed utterly to achieve the basic requirements of economic unification: relative convergence of the backward region with its Western counterpart and the neutralisation of the fiscal burden of political union on the public purse and on para-public institutions like the pensions and unemployment insurance funds. The 1995 Solidarity Pact had set the goal of convergence (and, by implication, the end of dependency) as its main objective by 2004. It became plain some time before the 'completion date' that the objective would not be realised. As a result, the Second Solidarity Pact of 2001 was agreed with a significantly longer timescale for convergence/ nondependency stretching forward to 2019. There is considerable doubt as to whether even this modified ambition is in any way realistic, as the concluding chapter will seek to demonstrate.

COPING WITH STAGNATION: THE PERSISTENT CONTRADICTIONS OF ECONOMIC ORTHODOXIES IN GERMANY AND EUROPE

On 22 November 2005, two months after Germany's federal elections, Angela Merkel (CDU) became the first woman chancellor of the Federal Republic at the head of its second Grand Coalition involving the 'Union-Parties' of CDU/CSU and Social Democrats. Grand Coalitions have been rare in Germany's democratic history and often associated with controversy, as in the case of the ill-fated government under Müller that preceded the collapse of the Weimar Republic; the 1966–69 administration under Kiesinger had been a surprisingly successful one in terms of policy but generated parliamentary (and extra-parliamentary) side-effects reflecting the disappearance of an effective democratic opposition. The formation of the Merkel administration was in many respects unremarkable, even though the election of a woman chancellor from the East of the reunited nation clearly represented a break with tradition. In other respects, the transition from Red–Green to Black–Red reflected a continuation of what was already going on at parliamentary level and of the policy mix at federal level. The parliamentary foundation of the Schröder administrations for most of their eight years had been a kind of Grand Coalition between a Red–Green Bundestag and a CDU-dominated Bundesrat but without a formal agreement and without the rhetoric of harmony and good will characteristic of 'national governments' in a situation of crisis management – a rose by any other name. The legislative results of the federal parliament between 1999 and 2005 were clearly codetermined by opposition preferences and characterised by a surprising speed of conception, formulation and implementation. The effective corresponsibility of CDU/CSU for Schröder's extensive reform programme made the 2005 electoral campaign in many ways stranger than the transition to a formal Grand Coalition under a Merkel chancellorship.

The Merkel cabinet has parity representation for CDU/CSU and SPD, with eight ministerial posts each, and with a similar balance of key posts to Kiesinger's cabinet in the 1960s. Merkel's Foreign Minister and vice-chancellor is Franz Müntefering (SPD) (1966–69: Brandt), the Finance Minister is Peer Steinbrück (SPD) and Economics Minister Michael Glos (CSU), mirroring the partnership between Strauss (CSU) and Schiller (SPD) in the 1960s. It is significant that Steinbrück has inherited the Finance portfolio from his SPD colleague, Hans Eichel. The latter had been responsible for the radical reforms of personal and corporate income tax after 1999 which had reduced marginal rates for top earners from 53 per cent to 42 per cent and created a standard level of corporation tax of 25 per cent. After the 3 percentage point rise in VAT at the beginning of 2007, Steinbrück's taxation reform proposals include a further reduction in corporation tax from 25 per cent to 15 per cent and reduction of assessed income tax for retained profits in non-incorporated businesses from 42 per cent to 28.5 per cent, along with the abolition of degressive depreciation allowances and other offset facilities. In combination with the repeated commitment to pursue budgetary consolidation in line with the Stability and Growth Pact, federal fiscal policy thus differs very little from the trend established under Kohl and accelerated under Schröder. It persists with the supply-side logic recommended by OECD, EC, the Academic Subcommittees of the Finance and Economics ministries, the Council of Economic Experts (with the exception of Peter Bofinger) and the Bundesbank.

There are some voices which urge the German state to go further. In 2004 the president of the *Ifo* economics research institute in Munich, Hans-Werner Sinn, produced a best-selling volume with the title: *Can Germany Yet be Saved?* (*Ist Deutschland noch zu retten?*). Seven reprints in 2004 alone were followed by audio-CD versions; Sinn was awarded the *Corine* book prize in 2005 and declared 'our best economics professor' by both *Bild* and the *Frankfurter Allgemeine Sonntagszeitung*. Sinn's central hypothesis is that Germany has become a 'bazaar-economy' (Sinn 2005: 71ff) in which the country's much extolled exports are seen to contain increasing proportions of foreign components, provided by cheaper production plants abroad, and where the domestic contribution to the end product is seen to be dwindling. The result is a disparity between the rise in the volume of industrial production and a (lower) level of domestically added value in manufacturing. Sinn interprets this trend as a potentially fatal weakening of Germany as the workshop of the world, as an innovative industrial powerhouse and its degeneration to a nation of shopkeepers. Responsibility for the migration of labour-intensive production processes to foreign, cheaper locations is laid predictably on Germany's trade unions and on Germany's state authorities (Sinn 2005: 14

etc.): excessive wage costs (direct and indirect), excessive employment protection, excessive taxation, excessive business regulation – the standard fare of neoliberal and business critics of Germany's political economy since the opening of the *'Standort-Debatte'* in the 1980s. Sinn's recommendation – in line with the official view of the *Ifo* institute (Sinn et al. 2006) – is that wages and welfare benefits should be reduced beyond the levels achieved with Hartz IV in order to lure back investors to *Standort-Deutschland*; more precisely Sinn argues for the promotion of a low-wage sector which is predicated on the reduction of welfare benefits below the new low levels of market incomes (Sinn et al. 2006: 180ff). The state is called upon to provide temporary wage subsidies – as a better way of using taxpayers' money than paying people to do nothing – as part of a refined strategy of 'activation', of weaning the jobless off welfare.

It is not the purpose of this chapter to subject the Sinn / *Ifo* hypotheses to a closer examination; others have already provided convincing rebuttals (Horn and Behnke 2004; Hickel 2004a). Rather, it is used to illustrate the astonishing resilience of neoliberal economic ideology despite its manifest failure to solve both the general problems of Germany's mature political economy and the very specific problems of unification. Since the beginning of the 1980s, German economic policy has instituted supply-side measures of cost-relief for private companies which have resulted in an historically unprecedented redistribution of national income in favour of the owners of capital as inducements to invest. The profitability of German enterprises has been consistently enhanced in the hope that enterprises might deploy their additional profits in additional capacity and additional jobs. The twenty-five-year experiment has failed: the profits ratio has risen, but the investment ratio has declined. And yet, Sinn and commentators like him insist that the failed process must continue, that corporate incomes and profits must be further boosted and incomes from salaries, wages and unemployment benefits kept under control or significantly reduced.

Those who assert that German reformers have just 'not gone far enough' are guilty of a crude syllogism, which is in turn rooted in a crude, mechanistic view of how 'the' market operates. The notion that a society of 82 million, a region of 720 million or a planet of 6 billion citizens can achieve an optimal allocation of social resources by favouring the decision making powers of the suppliers of goods and services, neglects the extraordinarily complex interdependence of modern human existence, where the distribution of resources at any given time is not simply the result of market or state but of climate, terrain, war, famine, demography, disease, conflict, gender relations, inheritance, established hierarchies of wealth and power, culturally embedded norms, to name but a few. These and other factors interfere with and overdetermine the processes of both market and state allocation, suggesting above all that the value placed on an individual's labour – the individual's material rewards – is almost entirely arbitrary: the machinist, the policeman, the nurse, the bricklayer, the teacher, the foundry worker, the laboratory assistant in China or Mexico or Estonia may be as skilful and dedicated as their counterparts in Europe, but their rewards and their social expectations are very different. Recent attempts to calculate the value to society of unpaid parental or household 'labour' – and the corresponding acknowledgement of this in Scandinavian and other pension systems – cast even greater doubt on the market 'valuation' of work in general.

The complex interdependence of the economic processes of chains of production and service provision – providing the cup of coffee in Starbucks, the digital radio in the hypermarket or the famous fruit yoghurt on its epic journey around Europe – implies a degree of cooperation and social integration that the individualised models of rational resource allocation (wage, salary, bonus, social benefit, pension entitlement) underplay or even deny. Nevertheless, the rhetoric of rational, individually justifiable rewards is extremely persuasive. It permeates not just meritocratic thinking but also liberal theories of social justice like those of John Rawls, who was able to justify social and economic inequalities so long as they benefited the least well-off (Rawls 1971: 303); this in turn has been used to underpin neoliberal economics.

More significantly for German and other European societies is the related modification of views of social justice away from quantitative notions of distributive fairness towards more opaque formulations like 'participatory justice', the 'justice of opportunity'. Gerhard Schröder, in the name of social democracy, makes the explicit distinction: 'We cannot limit ourselves any longer to distributional justice. This is no longer feasible because an expansion of social budgets cannot be anticipated and, by the way, is also not worth striving for. In order to achieve social justice in the knowledge and information society it is above all of decisive importance to create the justice of opportunity' (Schröder 2000: 203). Peer Steinbrück, Schröder's party colleague and the current Federal Finance Minister in Angela Merkel's Grand Coalition, aligns social justice even more with the performance principle:

> Social justice in the future has to mean pursuing policy for those who do something for the future of our country: who learn and gain qualifications, who work, who have children and bring them up, who start an enterprise and create jobs, who achieve success for themselves and our society. Politics must concern itself with them – and only with them. (*Die Zeit*, 11 November 2003)

The proximity of this new social democratic 'justice based on performance' to the views of CDU and CSU – the views were expressed two years before the 2005 elections – makes the subsequent formation of the Grand Coalition in November 2005 easy to understand and the seemingly seamless continuity of policy preferences from Red–Green to Red–Black. As Merkel and Steinbrück steer the German economy through rises in indirect (mass) taxation and towards further reductions in capital taxation, it is worth considering the evidence of increasing inequalities and the associated dangers for the cohesion of German society.

Two important indicators of income distribution are the wages and profits ratio, i.e., the share of wages and profits in national income. These are variously calculated, but the gross ratios for both wages and profits show the results of the primary (market) allocation of national income to wage and salary earners on the one hand and owners of capital on the other. The net ratios show the results of the secondary (state) allocation of resources through revenue and expenditure in the form of disposable household income for the same two categories. The validity of this functional distribution (according to the functional categories of capital and labour) is only partly qualified by the fact that wage and salary earners derive a small proportion of their household income from interest on bank savings accounts, fixed interest securities and dividends. The trend is unmistakable and continues that of the 1980s (see Chapter 3, Figure 3.5). The proportion of national income allocated to wage and salary earners fell from 71 per cent in 1991 to 69 per cent in 2005 (66.8 per cent in the first six months of 2006), while the ratio of gross profits to national income rose from 27.1 per cent in 1993 (the year of recession in West Germany) to 32.6 per cent in 2005 (36 per cent in the first half year of 2006). The columns in the graph do not really show the huge macroeconomic significance of this shift in primary distribution. The two percentage point drop between 1991 and 2005 means that wage and salary earners received €33.5 billion less than if the distribution ratios had remained the same; cumulatively the fall in the gross wages ratio signified a considerable decline, firstly, in readily taxable income – in contrast to income from capital that was historically more adept at reducing

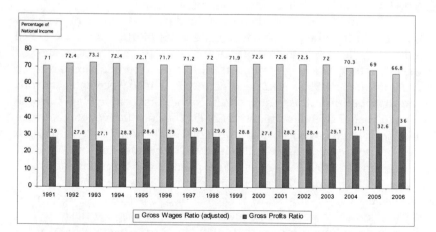

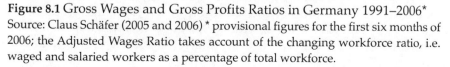

Figure 8.1 Gross Wages and Gross Profits Ratios in Germany 1991–2006*
Source: Claus Schäfer (2005 and 2006) * provisional figures for the first six months of 2006; the Adjusted Wages Ratio takes account of the changing workforce ratio, i.e. waged and salaried workers as a percentage of total workforce.

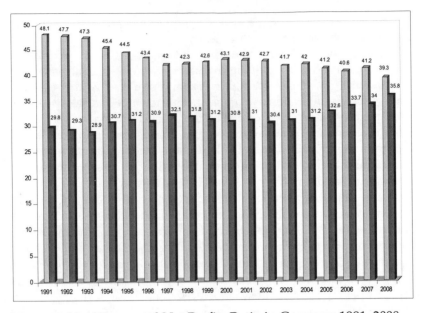

Figure 8.2 Net Wages and Net Profits Ratio in Germany 1991–2008
Source: Claus Schäfer (2008: 588)

tax liabilities and was, in any case, the beneficiary of targeted reductions in corporation and assessed income tax. Secondly, it signified a corresponding fall in post-tax disposable income. Figure 8.2 shows the net distribution of national income, after subtraction of direct taxes and social insurance contributions and after state fiscal transfers to individuals and households.

Figure 8.2 shows the combined effect of the downward trend of the gross wages ratio and the unequal effects of state redistribution measures since unification. The decline in the net wages ratio is considerably more marked than the fall in the gross wages ratio – from 48.1 per cent of national income (net social product) in 1991 to 41.2 per cent in 2005, a full 6.9 percentage points. Had the distribution ratios remained the same, disposable wage income would have been €115 billion higher in 2005. The cumulative total between 1991 and 2005 would have been in the order of €985 billion. The redistribution favoured net profits, although the cumulative volume of additional national income accruing to capital as a result of the changing distribution ratios was 'only' some €266 billion (27 per cent of the cumulative €985 billion which wage and salary earners forewent); the remaining 73 per cent were absorbed one way or another by the state through increases in statutory social insurance contributions, the Solidarity Surcharge and other changes to income tax statutes. The magnitude of the reduction in the net wages ratio of 6.9 percentage points in the fifteen years (1991–2005) becomes apparent if it is compared to the 5.2 per cent drop over thirty years between 1960 and 1990

(Schäfer 2006: 584). It above all constitutes an endogenous shock to the structure of demand within the German economy.

It is fatal in terms of both cyclical and growth policy that the purchasing power potential of the two income ratios have asymmetrical effects. Income from profits and wealth which at the micro-economic level tend to be associated with high incomes also manifest strong tendencies towards savings which do not have an effect on demand; the tendency to consume which is largely associated with wage incomes and which has strong demand effects, is unable to develop because of stagnating, indeed falling incomes at micro-economic level'. (Schäfer 2005: 605f)

The stagnation/reduction of recurrent state transfers through pensions, unemployment and other social benefits (Schäfer 2006: 584) – which have strong demand effects – reinforce the shock effect of the fall in gross and net wages ratios. Crucially, there is no evidence of weak consumer demand being compensated by a corresponding rise in investment demand. The trend identified for the 1980s and 1990s (Chapters Three to Six) continued after unification. As Figure 8.3 indicates, the ratios of both gross investments and investments in equipment (normally a key indicator of extended capacity and employment) fell between 1991 and 2005, while the profits ratio rose.

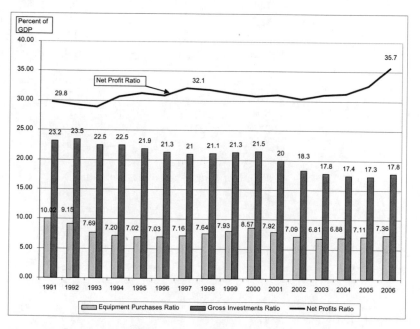

Figure 8.3 Investment Ratio and Profits Ratio 1991–2006
Sources: Claus Schäfer (2006); Statistisches Bundesamt

Figures 8.2 and 8.3 demonstrate the failure of state policy outlined in preceding chapters. They also indicate growing income inequality in Germany, and they provide an important background for an understanding of the deterioration of other aspects of social deprivation. The second Poverty Report of the federal government (Bundesregierung 2005: 15) revealed that the number of households below the official EU poverty line (60 per cent of median income of all households) had risen to 13.5 per cent in 2003 from 12.1 per cent in 1998 and, continuing the trend from 1983, the figures for East Germany show almost a fifth of the population (19.3 per cent) below the poverty line in 2003 (1998: 17.1 per cent). It is important to note that these figures refer to individuals and households *after* state transfers are factored

Table 8.1 Group-specific poverty ratios (below 60 per cent of median income) in Germany

Population Group	1998	2003
	Gender differentiation	
Men	10.7	12.6
Women	13.3	14.4
	Differentiation according to age	
0-15	13.8	15.0
16-24	14.9	19.1
25-49	11.5	13.5
50-64	9.7	11.5
65 and above	13.3	11.4
	Differentiation according to occupational status	
Self-employed	11.2	9.3
Employee	5.7	7.1
Unemployed	33.1	40.9
Pensioner	12.2	11.8
	People in single-person households	
Total	22.4	22.8
Men	20.3	22.5
Women	23.5	23.0
	People in households with children	
Single Parents	35.4	35.4
Two Parents with children	10.8	11.6
Overall Poverty Ratio	12.1	13.5

Source: Bundesregierung 2005: 17

in. The Poverty Report also shows that particular groups are more exposed to poverty than others. The self-employed, pensioners and those in full-time work are less vulnerable, whereas children up to the age of fifteen, young adults (sixteen to twenty-four), the unemployed, single parents and single householders have higher poverty ratios (see Table 8.1). The increased levels of poverty correspond to increased levels of affluence at the other end of the scale; the trend towards a wider 'spread' in the distribution of income is evident (Bundesregierung 2005: 12). While the richest 10 per cent of the population enjoyed 17.8 per cent of net household income in 1999, by 2003 this had risen to 21.6 per cent; the share of the poorest decile fell from 4.2 per cent to 3.9 per cent in the same period.

It is noteworthy that the figures derive from the period before the introduction of the Hartz IV measures, reducing benefits to the long-term unemployed, one of the most vulnerable groups in the Table 8.1; the likelihood of an increased widening of wage and income disparities has arguably increased (Seifert 2006: 604).

The distribution of wealth has also seen a widening of the disparities between rich and poor (Table 8.2); the bottom 10 per cent of all households has higher debts than assets and their position worsened in the decade between 1993 and 2003 from -0.2 per cent to -0.6 per cent of total wealth, while the share of the top 10 per cent has risen by 2.1 percentage points to 46.8 per cent. The top two deciles own over two thirds (67.5 per cent) of all private assets; the bottom five deciles only 3.8 per cent.

Table 8.2 Distribution of Wealth in Germany 1993–2003

Decile	Median Values in € 1000			Proportions of total wealth in percent		
	1993	1998	2003	1993	1998	2003
1	-2.1	-3.9	-7.9	-0.2	-0.3	-0.6
2	2.4	1.3	0.8	0.2	0.1	0.1
3	6.3	5.9	6.1	0.6	0.5	0.5
4	12.5	13.4	16.2	1.2	1.2	1.2
5	23.9	27.3	34.9	2.3	2.4	2.6
6	50.7	58.5	70.5	4.8	5.1	5.3
7	105.7	112.1	123.6	10	9.9	9.3
8	160.3	171.2	190.0	15.1	15.1	14.2
9	227.3	247.0	275.8	21.4	21.7	20.7
10	474.7	504.3	624.1	44.7	44.4	46.8

Source: Bundesregierung 2005

Income and wealth inequalities and income poverty have significant ramifications beyond the standard of living of poor households.

- Dietz and Ludwig (2006: 108) provide the crassest correlation between poverty and life expectancy in Germany, when they point out that men with a gross income of less than € 1,500 a month draw a pension (i.e., live beyond retirement) for an average of 10.8 years, whereas a man on more than € 4,500 a month can expect to live a further 18.2 years.
- The linkage between inequality, poverty and criminality has been well demonstrated (Entorf and Spengler 2002). Crime levels in Germany – measured per 100,000 members of the population – rose from under 3,000 incidents per year in the years of full employment to some 7,000 in the early 1980s to around 8,000 from the 1990s onward. Young males continue to be overrepresented in terms of the volume of cases, but now at higher levels than between 1960 and 1980 (Heinz 2005). Some three-quarters of young criminals have low educational qualifications. One regional survey showed that the ratio of young offenders, at least one of whose parents had been affected by unemployment, rose from 16.3 per cent in 1990 to 27.5 per cent in 1996 (Pfeiffer and Wetzels 2001). The robust correlations between a higher Gini-Coefficient and high prison populations and the fact of the higher representation of lower social classes within prison populations would imply increasing problems if income disparities in Germany widen further.
- Drug abuse is associated with both social deprivation and overall crime rates (Entorf and Spengler 2002); a high proportion of burglaries and robberies are driven by the need to feed a drug habit. Entorf and Winker (2001: 8) show a significant rise in drug offences between 1984 and 1999 from around 100 per 100,000 inhabitants to around 300, with a sharp rise in East Germany from almost zero in 1993 to around 170 in 1999.
- The correlation between poverty and education is acknowledged by the federal government (Bundesregierung 2005: 40, 58 etc) and many others; the proportion of social benefit recipients with no or only basic school qualifications stood at 63.4 per cent in 2002. Several studies, including the comparative PISA study, have confirmed the linkage between educational success and the social background of children (see: Dietz and Ludwig 2006: 105; Kaßebaum 2006: 193). According to the educational trade union *Gewerkschaft Erziehung und Wissenschaft* (GEW) '(t)here is no other comparable state in the world where school success is so heavily dependent on the income and educational attainments of the parents as in Germany' (GEW 2005). Both the Red–Green and the current Grand Coalition have thus stressed the improvement of educational opportunity as a key policy objective. However, according to Schäfer both administrations have ignored the danger that the young people affected may not be helped or be able to help themselves 'if the material preconditions for seizing and exploiting educational opportunities are not given, but taken away', i.e., if households remain poor and disadvantaged or benefits are cut in the manner of Hartz IV (Schäfer 2006: 589).

Social capital theory also asserts that there is a correlation between relatively narrow disparities of income distribution and greater 'social connectedness and civic engagement' (Putnam 2000: 359) and that wider disparities erode social cohesion, reducing the social capital (parental, group, community experience and understanding) that could have been deployed to support disadvantaged elements within society. This reinforces the argument that demands more than the enhancement of opportunity, as recommended by the popularisers of 'activation' in employment and social policy (e.g., Schröder and Steinbrück). Activation – focusing on the qualifications and skills of the unemployed individual as 'supply-side' factors of employability through personal consultations with employment advisors etc., – can only be sustained as a policy strategy if it is combined with policies that address other features of social deprivation, including the communities within which the individuals live, the quality of the local environment, of accommodation, the physical extent of the living space available, the level of crime, the general levels of health, the availability of leisure, sporting and social facilities, levels of civic engagement and trust in social and political institutions. More obviously, 'activation' will only be sustainable if at the end of the process the individual finds regular and rewarding employment. In a labour market where the ratio of vacancies to registered unemployed (without the unregistered reserve) is 1:6.5 in the whole country and 1:8.6 in the East, there is a clear and obvious danger of failing to fulfil expectations on a grand scale, of reinforcing exclusion and the feeling of exclusion. In a social culture which places so much stress on material success, on conspicuous consumption and 'performance' (*Leistung*), and where top salaries and annual bonuses frequently stand in crass contrast to stagnating real wages and reduced social benefits, the danger of increasing social exclusion, of persistent intergenerational poverty (PROFIT 2007) of 'de-solidarisation' (Eissel 2006: 266ff) and brutalisation of social relations, is very real.

Issues of social justice and the distribution of social resources are not confined to within Germany's borders. Indeed the intensity of the current debates in Germany about distribution and the semantics of social justice are inextricably linked to the processes of global redistribution that have been taking place at such a breathtaking speed over the last quarter of a century, the period covered in this book. A central tenet of this book is of the continuity of neoliberal, supply-side preferences in economic policy before and after unification, through the Kohl and Schröder eras to the current Merkel administration. The Grand Coalition – for all the self-demarcating rhetoric of CDU/CSU and SPD before the coalition agreement – reflects this continuity. It also reflects the apparent sense of inescapability from the global developments in technology, investment, production and trade that have caught all states in its maelstrom, even the most powerful; the poor growth records of Japan and Germany, the second and third largest economies in the world, and the chronic trading and payments deficit of the United States certainly suggest that the self-adequate 'Westphalian' nation state is dead. Nevertheless, as stated on several occasions in this book, neoliberal globalisation was in large measure the result of political decisions by representatives of leading nation states, including the United States, Japan and Germany; it was not just the result of the revolution in communications technology. The abandonment of fixed exchange rates and exchange controls, the deregulation of financial markets ('big bang'), the intra- and interregional liberalisation of trade, of investment and state procurement, the institutionalisation of monetarism through the establishment of independent central banking throughout most of the OECD, the deregulation of labour markets, the privatisation of public assets (including natural monopolies) and the adoption in Europe of fiscal austerity measures – all these decisions were made with the approval of sovereign parliaments. Secondly, while globalisation has undoubtedly produced common and similar political reactions to the behaviour of 'the markets' by most nation states, there have been clear differences in significant areas of macroeconomic policy.

The relative success of both the United States and the United Kingdom economies in recent years is ascribed by neoliberal critics of 'euro-sclerosis' as a function of the largescale removal of employment protection statutes in these two economies under successive regimes and the corresponding moderation of wage levels (Sinn 2005: 27ff; 123ff). In contrast, other economists point to the distinctive pattern of fiscal and monetary policy in the United States and the United Kingdom. Schulmeister (2005: 100ff) goes as far as describing US economic policy as 'Keynesian' – albeit of a 'bastard' variety – firstly in its rejection of prescriptive rules and secondly in its marked anti-cyclical character. Thus the reaction of the Federal Reserve to the cyclical downturn of 2000 was to reduce central bank rates from 6.5 per cent to 1.75 per cent and then to 1 per cent, stimulating both corporate investment and consumer spending, while fiscal policy produced tax reductions for private households between 2000 and 2002 of the order of 3.8 per cent of disposable income. The OECD notes that the Umited Kingdom's 'expansionary fiscal policy has been an important factor supporting demand since the global downturn' (OECD 2005c: 29–30). In contrast, the eurozone states committed themselves to a rules-based economic policy regime which firstly set monetary stability and thus monetary policy above all other policy fields, secondly established a policy architecture which produced the most extreme degree of central bank independence and thirdly embarked on programme of fiscal austerity which largely ignored the progress of the economic cycle. The deflationary continuum, perfected under the Bundesbank in Germany (Leaman 2001: 241f), was reproduced in the framework of both qualification for EMU between 1992 and 1998 and, with the Stability and Growth Pact of 1997, in the management of national fiscal affairs since the introduction of the euro in 1999. While most eurozone states avoided the worst effects of pro-cyclical budgetary consolidation, Germany – as the author of the SGP and with the colossal burden of unification – manoeuvred itself into pro-cyclical deflationary stagnation: between 2000 and 2004 state investments in the United States were expanded by 17.3 per cent, in the eurozone by 11.2 per cent, but were cut back by -17.3 per cent in Germany. Public sector employment rose in both the United States and the eurozone (+3.9 per cent and +4.8 per cent) but was reduced in Germany by 4.3 per cent. State expenditure in Germany rose by only 6.5 per cent but by 23.6 per cent in the United States. German transfer payments to private households rose by only 10.6 per cent in this period, but corresponding expenditure rose by 30.7 per cent in the United States and by 22.5 per cent in the eurozone (even though unemployment in Germany had risen by 27.6 per cent) compared to the eurozone's +1.5 per cent (Schulmeister 2005: 105).

The comparison between the stance of policymakers in the United States, the United Kingdom, the eurozone (without Germany) and Germany reveals above all that there *are macropolitical alternatives in the process of adapting to globalisation*. States – notably powerful states – have political choices. What it also indicates is the very particular position of Germany's political economy at the very particular historical juncture where it finds itself. As a technologically and socially advanced capitalist economy it manifests a number of common critical features:

- It has reached a level of affluence which makes the achievement of additional increments of growth more problematic in volume terms, in terms of the satisfaction of material needs and in terms of the ecological effect on finite resources. The relative saturation of demand (as well as a growing environmental sensitivity) produces both lower exponential growth in GDP – the primary vehicle of employment – and a greater elasticity of demand; in periods of economic insecurity, of low growth and higher unemployment the demand for nonessential goods is likely to fall with corresponding pro-cyclical effects.
- It has established a pattern of social reproduction where female fertility is insufficient to maintain a stable population, i.e., below 2.1 children per adult woman. The resulting demographic asymmetry weakens the future potential demand for goods and services and alters the potential patterns of demand between generational groups (pensioner households will have significantly different patterns of expenditure and need compared to younger generations). This demographic imbalance will compound the saturation effects of affluence.
- It is increasingly dependent on exports as a vehicle for sustaining domestic economic activity and domestic employment but, at the same time, increasingly dependent on the cost advantages of imported pre-

products from foreign companies or of imported goods and services from the foreign affiliates of German companies abroad. These cost advantages are exaggerated by both the relative cheapness of energy – oil price inflation since the 1970s has in fact been lower than overall consumer price inflation – and the specific anomaly of most trading nations not taxing aircraft fuel (kerosene) despite its extreme polluting effect (a key 'nondecision' of major world states over the last quarter of a century).

- The dependence on new markets for both goods and FDI has produced strong measures of trade liberalisation – through the auspices of GATT and its successor, the WTO – but much less attention to the social and economic conditions of the working populations in the economies, newly integrated into the global trading system. The deficiencies in the regulatory systems governing employment law, social welfare, health, accidents, invalidity and old age in many emerging economies have produced strong calls from the International Labour Organisation (ILO 2004), the European Trade Union Confederation (ETUC 2006) and human rights NGOs for countries like China to improve their employment rights. In response, and clearly mindful of the need to present a better human rights face to the world ahead of the 2008 Olympics, China drafted a law in 2006 to end sweatshop labour and strengthen trade union rights, but this has 'set off a battle with American and other foreign corporations that have lobbied against it by hinting that they may build fewer factories here' (*New York Times*, 16 October 2006).

- The global division of labour is changing rapidly; technological developments and productivity growth, when combined with global population growth, will produce a permanent surplus of labour worldwide and allow global corporations to provide goods and services, using a fraction of the available labour force and thus at low cost. Market allocation of labour cannot solve the problem, because of the opposing logics of microeconomic profit maximisation and macrosocial management of human existence. Allowing corporations to dictate the framework of political and social governance in a global political economy that is characterised above all by unequal development has catastrophic potential for the future of democracy and human welfare. In the absence of international regulation of the behaviour of TNCs, there is a real danger of the 'race to the bottom' – of reducing welfare and employment protection standards to the lowest common denominator.

- The nature of TNC and other 'investment' worldwide confirms the view that it cannot be relied upon to satisfy the political need of nation states for structural unemployment to be reduced. Firstly, 90 per cent of FDI is not in greenfield operations – involving the establishment of new capacity – but in the acquisition of existing capacity through mergers and acquisitions (UNCTAD 2005). Figure 8.4 shows the recent surge in global merger and acquisition activity – predominantly acquisitions by large companies of other companies and not the merger of equals through equity swaps. The data from Dealogic indicate that the value of takeovers in 2006 reached $4 trillion, overtaking the previous record of $3.8 trillion in 2000. A full 18.4 per cent of the $4 trillion – $725.3 billion – was deployed by 'private equity' companies that operate by shorter time horizons than ordinary TNCs and focus on maximising shorter-term 'shareholder value', often at the expense of the workforce through asset stripping and increased debt burdens (UNCTAD 2005: 19). However, in its World Investment Report for 2005, the United Nations Council for Trade and Development noted that 'more recently, TNCs have also increasingly been driven by short-term performance targets to meet shareholders' expectations for high and rapid returns' (UNCTAD 2005: 19). Germany, which had historically resisted hostile takeovers, has recently become a target for private equity and hedge fund operators, including the acquisition of a controlling interest in the Frankfurt stock exchange (*Deutsche Börse*) by Atticus, a US private equity company, and TCI, a UK-based hedge fund in 2004. In 2005 the German property market – deemed undervalued by international investors – was also the subject of several private equity acquisitions, notably of Deutsche Viterra AG by Terra Firma from E.ON; this deal was marked out, firstly because it was a heavily 'leveraged' buyout, i.e., the $8.8 billion deal was financed predominantly by loans, but secondly because the loans were raised in Germany, such that the deal could not be categorised as a cross-border takeover.

• Reliance on the 'invisible hand' of global FDI markets is thus a perilous speculation for all nation states, when the market operators seek the 'efficiencies' of cheap labour, oligopolistic market shares and short-term asset stripping. Some leading German statesmen, including the current Vice-Chancellor Franz Müntefering, have, it should be said, raised serious concerns about the activities of the anonymous 'locusts' and 'vultures'. Alfred Mechtersheimer's *Handbuch Deutsche Wirtschaft* (Mechtersheimer 2007) includes a whole section on the 'strategy of the locusts' and Peer Steinbrück has used the 2007 German presidency of the EU to highlight the need to regulate hedge funds (Münchau 2007: 19).

These common problems require common regulatory solutions, based on supranational, multilateral agreement, just as the eurozone requires consistent and long-term processes of policy coordination (Heise 2002: 8ff). However, on top of the critical problems that Germany shares with the advanced welfarist democracies in the OECD, its predicament is compounded by unique structural economic and structural political factors which deserve the most urgent attention from its political and economic elite, from German civil society, from the EU Commission and fellow member states and from the institutions of global economic governance like the WTO, the IMF and the World Bank. The attention is urgent because

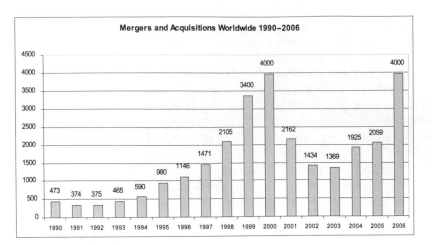

Figure 8.4 Mergers and Acquisitions Worldwide 1997–2006
Sources: Dealogic

the weakening of Germany's political economy weakens Europe even further than its demographic fate forebodes, and with it the development of the global economic system.

The most obvious *structural economic* factor, examined in detail in this book, is the reverberating shock of unification – the 'greatest imaginable accident' (*größter anzunehmender Unfall*; GAU), as it has been described in the sensational but no less convincing account by Uwe Müller (2006). It is no longer idly alarmist to assert that the long-term effect of unification will be considerably worse than the effect of the Second World War on Germany's development. After all, within fifteen years of *Stunde Null* in 1945 and just twelve years after the currency reform, the Federal Republic had undergone a dramatic reconstruction of its infrastructure, both civilian and economic; had achieved full employment for a population that had grown from 42.9 million in 1939 to 55.9 million in 1960; and achieved a public sector fiscal surplus in both 1960 and 1961. The seventeen years since unification have certainly seen improvements in the East's infrastructure and significant pockets ('clusters') of growth, but average real growth has been well below 2 per cent, unemployment – despite the improvement in the winter of 2006/07 – has risen from cycle to cycle in both West and East Germany (January 2007: 11.4 per cent [West: 9.5 per cent; East: 18.8 per cent]) and the public sector borrowing requirement has exceeded the SGP ceiling of 3 per cent in eight of the seventeen years, averaging 2.89 per cent in the whole period. For the last ten years (since 1997) the East–West disparity has been widening, when it is incontestably only through the narrowing of that disparity that 'the future viability of our country' can be assured (Helmut Schmidt in 2005, cited in Müller 2006: 36). The prospect of the East as a 'Mezzogiorno without the Mafia' (ibid.) represents a burden that will drain the coffers of the German state and the dynamic energy of the population if remedial action is not forthcoming.

A second unique structural economic feature is Germany's geoeconomic centrality within the reunited and now extensively integrated Europe. It is the largest European economy, the third largest economy in the world; it is the biggest exporter in Europe and in 2005 with $1.133 trillion of exports the largest exporter in the world (United States: $1.024 trillion). It is the dominant trading partner within the EU, the main export market for thirteen out of the twenty-six other EU member states and the main source of imports for sixteen of the twenty-six (see Table 8.3), most notably of investment goods. As a key advocate of the EU's eastward expansion, it is

Table 8.3 Germany's Centrality as European Trading Partner 2005

	Proportion of Exports to Germany in %	Proportion of imports from Germany in %
Austria	31.2 (1)	45.9 (1)
Belgium	19.4 (1)	17.2 (2)
Bulgaria	9.8 (3)	13.6 (2)
Cyprus	6.0 (4)	8.4 (4)
Czech Republic	33.5 (1)	30.0 (1)
Denmark	17.6 (1)	20.5 (1)
Estonia	6.2 (5)	13.9 (2)
Finland	10.5 (3)	16.2 (1)
France	14.7 (1)	18.9 (1)
Greece	12.4 (1)	12.7 (1)
Hungary	30.2 (1)	27.5 (1)
Ireland	7.4 (4)	9.2 (3)
Italy	13.1 (1)	17.2 (1)
Latvia	10.2 (3)	13.9 (1)
Lithuania	9.4 (3)	15.1 (2)
Luxembourg	21 (1)	21.8 (2)
Malta	11.2 (5)	8.0 (4)
Netherlands	24.9 (1)	16.6 (1)
Poland	28.2 (1)	29.6 (1)
Portugal	11.9 (3)	13.4 (2)
Romania	14.0 (2)	14.0 (2)
Slovakia	26.2 (1)	25.1 (1)
Slovenia	19.8 (1)	19.5 (1)
Spain	11.4 (2)	15.3 (1)
Sweden	10.2 (2)	17.6 (1)
United Kingdom	10.5 (2)	12.8 (1)

Source: CIA World Factbook; figures for 2005

a key bridge for trade, investment, credit and economic diplomacy as well as the physical bridge for oil (the Northern Druzhba) and gas pipelines (Yarnal-Europe and Transgas). Whatever metaphor one employs, Europe's development depends very heavily on Germany's leading (hegemonic) position; Imanuel Geiss describes postunification Germany as 'the capstone in the delicately vaulted arch' of Europe (Geiss 1997); too heavy, too light or weakened by erosion, that capstone threatens the integrity of the whole edifice. Reinhard Rode's early reflections on the greater danger of a weakened Germany (Rode 1993: 203ff) – as opposed to the revitalised regional hegemon à la neo-realist school (Mearsheimer 1990) – would be well heeded by the architects of European and global governance.

A *structural political* factor confronting Germany in particular is indeed the policy architecture of the EU – not because other member states are not bound within it, but because it makes greater and contradictory demands on Germany. As noted in earlier chapters, the institutions of the EU place a disproportionately large burden on its largest member state, firstly as paymaster, secondly as crisis manager and growth locomotive; the size of Germany's domestic economy renders its demand for goods and services within the single market critical to the success of that economy. At the same time the ambitions of the Stability and Growth Pact limit the potential for expanding German demand for imports from other EU countries by imposing not just ceilings for PSBR and overall state debt but by demanding the reduction of borrowing and debt to zero in the medium term. Whether this ambition is appropriate for the optimal fiscal management of the normal state – the other eurozone member states, for example – can be set aside here precisely because Germany is not a normal state in a normal historical context. It is a markedly abnormal state in an abnormal context, seeking to resolve the abnormal problem of economic and social unification. Jean-Philippe Cotis, chief economist at the OECD, praised the daring of the German state for taking such a doughty approach to budgetary consolidation (quoted in *Die Welt*, 5 January 2007) but was clearly blind to Germany's abnormality and, more importantly, to the damage a one-eyed approach to fiscal policy is doing to Germany's and Europe's fortunes. The policy architecture of budgetary consolidation, market liberalisation and a reduced state involvement in the allocation of social resources is *entirely inappropriate* for Germany's extreme predicament. Arne Heise (2002c: 8) sees no virtue in the zero-deficit ambitions of 'the neo-liberal world' and argues convincingly for a flexible adjustment of the SGP rules, prioritising the growth element of the pact, without taking one's eye off the dangers of budgetary extravagance. The 'austerity straitjacket' of the current SGP is, according to Heise and others, dysfunctional and unnecessary; with the weakness of the dollar 'the international finance markets view a one per cent growth boost more favourably than a one per cent reduction in inflation' (ibid.). If orthodox economists were to take the negative growth effects of the SGP's regulatory framework as seriously as they take the supposed negative effects of environmental regulation on growth and investments (Haythornthwaite 2007: 17) there would be less to worry about.

Taken together, the challenges of global location, competition and national unification represent exogenous shocks which will have a far greater effect on the economic development and welfare of German citizens than the brutal interruption of a genocidal, industrialised war. Very soon, Germany and its European partners will also have to face the challenge of slow, zero or even negative growth, particularly if the forecast trend of major population decline continues. Neoliberalism, in particular the deflationary eurozone variant of neoliberalism, is probably one of the worst vehicles for such a challenge. It is ironic that, as German corporations and their academic allies demand the weakening of trade union power and the institutions of codetermination (*Mitbestimmung*), the German political economy may lose a set of consensus seeking institutions that could contribute (could have contributed) to the challenge of an economic culture that physically, mathematically and ecologically is incapable of growing as fast as the laws of capitalist accumulation currently demand.

Neoliberalism does not simply have to account for the failure of its *deliberate* supply-side measures to generate the profit-investment-growth-employment cycle and for its responsibility in increasing income and wealth disparities nationally and globally. As culpable as the deliberate measures of neoliberal regimes in Germany and elsewhere, are the *nondecisions* to counteract economic activities which are both destabilising and ethically unsupportable. There have been sporadic attempts to reintroduce exchange controls to neutralise the volatility of international financial transactions, but no serious consideration has been given to the idea of a 'Tobin-Tax' on short-term international financial transactions. European Monetary Union has halted the intraregional currency speculation that blighted Europe in the 1980s and 1990s, but globally currency and equity markets remain hyperactive. Megamergers at national, regional or international level continue to be tolerated in the main by so-called competition authorities. States and supranational bodies choose to ignore the deliberate acquisition of monopolistic and monopsonistic market power and its systematic abuse. As in sport – the semantic home of competition – if the referee fails to penalise foul play, players will continue to commit fouls. Most culpable is the continuing toleration of 'offshore' tax havens by the global political community. Tax havens provide the corporate sector and wealthy members of the economic *and political* elites with the facility to avoid tax liabilities in the countries where their operations benefit from collectively financed economic and social infrastructures. This is an intolerable anomaly in a global political economy which demands such high standards of commercial probity in contract law, which punishes insider dealing, embezzlement and fraud and agrees extradition treaties for the prosecution of commercial crime. Tax havens, as they are exploited today, are scandalous facilitators of larceny on a grand scale. The world would not tolerate the existence of an island to where pirates and thieves can retreat with impunity. Why should it tolerate financial offshoring and the ruinous taxation competition that ensues between increasingly weakened nation states?

Germany's singular neoliberal sin of omission was to ignore the implications of a premature and ill-conceived currency union and to continue with a policy of 'business as usual'. Having taken the bold (and probably unavoidable) decision to introduce the DM into the East and to favour savers over debtors with a generous conversion rate, the failure to pursue a coordinated structural policy aimed at the rapid convergence of Eastern productivity with that of the West, was a *disastrous nondecision*. As Lange and Pugh (1998: 111f) point out, German economic and monetary union, which dictated that East German wages be converted at a rate of 1:1 had to be supported by a high-wage, high-technology strategy. For such a strategy to succeed, however, in the speediest manner possible, nothing short of a wartime command economy with the tightest coordination of macroeconomic policies was required to help Eastern enterprises survive along with their Western counterparts. This coordination was not forthcoming. Policy remained fragmented, wastefully uncoordinated and – worst of all – ideologically complacent and intellectually lazy. It would be a tragedy if the legacy of the 1982 *Wende* – a sluggish national economy with its permanent crisis region in the East, and a weakened polity – cannot be reversed. For this to happen, the paralysis of German and European politicians, who remain largely in denial, has to end.

POSTSCRIPT

The manuscript for this book was completed before the collapse of the global banking system in the autumn of 2008 and the subsequent desperate attempts by state authorities within the developed world to mitigate the effects of this economic 'tsunami', as Alan Greenspan and Axel Weber, among many others, have dubbed it. Given the scale of the current crisis and the particular effects it is having on Germany's political economy, a short postscript is therefore in order.

In contrast to the real tsunami of December 2004, however, the 2008 crisis of global capitalism was entirely predictable; it was not a manifestation of the cruel, capricious forces of nature, but a man-made disaster, presided over by the political and economic elites of the world's leading nations with the active or tacit support of mainstream economists in the universities and research institutes of these nations. The helter-skelter speed with which neo-liberalism was embraced as the paradigm of economic management replacing Keynesianism by these elites is explicable in terms of (short-term and short-sighted) economic interest and political fashion. What is less explicable and much less excusable was the intellectual abandonment – by the majority of academic economists in the OECD – of the principles of scepticism and caution when assessing the credentials of the new orthodoxy. The critical questioning of received wisdom, demanded ad nauseam of all social science undergraduates, was largely set aside and replaced by either a triumphalist celebration of 'the' market and its 'self-healing' properties or a fatalistic acceptance of the 'natural' (economic) order in which the market prevails, whether we like it or not. There were notable and honourable exceptions – some of whom are cited in this book – who continued to assert the inherent flaws of markets and the need to maintain, adapt or strengthen democratic state controls of their operations. There were several who focused on the accumulation and abuse of market power in the shape of oligopolies, monopsonies, cartels and other strategic gatekeepers in the global cycles of production, distribution and consumption. But there were many, many more who urged their respective states to 'roll back' the political controls of economic processes, to deregulate factor markets, to privatise state-owned natural monopolies and other utilities, to liberalise international capital markets and even to recommend tax havens and tax competition as 'welfare enhancing'[1]. The marginalising of economists of a Keynesian, socialist, development, green and other non-orthodox stripe in the neo-liberal gold-rush of the 1980s and 1990s went hand-in-hand with the absorption of the major 'social democratic' parties of the west – traditionally bastions of redistributive welfare Keynesianism – into the new consensus. The seamless transition from Kohl to Schröder and Thatcher to Blair demonstrated this very clearly; both the Schröder- and Blair-eras were characterised by vigorous and frequently more incisive neo-liberal reforms than their conservative predecessors. Social inequality – the primary target of Europe's original social democrats – worsened in Schröder's Germany and in Blair's Britain. Indeed in all advanced economies, the share of wages and salaries as a proportion of national income declined by 6.82 percentage points between 1980 and 2005; the redistribution of national income away from waged income to profit income was even greater in Europe at 9.36 percentage points (figures derived from IMF: World Economic Outlook 2007). Future economic historians will, I predict, stress the unprecedented scale of this redistribution in favour of profit income between 1980 and the present day. Notwithstanding that a proportion of profit income covers the income from the savings of wage- and salary-earners, the aggregate decline of 6.8 percentage points in the wages ratio represents a colossal reduction of potential demand from the world's major economies. It is worth speculating about the implications for GDP growth if the wages ratio had remained constant. A very basic (counterfactual) calculation would suggest that the 18 most advanced industrial economies, with a collective GDP of $29.8 trillion in 2005, would have enjoyed an additional $2.03 trillion in gross household income. The direct and indirect (multiplier) effects on domestic demand of the (even just partial) deployment of this income would have been prodigious.

The failure by ostensibly progressive administrations to reverse this historically unprecedented redistribution of social resources in favour of capital was a reflection not just of their powerlessness but also of their conversion to the seductive illusions of neo-liberal supply-sidism: award

---

1. The website of the 'Coalition for Tax Competition', coordinated in the US by the Center for Freedom and Prosperity, contains some extraordinary arguments in favour of tax competition and tax havens, including an appeal to the human rights of 'business owners in Venezuela, ethnic Chinese in Indonesia, Jews in France (sic), or homosexuals in Saudia Arabia', namely that '(w)ithout the ability to protect their assets in so-called tax havens, these people would be at even greater danger' (Daniel Mitchell, senior fellow of the Heritage Foundation, cited in a CTC press release from April 2005; see website: http://www.freedomandprosperity.org/press/p04-07-05/p04-07-05.shtml (accessed 25.2.09)

corporations and their executives with lower taxation, reduced welfare levies, new market freedoms and higher profits and they will repay you with higher investment, higher levels of full-time employment and higher levels of stable growth. The current state deployment of trillions of dollars, euros and pounds to ward off economic calamity is sad proof of the intellectual poverty that underpinned this faith in the virtuous circle. As this volume has attempted to show, higher profits produced not higher investment, nor higher levels of stable growth, but colossal capital reserves which in turn were deployed, along with vast volumes of cheap credit, to finance an unprecedented wave of global mergers and acquisitions, short-term portfolio investments, currency speculation and the plethora of gambling instruments which have subsequently brought the neo-liberal house of cards tumbling down. The most serious consequence of the decoupling of monetary accumulation from the real processes of investment, production, distribution and consumption has been the suspension of the enabling, fiduciary function of financial services – the destruction of trust in money assets as a store of value. The particular attention given to the Ponzi-schemes of Bernard Madoff and Allen Stamford runs the risk of diverting attention away from the more pernicious generalised speculation which was predicated on the assumption that the asset values, on which colossal borrowing levels were based, would continue rising, allowing debts to be easily repaid. This, together with the increasingly unrealistic corporate expectations of rates of return in excess of 20 per cent, produced a global system of accumulation as near as dammit to a Pyramid / Ponzi scheme as makes no difference. If the stability of global capitalism depended on the persistence of aggregate asset price inflation, the peddlers of this assumption and the various Emperors who bought it were guilty of criminal duplicity and / or criminal stupidity. Madoff and Stamford are thus convenient scapegoats for a generalised degeneration of economic and political good sense which spread across the intellectual landscape of the West like an epidemic in the 1980s. The reversal of that paradigm shift (described in Chapters One and Two) is now under way; the motley collection of Emperors – in central banks, finance ministries, regulatory quangos, credit rating agencies and international political agencies – are rediscovering the virtues of the vigilant, supportive, coordinating and security-conscious state and covering their embarrassing nakedness in dramatic and speedy fashion.

Germany's political economy was never going to be immune to global crises, even if its lower exposure to US sub-prime 'securities' persuaded the Bundesbank (c.f its Financial Stability Report of April 2008) to declare its confidence in Germany's continued growth prospects; even after the decisive collapse of Lehmann brothers in September 2008, the Merkel administration remained comparatively sanguine about Germany's economic position. The crisis was perceived as being predominantly sectoral: limited to financial services and therefore more critical in the US, the UK and Ireland than in the core economies of Europe. In retrospect, the denial can be interpreted partly as intending to avoid further panic. However, apart from failing to stem the rapid decline in business confidence, German reluctance to acknowledge the depth of the incipient slump contributed to the disappointing levels of unanimity at the EU-summit in mid-October 2008. Furthermore, Germany's €480 billion guarantee package in support of bank liquidity was launched with the confident view that it was merely a safety net that would not need to be extensively deployed.

The government's sanguine assessment was reinforced by the 2008 Autumn Report of Germany's economic research institutes, published on 14 October, which foresaw a downturn but predicted a recovery in the second half of 2009 and the avoidance of recession this year. Even after the G20 summit in November and the announcement of the Federal Government's First 15-Point Programme, Peer Steinbrück – the Social Democratic Finance Minister – lambasted Gordon Brown for his shift to 'crass Keynesianism' in early December.

The November 15-Point Programme was the subject of considerable criticism within the ranks of the parties of the governing coalition, including the Bavarian CSU as well as the SPD. With a further 10-point drop in the IFO-Index between September (92.8) and December (82.6), a 10 per cent drop in exports in November and a series of negative forecasts, the Federal Government finally began coalition talks about a more radical set of proposals which subsequently gained Bundestag approval. The stimulus package agreed in the Pact for Employment and Stability (PAS) amounted to €50 billion over two years: some €36 billion in 2009 (some 1.46 per cent of GDP at 2008 prices) and €14 billion (0.56 per cent) in 2010. The package was more than double the volume of the first crisis programme (€23 billion) agreed in parliament in December. With real GDP now forecast (by the Federal Economics Ministry as well as others) to fall by at least 4.5 per cent in 2009 alone, the package is relying on speedy multiplier effects to prevent further decline in 2010.

The regional and global situation in the Spring of 2009 is now such that an extended depression cannot be discounted. The fragile confidence in German recovery after two decades of disappointing growth, which emerged in the wake of the Hartz employment reforms, encouraged by marked falls in unemployment, has all but evaporated. Unemployment is rising rapidly, business confidence has plummeted and the already unrealistic ambitions of the federal state to achieve balanced budgets by 2011 have been effectively abandoned; the effects of the global downturn are threatening the growth prospects of Germany's export-dependent economy critically, but these effects are likely to be compounded by the political mistakes of the Kohl- and Schröder-eras covered in this book, in particular the failure to pursue coherent, coordinated structural policies aimed at ensuring the optimal integration of the five new Länder into the sophisticated political economy of the Federal Republic. Reliance on the allocatory efficiency of 'the' market has been calamitous for global economic governance as it has for the management of Germany's economic unification.

Nevertheless, and despite the damage incurred by naïve neo-liberal experimentation, Germany's institutional structures, its political and economic cultures retain invaluable resources for confronting both the immediate challenges of economic depression and the medium-term challenges of environmental crisis, demographic change and international conflict. These resources include the traditions of consensual conflict-resolution in both industrial relations and legislative politics, the sophisticated system of fiscal equalisation, a comparatively mature and dynamic culture of democratic participation and a deep-seated commitment to multi-lateral approaches to regional and global problems. In the short space of time since the absolute urgency of the current crisis has become apparent, Germany's institutions and leaders have also demonstrated a willingness to reassess global economic problems and to alter course away from neo-liberal complacency towards a more strictly regulated set of global economic relationships. The apparent preparedness of Merkel, Sarkozy and Obama to make common cause in combatting the long-standing nonsense of tax havens is promising. The broadening of crisis management to encompass the G20 nations bodes well for the reform of global economic governance, if only by preventing the destructive effects of great power unilateralism.

Whether the ongoing paradigm shift is radical enough to ensure the stable improvement in the living conditions of humankind is a matter of considerable doubt, however. The social and political fall-out from the economic slump has the potential to provoke frequent national and international conflicts, in particular over the distribution of scarce resources. It will not be sufficient to trust wise stateswomen and men with the task of restoring economic and social order. Well informed, open-minded democratic participation is utterly indispensable to the process. It is hoped that this book will contribute to the understanding of the complex politico-economic relationships affecting Europe's dominant industrial and trading economy and therefore support the efforts of future generations to distribute the world's resources sustainably and fairly.

Jeremy Leaman
March 2009

BIBLIOGRAPHY

Abelshauser, Werner (1983) *Wirtschaftsgeschichte der Bundesrepublik Deutschland 1945–1980*, Frankfurt am Main (Suhrkamp).

Abelshauser, Werner (2005a) *Deutsche Wirtschaftsgeschichte seit 1945*, Bonn (Bundeszentrale für politische Bildung).

Abelshauser, Werner (2005b) *The Dynamics of German Industry. Germany's Path toward the New Economy and the American Challenge*, New York/Oxford (Berghahn Books).

Albert, Michel (1991) *Capitalism against Capitalism*, Hoboken, NJ (Wiley).

Altvater, Elmar (1992) *Die Zukunft des Marktes*, Münster (Westfälisches Dampfboot Verlag).

Altvater, Elmar (1995) 'A Contest without Victors', in: *Journal of Area Studies*, 7.

Altvater, Elmar and Mahnkopf, Brigitte (1996) *Grenzen der Globalisierung. Ökonomie, Ökologie und Politik in der Weltgesellschaft*, Münster (Westfälisches Dampfboot Verlag).

Ambrosius, Gerald (1984) *Der Staat als Unternehmer*, Göttingen.

AngelouEconomics (2006) 'The Productivity Trap in Technology. How Increases in Output and Productivity Don't Translate into Jobs', www.angeloueconomics.com/technology-June2006.html.

Arbeitsgruppe Alternative Wirtschaftspolitik (AAW) (1984) *Memorandum '84. Gegen soziale Zerstörung durch Unternehmerherrschaft*, Cologne (Pahl-Rugenstein).

Arbeitsgruppe Alternative Wirtschaftspolitik (AAW) (1985) *Memorandum '85. Gegen die Unterwerfung der Arbeit und die Zerstörung der Umwelt – Mehr Arbeitsplätze, soziale Sicherheit und Umweltschutz*, Cologne (Pahl-Rugenstein).

Arbeitsgruppe Alternative Wirtschaftspolitik (AAW) (1986) *Memorandum '86. Für eine beschäftigungspolitische Offensive. Sofortmaßnahmen für zwei Millionen Arbeitsplätze*, Cologne (Pahl-Rugenstein).

Arbeitsgruppe Alternative Wirtschaftspolitik (AAW) (1988) *Memorandum'88: Im Abschwung: Gegensteuern statt Steuerreform*, Cologne (Pahl-Rugenstein).

Arbeitsgruppe Alternative Wirtschaftspolitik (AAW) (1989) *Memorandum'89: Gegen Unternehmermacht und Patriarchat*, Cologne (Pahl-Rugenstein).

Arbeitsgruppe Alternative Wirtschaftspolitik (AAW) (1990a) *Memorandum'90: Im deutsch-deutschen Umbruch*, Cologne (Pahl-Rugenstein).

Arbeitsgruppe Alternative Wirtschaftspolitik (AAW) (1990b) 'Sondermemorandum: Sozial-ökologisches Sofortprogramm – Risiken der deutschen deutschen Währungsunion', in: *Memo-Forum* 16.

Arbeitsgruppe Alternative Wirtschaftspolitik (AAW) (2006) *Memorandum 2006: Mehr Beschäftigung braucht eine andere Verteilung*, Cologne (Papyrossa).

Armingeon, K and M. Beyeler (2004) *The OECD and European Welfare States*, Cheltenham (Elgar).

Australian Stock Exchange (2005) *International Share Ownership*.

Balkhausen, Dieter (1992) *Gutes Geld und Schlechte Politik*, Düsseldorf.

Bandelow, Nils C. and Klaus Schubert (1998) 'Wechselnde Strategien und kontinuierlicher Abbau solidarischen Ausgleichs. Eine gesundheitspolitische Bilanz der Ära Kohl', in: Wewer, Göttrik (ed.) *Bilanz der Ära Kohl*, Opladen (Leske and Budrich).

Bandemer, Stephan von and John Haberle (1998) 'Wirtschaftspolitik im Zeichen des Primats der Politik oder der Ökonomie?', in: Wewer, Göttrik (ed.) *Bilanz der Ära Kohl*, Opladen (Leske and Budrich).

Barratt Brown, Michael (1993) *Fair Trade. Reform and Realities in the International Trading System*, London (Zed Books).

Barro, Robert and Sala-i-Martin, Xavier (1995) *Economic Growth*, New York (McGraw-Hill).

Beck, Dorothee and Hartmut Meine (1998) *Wasserprediger und Weintrinker*, Göttingen.

Bertelsmann-Stiftung (ed.) (2003) *Arbeitsmarktpolitik von 15 Ländern im Vergleich*, Gütersloh (Verlag Bertelsmann-Stiftung).

Besters, H. (1990) 'Hindernisse für Vollbeschäftigung', *aus politik und zeitgeschichte*, B/18.

Biedenkopf, Kurt and Miegel Meinhard (1979) *Die programmierte Krise. Alternativen zur staatlichen Schuldenpolitik*, Stuttgart (Bonn Aktuell).

Bispinck, Reinhard (1990) 'Tarifbewegungen im Jahr 1989', *WSI-Mitteilungen*, 3/90

Bispinck, Reinhard (2005) 'Betriebsräte, Arbeitsbedingungen undTarifpolitik', *WSI-Mitteilungen*, 6/301–307.

Bispinck, Reinhard (2006) 'Tarifpolitischer Jahresbericht 2005: Gemischte Bilanz – Reallohnverluste überwiegen', *WSI-Mitteilungen*, 2/63–70.

Blair, Tony and Gerhard Schröder (1999) *Der Weg nach vorne für Europas Sozialdemokraten*, Berlin/London.

Bofinger, Peter (2005) *Wir sind besser als wir glauben – Wohlstand für alle*, Munich (Pearson).

Borchardt, Knut (1966) 'Die Bundesrepublik Deutschland', in: Gustav Stolper, Karl Häuser and Knut Borchardt (eds), *Deutsche Wirtschaft seit 1870*, Tübingen (Mohr).

Borchardt, Knut (1990) 'Zäsuren in der wirtschaftlichen Entwicklung. Zwei, drei oder vier Perioden?', in: Martin Broszat (ed.), *Zäsuren nach 1945*, Munich (Oldenbourg), 21–33.

Bothfeld, Silke (2005) 'Aktiv und aktivierend: Grundzüge einer zukunftsfesten Arbeitsmarktpolitik', *WSI-Mitteilungen*, August 2005/419ff.

Bowles, S. and H. Gintis, (1994) *Democracy and Capitalism*, London (Routledge).

Brakman, Steven, Harry Garretsen and Charles van Marrewijk (2005) 'Cross-Border Mergers and Acquisitions: On Revealed Comparative Advantage and Merger Waves', CESIFO Working Paper No. 1602.

Brandt, Nicola, Jean-Marc Burniaux and Romain Duval (2005) 'Assessing the OECD Jobs Strategy: Past Developments and Reforms', OECD Economics Department Working Paper 429, Paris.

Bräuninger, Thomas and Thomas König (2000) *Regieren im Föderalismus*, Konstanz.

Breuel, Birgit (1994) 'Treuhandanstalt: Bilanz und Perspektiven', *Aus Politik und Zeitgeschichte*, B43.

Brittan, Samuel (2005) 'Why Long-term Bond Yields are Low', *Financial Times*, 4 February.

Bub, Kristin (2006) 'AEG, Siedlerstolz und Schwarzmarkt', in: Klaus Topitsch and Anke Brekerbohn, *"Der Schuß aus dem Bild": Für Frank Kämpfer zum 65. Geburtstag*, Virtuelle Fachbibliothek Osteuropa. Retrieved 11 September from http://epub.ub.uni-muenchen.de/558/2/bub-aeg-siedlerstolz-schwarzmarkt.pdf.

Büchs, Milene (2004) 'Asymmetries of Policy Learning? The European Employment Strategy and its Role in Labour Market Policy Reform in Germany and the UK', paper given to ESPAnet Conference, University of Oxford, September 2004.

Bulmer, Simon and Claudio M. Radaelli (2004) 'The Europeanisation of National Policy?', Queen's Papers on Europeanisation, No. 1.

Bundesagentur für Arbeit (2006) www.pub.arbeitsamt.de/hst/services/statistik.

Bundesbank (1979) *Monatsbericht*, March.

Bundesbank (1983a) *Geschäftsbericht für das Jahr 1982*, Frankfurt a.M.

Bundesbank (1986) *Geschäftsbericht für das Jahr 1985*, Frankfurt a.M.

Bundesbank (1987) *Geschäftsbericht für das Jahr 1986*, Frankfurt a.M.

Bundesbank (1988) *Geschäftsbericht für das Jahr 1987*, Frankfurt a.M.

Bundesbank (1989) *Geschäftsbericht für das Jahr 1988*, Frankfurt a.M.

Bundesbank (1990) 'Vorschläge des Zentralbankrats zu einem Umstellungsgesetz' (2 April 1990), *Auszüge aus Presseartikeln*, 28.

Bundesbank (1990) *Geschäftsbericht für das Jahr 1989*, Frankfurt a.M.

Bundesbank (1995) *Geschäftsbericht für das Jahr 1994*, Frankfurt a.M.

Bundesbank (2000) *Geschäftsbericht für das Jahr 1999*, Frankfurt a.M

Bundesbank (2004) 'Mehr Flexibilität am deutschen Arbeitsmarkt', in: *Monatsbericht*, September, 43–58.

Bundesbank (various), *Monatsbericht*, Frankfurt a.M.

Bundeskartellamt (1996) *Tätigkeitsbericht*, Berlin.

Bundeskartellamt (1998) *Tätigkeitsbericht*, Berlin.

Bundeskartellamt (2000) *Tätigkeitsbericht*, Berlin.

Bundeskartellamt (2002) *Tätigkeitsbericht*, Berlin.

Bundeskartellamt (2004) *Tätigkeitsbericht*, Berlin.

Bundesverband Deutscher Investmentbanken (BVI) (1998) *Jahresbericht*.

Bundesverfassungsgericht (1991) *BVerfGE 84, 239 – Kapitalertragssteuer*, Karlsruhe.

Busch, Ulrich (2005) 'Ostdeutschland: Wirtschaftspolitische Optionen für 2005 bis 2019', in: *UTOPIE kreativ*, 172, February, 135–46.

Bust-Bartels, Axel (1986) 'Stärken und Grenzen des realsozialistischen Sozialstaats', in: *Widersprüche*, 18, April.

Butterwegge, Christoph (2005) *Krise und Zukunft des Sozialstaates*, Wiesbaden (Verlag der Sozialwissenschaften).

Carnoy, Martin (1995) 'Structural Adjustment and the Changing Face of Education', *International Labour Review*, 653–73.

Christ, Peter (1991) *Kolonie im eigenen Land: die Treuhand, Bonn und die Wirtschaftskatastrophe der fünf neuen Länder*, Berlin.

Christlich-Demokratische Union (CDU) (1984a) *Deutschlands Zukunft als moderne und humane Industrienation. Stuttgarter Leitsätze für die 80er Jahre*, Bonn.

Christlich-Demokratische Union (CDU) (1949) *Düsseldorfer Leitsätze*. Reprinted in: Ernst Ulrich Huster et al. (1975) *Determinanten der westdeutschen Restauration 1945–49*, Frankfurt am Main (Suhrkamp).

Christliche-Demokratische Union (CDU) (1984b) *Erneuerung der Sozialen Marktwirtschaft. Materialien zur Diskussion der Stuttgarter Leitsätze*, Bonn.

Däubler, Wolfgang (1988) 'Deregulierung und Flexibilisierung im Arbeitsrecht', *WSI-Mitteilungen*, 8/88.

Deregulierungskommission (1991) *Marktöffnung und Wettbewerb*, Stuttgart (Poeschel).

Deutsche Bank Research (2004), 'Perspektiven Ostdeutschlands – 15 Jahre danach –', *Mitteilung*, 306, 10 November.

Dietz, Berthold and Carmen Ludwig (2006) 'Armut in Deutschland', in: Alexander Grasse, Carmen Ludwig and Berthold Dietz (eds), *Soziale Gerechtigkeit. Reformpolitik am Scheideweg*, Wiesbaden (VS Verlag für Sozialwissenschaften).

Ehrenberg, Herbert (1991) *Abstieg vom Währungsolymp. Zur Zukunft der deutschen Bundesbank*, Frankfurt am Main (Fischer).

EIRO (European Industrial Relations Observatory). Retrieved 11 September 2008 from http://www.eiro.eurofound.eu.int.

Eissel, Dieter (1997) 'Reichtum unter der Steuerschraube? Staatlicher Umgang mit hohen Einkommen und Vermögen', in: Ernst-Ulrich Huster, *Reichtum in Deutschland. Die Gewinner in der sozialen Polarisierung*, Frankfurt a.M. (Campus).

Eissel, Dieter (2004) 'Steuergerechtigkeit oder der Marsch in den Lohnsteuerstaat', *Gewerkschaftliche Monatshefte*, 2.

Eissel, Dieter (2006) 'Verteilungspolitik im Zeichen des Neoliberalismus', in: Katrin Ruhl, Jan Schneider, Jutta Träger and Claudia Wiesner (eds) *Demokratisches Regieren und politische Kultur*, Münster/Hamburg/Berlin (Lit).

Entorf, Horst and Hannes Spengler (2002) *Crime in Europe: Causes and Consequences*, Heidelberg (Springer).

Entorf, Horst and Peter Winker (2001) 'The Economics of Crime: Investigating the Drugs-Crime Channel'. Retrieved 11 September from http://129.3.20.41/eps/le/papers/0108/0108001.pdf.

Erhard, Ludwig and Alfred Müller-Armack (1972) *Die Soziale Marktwirtschaft: Manifest '72*, Frankfurt.

Esping-Andersen, Gøsta (1990) *The Three Worlds of Welfare Capitalism*, Cambridge (Polity Press).

Esser, Josef (1989) 'Symbolic Privatisation: The Politics of Privatisation in West Germany', in: John Vickers and Vincent Wright, *The Politics of Privatisation in Western Europe*, London (Frank Cass).

Esser, Josef (1998) 'Privatisation in Germany: Symbolism in the Social Market Economy', in: David Parker (ed.), *Privatisation in the European Union. Theory and Perspectives*, London (Routledge).

Eucken, Walter (1955) *Grundsätze der Wirtschaftspolitik*, Tübingen.

European Trade Union Confederation (ETUC) (2006) 'Europe's Trade and Investment with China: Challenges and Choices', Statement, 7 July.

Fischer, Manfred (2004) 'Deutsche Unternehmer schätzen die Heimat', *Die Welt*, 8 August.

Freie Demokratische Partei Deutschlands (FDP) (1985) *Liberales Manifest 1985* (Archive of the Friedrich Naumann Stiftung).

Friedrich Ebert Stiftung (ed.) (2006) 'Deutschland: Exportweltmeister von Arbeitsplätzen – Mythos oder Wirklichkeit?', Series: *Europäische Wirtschafts- und Sozialpolitik*, No. 2.

Friedrich Ebert Stiftung (ed.) (2005) *Mitbestimmung in Zeiten der Globalisierung. Bremsklotz oder Gestaltungskraft?*, Bonn (Arbeitskreis Arbeit, Betrieb, Politik).

Galbraith, John Kenneth (1992) *The Culture of Contentment*, London (Sinclair-Stevenson).

Galbraith, John Kenneth (1994) *The World Economy since the Wars. A Personal View*, London (Mandarin).

Geiss, Imanuel (1997) *The Question of German Unification*, London.

Gesamtverband der deutschen Textil- und Modeindustrie (GDTM) (2005) *Jahresbericht 2005*, Eschborn.

Gewerkschaft Erziehung und Wissenschaft (GEW) (2005) 'Deutschland spielt weiter in der zweiten Liga', press statement, http://www.gew.de/122004_PISA_II.html.

Giddens, Anthony (2000) *The Third Way and its Critics*, Oxford (Blackwell).

Giegold, Sven (2005) 'Steuerflucht und Steuervermeidung als Hebel für Sozialabbau', www.bewegungswerkstatt.org/giegold.

Gilder, George (1982) *Wealth and Poverty*, London (Buchan and Enright).

Glastetter, Werner, Günter Högemann and Ralf Marquardt (1991) *Die wirtschaftliche Entwicklung in der Bundesrepublik Deutschland 1950–1989*, Frankfurt a.M. (Campus).

Glastetter, Werner, Rüdiger Paulert and Ulrich Spörel (1983) *Die wirtschaftliche Entwicklung in der Bundesrepublik Deutschland 1950–1980. Befunde, Aspekte, Hintergründe*, Frankfurt a.M. (Campus).

Goldman Sachs International (1992) *Borrowed Prosperity: Medium Term Outlook for the East German Economy*, London (Goldman Sachs).

Görgens, Hartmut (1990) 'Gewinnexplosion seit 1983 – Zur Entwicklung von Gewinnen und Kapitalrentabilität in der Bundesrepublik Deutschland', *WSI-Mitteilungen*, Issue 3, March.

Harvey, David (2007) *A Brief History of Neoliberalism*, Oxford (Oxford University Press).

Haselbach, Dieter (1991) *Autoritärer Liberalismus und soziale Marktwirtschaft*, Baden-Baden.

Hassel, Anke, M. Höpner, A. Kurdelbusch, B. Rehder, and R. Zugehör (2000) 'Dimensionen der Internationalisierung: Ergebnisse der Unternehmensdatenbank "Internationalisierung der 100 größten Unternehmen Deutschlands"', MPIfG Working Paper No. 1.

Friedrich August von Hayek, F.A. (1989) 'The Pretence of Knowledge', *American Economic Review*, 79: 6, December.

Haythornthwaite, Rick (2007) 'Beware of Reckless Regulation on Climate Change', *Financial Times*, 5 February 5.

Hein, Eckhard and Achim Truger (2004) 'What ever happened to Germany? Is the Decline in the Key Currency Country Caused by Structural Sclerosis or by Macroeconomic Mismanagement?', *Arbeitspapiere des Instituts für Volkswirtschaftslehre*, Technical University of Darmstadt, No. 134.

Heinz, Wolfgang (2005) 'Kriminalität in Deutschland unter besonderer Berücksichtigung der Jugend- und Gewaltkriminalität', *Konstanzer Inventar Kriminalitätsentwicklung*, Konstanz.

Heise, Arne (2002a) 'Off with the Austerity Straitjacket: Germany and the Stability and Growth Pact', *Debatte*, 10/1: 93–97.

Heise, Arne (2002b) 'Promised and Kept? An Assessment of the Modernisation Concepts of the Red-Green Coalition in relation to Economic and Employment Policy', *Debatte*, 10/2: 157–78.

Heise, Arne (2002c), 'Währungsunion und Koordinierung', *Berliner Debatte Initial*, 13/1: 1–10.

Heisenberg, Dorothee (1999) *The Mark of the Bundesbank. Germany's Role in European Monetary Cooperation*, Boulder, CO (Lynee Reiner).

Hickel, Rudolf (2000) 'Steuerpolitik für Shareholder', *Blätter für deutsche und internationale Politik*, 2, February.

Hickel, Rudolf (2001) 'Widersprüchlicher Prozess der ostdeutschen Transformation', www.memo.uni-bremen.de/docs/m1901.

Hickel, Rudolf (2004) Die Republik im Steuersenkungsrausch, www.memo.uni-bremen.de/docs/m0804.pdf.

Hickel, Rudolf (2004a) 'Deutschland – keine Basarökonomie', *Blätter für deutsche und internationale Politik*, 12, December.

Hickel, Rudolf (2005) 'Flat Tax: einfach ungerecht', *Blätter für deutsche und internationale Politik*, 10, 1165–7.

Hobsbawm, Eric (1994) *The Age of Extremes. The Short Twentieth Century 1914–1991*, London (Penguin).

Hombach, Bodo (2000) *The Politics of the New Centre*, Cambridge, Polity Press.

Hoppmann, Erich (1973) 'Soziale Marktwirtschaft oder Konztruktivistischer Interventionismus', in: Egon Tuchtfeldt (ed.), *Soziale Marktwirtschaft im Wandel*, Freiburg i.B (Rombach).

Horn, Gustav and Stefanie Behnke (2004) 'Deutschland ist keine Basarökonomie', *DIW-Wochenbericht*, 40.

Huffschmid, Jörg (1972) *Die Politik des Kapitals*, Frankfurt (Suhrkamp).

Huffschmid, Jörg (2002) *Politische Ökonomie der Finanzmärkte*, Hamburg (VSA).

Humphreys, Peter (1989) 'Policies for Technological Innovation and Industrial Change', in: Simon Bulmer (ed.) *The Changing Agenda of West German Public Policy*, Aldershot (Dartmouth).

Huster, Ernst-Ulrich (1985) 'Struktur und Krise kommunaler Sozialfinanzen', in: Stefan Leibfried and Florian Tennstedt, *Politik der Armut und die Spaltung des Sozialstaats*, Frankfurt am Main (Suhrkamp).

Huster, Ernst-Ulrich (ed.) (1997) *Reichtum in Deutschland. Die Gewinner der sozialen Polarisierung*, Frankfurt a.M./New York (Campus).

Hüttenberger, Peter (1974) *Die Entstehung der Bundesrepublik Deutschland*, Bonn (Informationen zur politischen Bildung).

Hutton, Will (1995) *The State We're In*, London (Jonathan Cape).

Institut der deutschen Wirtschaft (ed.) (2008) 'Mitbestimmung. Mehr geregelt als anderswo', *iwd* 27, March.

International Labour Organisation (ILO) (2005) *Key Indicators of the Labour Market*, Geneva.

International Labour Organisation (ILO) (2004) *A Fair Globalization: Creating Opportunities for All*, Geneva.

International Monetary Fund (IMF) (2006) *World Economic Outlook*, September.

International Monetary Fund (IMF) (various) *Direction of Trade Statistics*.

Jäger, Hans (1988) *Geschichte der Wirtschaftsordnung in Deutschland*, Frankfurt a.M. (Suhrkamp).

Kaßebaum, Bernd (2006) 'Bildung und soziale Gerechtigkeit', in: Alexander Grasse, Carmen Ludwig and Berthold Dietz (eds), *Soziale Gerechtigkeit. Reformpolitik am Scheideweg*, Wiesbaden (VS Verlag für Sozialwissenschaften).

Kennedy, Ellen (1991) *The Bundesbank. Germany's Central Bank in the International Monetary System*, London (Pinter).

Keuchel, M. (1989) *Kann der Arbeitsmarkt dem Wettbewerb unterworfen werden?*, Cologne (University of Cologne Institute of Economic Policy).

Kitchen, Martin (1978) *The Political Economy of Germany 1815–1914*, London (Croom Helm).

Knuth, Matthias, Oliver Schweer and Sabine Siemes (2004) *Drei Menüs und kein Rezept. Dienstleistungen am Arbeitsmarkt in Großbritannien, in den Niederlanden und in Dänemark*, Friedrich Ebert Stiftung, March.

Kohl, Helmut (1998) Interview, *Neue Bundesländer Illustrierte* (CDU Election Newspaper).

Kowalski, Reinhold (2007) 'Abstieg Ost trotz Aufschwung West', *Blätter für deutsche und internationale Politik*, Issue 2, February.

KPMG (ed.) (2006) *Ostdeutschland als Standort für Direktinvestitionen: Ein Vergleich mit ausgewählten osteuropäischen Städten*.

Kreutz, Daniel (2002) 'Neue Mitte im Wettbewerbsstaat. Sozialpolitische Bilanz von Rot-Grün', *Blätter für deutsche und internationale Politik*, 4, 463–72.

Kühn, Hagen (2003) 'Leere Kassen. Argumente gegen einen vermeintlichen Sachzwang', *Blätter für deutsche und internationale Politik*, 6, 731–40.

Lahusen, Christian and Carsten Stark (2003) 'Integration: Vom fördernden und fordernden Wohlfahrtsstaat', in: Stephan Lessenich (ed.) *Wohlfahrtsstaatliche Grundbegriffe*, Frankfurt a.M.

Lambsdorff, Otto von (1980), *Bewährung. Wirtschaftspolitik in Krisenzeiten*, Düsseldorf / Vienna (Econ).

Lambsdorff, Otto von and Hans Tietmeyer (1982) *Konzept für eine Politik zur Überwindung der Wachstumsschwäche und zur Bekämpfung der Arbeitslosigkeit*, Archiv des Liberalismus, Friedrich Naumann Stiftung.

Lange, Thomas and Geoffrey Pugh (1998) *The Economics of German Unification*, Cheltenham / Northampton MA (Elgar).

Leaman, Jeremy (1988) *The Political Economy of West Germany 1945–1985 – An Introduction*, London (Macmillan).

Leaman, Jeremy (1993) 'The Rhetoric and Logic of the *Wende*', *German Politics*, 2: 1, 124–35.

Leaman, Jeremy (1994) 'Regulatory Reform and Privatization in Germany', in: Michael Moran and Tony Prosser (eds), *Privatization and Regulatory Change in Europe*, Buckingham (Open University Press).

Leaman, Jeremy (1995) 'Central Banking and the Crisis of Social Democracy – A Comparative Analysis of British and German Views', *German Politics*, 4: 3, 22–48.

Leaman, Jeremy (2001) *The Bundesbank Myth. Towards a Critique of Central Bank Independence*, London/New York (Palgrave).

Lessenich, Stephan (ed.) *Wohfahrtstaatliche Grundbegriffe. Historische und aktuelle Diskurse*, Frankfurt a.M.

Liedtke, Rüdiger (2001) *Wem gehört die Republik? 2002. Die Konzerne und ihre Verflechtungen*, Frankfurt a.M. (Eichborn).

Luttwak, Edward (1997) 'Central Bankism', in: Peter Gowan and Perry Anderson, *The Question of Europe*, London (Verso).

Mai, Karl (2006) 'Ostdeutscher Produktivitätsrückstand', www.memo.uni-bremen.de/docs/m0406.pdf.

Marsh, David (1992) *The Bundesbank. The Bank that Rules Europe*, London (Mandarin).

Mearsheimer, John (1990) 'Back to the Future. Instability in Europe after the Cold War', *International Security*, 15/1.

Mechtersheimer, Alfred (2007) *Handbuch Deutsche Wirtschaft – 5000 Firmen und die Heuschrecken*, Starnberg (Unser Land – Wissenschaftliche Stiftung e.V.).

Mehrländer, Ursula and Günther Schultze (1992) *Einwanderungskonzept für die Bundesrepublik*, Bonn (Friedrich Ebert Stiftung: Digitale Bibliothek).

Merklein, Renate (1985) 'Die Sklerose der deutschen Wirtschaft', in: *Der Spiegel*, 1/1985.

Miegel, Meinhard (1983) *Die verkannte Revolution (1), Einkommen und Vermögen der privaten Haushalte*, Stuttgart.

Mierzejewski, Alfred C. (2004) *Ludwig Erhard*, Chapel Hill (N. Carolina University Press).

Möller, Carola (1988) 'Flexibilisierung – Eine Talfahrt in die Armut – Prekäre Arbeitsverhältnisse im Dienstleistungssektor', *WSI-Mitteilungen*, 8/88.

Monopolkommission (2006) *Sechzehntes Hauptgutachten der Monopolkommission 2004/2005*, Berlin (Bundesdrucksache 16/2460).

Moran, Michael (1989) 'A State of Inaction: the State and Stock Exchange Reform in the Federal Republic of Germany', in: S. Bulmer (ed.) *The Changing Agenda of West German Public Policy*, Aldershot (Dartmouth).

Müller, Gernot and Hartmut Seifert (1991) 'Deregulierung aus Prinzip? Ein Diskussion der Vorschläge der Deregulierungskommission zum Arbeitsmarkt', *WSI-Mitteilungen*, 8/91.

Müller, Uwe (2006) *Supergau Deutsche Einheit*, Hamburg (Rowohlt).

Münchau, Wolfgang (2007) 'The Germans Have the Right Idea on Hedge Funds', *Financial Times*, 12 February 2007.

Münchau, Wolfgang (2008) 'Two Nails in the Coffin of German Corporatism', *The Financial Times*, February 17 2008.

Nick, Harry (1995) 'An Unparalleled Destruction and Squandering of Economic Assets', in: H. Behrend (ed.) *German Unification. The Destruction of an Economy*, London/East Haven (Pluto Press).

Nunnenkamp, Peter (2005) 'The German Automobile Industry and Central Europe's Integration into the International Division of Labour: Foreign Production, Intra-industry Trade and Labour Market Repercussions, Euroframe Publications.

OECD (1983) *Positive Adjustment Policies: Managing Structural Change*, Paris (OECD).

OECD (1990) *Progress in Structural Reform*, Paris (OECD).

OECD (2002) *Policy Brief: Economic Survey of Germany*, Paris (OECD).

OECD (2003) *Employment Outlook. Towards more and better jobs*, Paris (OECD).

OECD (2005) *Employment Outlook. 2005*, Paris (OECD).

OECD (2005) *E-Commerce: Transfer Pricing and Business Profits Taxation*, OECD Tax Policy Studies No. 10, Paris (OECD).

OECD (2005c) *Economic Survey of the United Kingdom*, Paris (OECD).

OECD (various), *Economic Outlook*, Paris (OECD).

OECD (various), *Economic Survey: Germany*, Paris (OECD).

Palley, Thomas (2005) 'From Keynesianism to Neoliberalism: Shifting Paradigms in Economics', in: Alfredo Saad-Filho and Deborah Johnston (2005) *Neoliberalism. A Critical Reader*, London (Pluto Press).

Pelinka, Anton (1983) *Social Democratic Parties in Europe*, New York (Praeger).

Pfeiffer, Christian and Peter Wetzels (2001) 'Zur Struktur und Entwicklung der Jugendgewalt in Deutschland', in: R. Oerter and S. Höfling (eds) *Mitwirkung und Teilhabe von Kindern und Jugendlichen*, Munich (Hanns-Seidel Stiftung).

Polanyi, Karl (1954) *The Great Transformation*, Boston (The Beacon Press).

Prantl, Heribert (2005) *Kein schöner Land. Die Zerstörung der sozialen Gerechtigkeit*.

Presse- und Informationsamt der Bundesregierung (1978) *Tatsachen über Deutschland*, Bonn.

Priewe, Jan (no date) 'Fünf Keynesianismen – zur Kritik des Bastard Keynesianismus' (download from author's personal website).

Prokla-Redaktion (1995) 'Verteilungsfragen', *PROKLA* 99, 1995 Nr.2.

Pugh, Geoff (1998) 'Economic Reform in Germany. The 1948 Currency and Economic Reforms in Comparison with the 1990 Economic and Monetary Union', in: Thomas Lange and J.R. Shackleton (eds) *The Political Economy of German Unification*, Providence/Oxford (Berghahn).

Putnam, Robert (2000) *Bowling Alone: the Collapse and Revival of American Community*, New York (Simon and Schuster).

Ragnitz, Joachim (2005) 'Zur Diskussion um den Produktivitätsrückstand Ostdeutschlands', IWH-Internetpublikation, March 2005.

Rawls, John (1971) *A Theory of Justice*, Harvard (Belknap).

Reissig, Rolf (2000a) 'Die Wirtschaftsentwicklung in Ostdeutschland. Legenden und Versuche einer Annäherung an die Wirklichkeit', in: Wolfgang Thierse, Ilse Spittmann-Rühle and Johannes L. Kuppe (eds) *Zehn Jahre deutsche Einheit, Eine Bilanz*, Opladen (Leske and Budrich), 49–58.

Reissig, Rolf (2000b) *Die gespaltene Vereinigungsgesellschaft*, Berlin (Dietz).

Richter, Edelbert (2006) 'Neomerkantilismus – ein deutscher Sonderweg', *Blätter für deutsche und internationale Politik*, 8, August, 995–1005.

Rode, Reinhard (1992) 'Deutschland: Weltwirtschaftsmacht oder überforderter Euro-Hegemon', in: Bruno Schoch (ed.) *Deutschlands Einheit und Europas Zukunft*, Frankfurt (Suhrkamp).

Rödl, Helmut (2003) 'Zur Stabilität mittelständischer Unternehmen vor dem Hintergrund bankwirtschaftlicher Entscheidungsprozesse', http://www.ecfs.de/pdf/Roedl.pdf.

Röpke, Wilhelm (1966) *Jenseits von Angebot und Nachfrage*, Erlenbach-Zürich/Stuttgart.

Roth, Karl Heinz (1990) 'Nach dem Anschluß', in: *Konkret*, September 1990, 10–15.

Sachverständigen Rat zur Begutachtung der Wirtschaft [SVR] (1978/79) *Jahresgutachten*. Bundestagsdrucksache 8/2313, Bonn.

Sachverständigen Rat zur Begutachtung der Wirtschaft (1991) Special Report: *Marktwirtschftlichen Kurs halten. Zur Wirtschaftspolitik für die neuen Bundesländer*, Bonn (April 13).

Sarrazin, Thilo (1985) 'Die Finanzpolitik des Bundes 1970–1982', in: Helmut Schmidt and Walter Hesselbach (eds) *Festschrift für Hans Matthöfer*, Bonn.

Schäfer, Claus (1990) 'Die Früchte in einem reichen Land werden immer ungleicher verteilt – Zur Entwicklung der Einkommensverteilung 1989', *WSI-Mitteilungen*, 9.

Schäfer, Claus (2004) 'Mehr soziale Ungleichheit – weniger ökonomischer Erfolg: Zur Verteilungsentwicklung in 2003 und den Vorjahren', *WSI-Mitteilungen*, 11, 583–95.

Schäfer, Claus (2005) 'Weiter in der Verteilungsfalle – Die Entwicklung der Einkommensverteilung in 2004 und davor', *WSI-Mitteilungen*, 11, 603–15.

Schäfer, Claus (2006) 'Unverdrossene "Lebenslügen-Politik" – Zur Entwicklung der Einkommensverteilung', *WSI-Mitteilungen*, 11, 583–91.

Schäfer, Claus (2008) 'Anhaltende Verteilungsdynamik – WSI-Verteilungsbericht 2008, *WSI-Mitteilungen*, 11/12, 587–96.

Scharpf, Fritz (1987) *Crisis and Choice in European Social Democracy*, Ithaca and London.

Schäuble, Wolfgang (1991) *Der Vertrag. Wie ich über die deutsche Einheit verhandelte*, Stuttgart.

Schmidt, Helmut (1994) *Handeln für Deutschland. Wege aus der Krise*, Hamburg.

Schratzenstaller, Margit (2000) 'Corporation Tax in Europe: Possibilities, Problems and Options for Reform', http://www.memo-europe.uni-bremen.de/downloads/Schratzenstaller.

Schratzenstaller, Margit (2004) 'Aktuelle Entwicklungen der Unternehmensbesteuerung im europäischen Kontext', *WSI-Mitteilungen*, December (669–76).

Schröder, Gerhard (2000) 'Die zivile Bürgergesellschaft. Anregungen zu einer Neubestimmung der Aufgaben von Staat und Gesellschaft', *Neue Gesellschaft/Frankfurter Hefte*, 4.

Schulmeister, Stephan (1997) 'EURO-Projekt – Selbsterhaltungsdrang der Bundesbank und das Finale Deutschland gegen Italien', *WSI-Mitteilungen*, 5, 298–309.

Schulmeister, Stephan (2005) 'Die "ausgeblendeten" Ursachen der deutschen Wirtschaftskrise. Die Entwicklung seit 1991 in den USA, in Deutschland und in der übrigen Eurozone', in: Günther Chaloupek, Arne Heise, Gabriele Matzner-Holzer and Wolfgang Roth (eds), *Sisyphus als Optimist. Versuche zur zeitgenössischen politischen Ökonomie. In Memoriam Egon Matzner*.

Schulten, T. (2006) 'Europäischer Tarifbericht des WSI -2005/2006', *WSI-Mitteilungen*, 7, 365–73.

Seifert, Hartmut (2006) 'Was hat die Flexibilisierung des Arbeitsmarktes gebracht?', *WSI-Mitteilungen*, 11, 601–8.

Sinn, Hans-Werner (2004) *Ist Deutschland noch zu retten?*, Hamburg (Ullstein).

Sinn, Hans-Werner (2005) *Die Basar-Ökonomie. Deutschland: Exportweltmeister oder Schlusslicht?*, Berlin (Econ-Verlag).

Sinn, Hans-Werner, et al. (2006) *Redesigning the Welfare State. Germany's Current Agenda for an Activating Social Assistance*, Cheltenham (Edward Elgar).

SPD (1975) *Zweiter Entwurf eines ökonomisch-politischen Orientierungsrahmens für die Jahre 1975–1985*, Bonn.

SPD (1986) *Entwurf für ein neues Grundsatzprogramm der Sozialdemokratischen Partei Deutschlands*, Irsee.

SPD (1987) *Zukunft für Alle. Arbeiten für soziale Gerechtigkeit und Frieden* (Election Programme for 1987 Federal Elections), Bonn.

Staack, Michael (2000) *Handelsstaat Deutschland. Deutsche Aussenpolitik in einem neuen internationalen System*, Paderborn (Schöningh).

Stoltenberg, Gerhard (1997) *Wendepunkte: Stationen deutscher Politik 1947 bis 1990*, Berlin (Siedler).

Strange, Susan (1986) *Casino Capitalism*, Oxford (St Martin's Press).

Streeck, Wolfgang and Yamamura, Kozo (eds) (2001) *The Origins of Nonliberal Capitalism. Germany and Japan in Comparison*, Ithaca and London (Cornell University Press).

Sturgeon, Timothy (1997) 'Globalization and the Threat of Overcapacity in the Automotive Industry', MIT, http://ipc-lis.mit.edu/globalization/Overcapacity.pdf.

Sturm, Roland and Heinrich Pehle (2001) *Das neue deutsche Regierungssystem. Die Europäisierung von Institutionen, Entscheidungsprozessen und Politikfeldern in der Bundesrepublik*, Opladen (Leske and Budrich).

Suhr, H. (1990) *Der Treuhandskandal. Wie Ostdeutschland geschlachtet wurde*, Frankfurt a.M.

Thalheim, Karl (1978) *Die wirtschaftliche Entwicklung der beiden deutschen Staaten in Deutschland*, Berlin.

Thatcher, Margaret (1993) *The Downing Street Years*, London (Harper Collins).

Tober, Silke (1997) 'Monetary Reform and Monetary Union: A Comparison between 1948 and 1990', in: Stephen Frowen and Jens Hölscher (eds) *The German Currency Union of 1990. A Critical Assessment*, London (Macmillan), 227–45.

Tobin, James (1999) 'Supply Constraints on Employment and Output', in: Giancarlo Gandolfo and Ferruccio Marzano (eds) *Economic Theory and Social Justice*, Basingstoke (Macmillan), 35–50.

Trampusch, Christine (2006) 'Postkorporatismus in der Sozialpolitik – Folgen für Gewerkschaften, *WSI-Mitteilungen*, 6, 347–52.

Trube, Achim (2005) '"Besser irgendeine Arbeit als keine Arbeit?" – Kritik einer qualitätsblinden Arbeitsmarkt- und Sozialpolitik', *WSI-Mitteilungen*, April, 179ff.

Truger, Achim (2004) 'Rot-grüne Steuerreformen, Finanzpolitik und makroökonomische Performance – was ist schief gelaufen?', in: Eckhard Hein, Arne Heise, Achim Truger (eds) *Finanzpolitik in der Kontroverse*, Marburg (Metropolis).

Tuchtfeldt, Egon (1973) 'Soziale Marktwirtschaft und Globalsteuerung', in: Egon Tuchtfeldt (ed.) *Soziale Marktwirtschaft im Wandel*, Freiburg i.B. (Rombach).

UNCTAD (1998) *World Investment Report 1998*, New York (United Nations).

UNCTAD (2003) *World Investment Directory Vol. VIII: Central and Eastern Europe*, New York (United Nations).

UNCTAD (2005) *World Investment Report 2005*, New York (United Nations).

UNCTAD (2006) *World Investment Report 2006*, New York (United Nations).

Verheugen, Günter (1984) *Ausverkauf. Macht und Verfall der FDP*, Reinbek (Rowohlt).

Vesper, Dieter (1995) 'Steuern, Staatsausgaben und Umverteilung', *PROKLA*, 99, 165–92.

Vesper, Dieter (2006) 'Was läuft falsch in der Finanzpolitik?', *WSI-Mitteilungen*, 9.

Vilmar, Fritz and Wolfgang Dümcke (1996) 'Kritische Zwischenbilanz derVereinigungspolitik. Eine unerledigte Aufgabe der Politikwissenschaft', in: *Aus Politik und Zeitgeschichte*, B40, 35–45.

Wallerstein, Immanuel (1983) *Historical Capitalism and Capitalist Civilization*, London.

Weltalmanach-Redaktion (1999) *Deutschland '49 –'99*, Frankfurt (Fischer).

Welteke, Marianne (1976) *Theorie und Praxis der Sozialen Marktwirtschaft*, Frankfurt a.M (Campus).

Welzk, Stefan (2006) 'Die "Alterskatastrophe" und der Absturz der Renten', *Blätter für deutsche und internationale Politik*, June, 707–21.

Wolf, Martin (1999) 'Greenspan's big experiment', *Financial Times*, November 3.

Wolff, Robert Paul (1969) *The Poverty of Liberalism*, New York (Beacon).

Woolcock, S., Hodges, M. and Schreiber, K (1991) *Britain, Germany and 1992. The Limits of Deregulation*, London (Pinter).

World Federation of Exchanges (1980) Annual Report.

World Federation of Exchanges (1990) Annual Report.

World Federation of Exchanges (2000) Annual Report.

World Federation of Exchanges (2005) Annual Report.

Young, Arthur (1771) *The Farmer's Tour through the East of England*, London.

Zatlin, Jonathan (2007) *The Currency of Socialism*, Cambridge (Cambridge University Press).

Zohlnhöfer, Reimut (2005) *The Politics of Budget Consolidation in Britain and Germany*, Harvard Center for European Studies, Working Paper No. 05.2.

Zweig, Konrad (1976) *Germany through Inflation and Recession: an Object Lesson in Economic Management*, London.

INDEX

General

accumulation, monetary, 65, 73ff, 84ff, 88, 94

Audi AG, 147, 148f

'*Aufbau Ost*' (Development East), 115, 118, 120, 139, 145

Austria, 65, 162, 174, 178, 180, 199

BASF AG, 34, 153, 155

Bayer AG, 34, 153, 155

Belgium, 25, 70, 114, 123, 162, 174, 180, 199

BMW AG, 147, 150, 153, 155

Britain, xiv, 26, 28, 51, 52, 63, 65, 68, 70, 105, 106, 134, 140, 162, 171, 180

Bulgaria, 145, 199

Bundesbank (Federal Bank), xv, xvi, 4f, 7ff, 10, 12, 24ff, 27ff, 30, 43, 49f, 83, 84–99, 104, 106–10, 112, 119, 121f, 123ff, 129–34, 137, 154, 158f, 164, 173, 184, 194

capital accumulation, 64

capital concentration, xviii, 2, 34

capitalism, 42, 52, 65, 68, 69, 71, 78, 94, 100, 106, 113, 117

casino capitalism, 65, 71, 78, 94

central and eastern European countries (CEECs), 100, 101, 128, 145, 146, 151, 152

'flat taxes' in, 152

German FDI in, 145

German trade with, 146

passenger car production in 147, 148

China, xi, 147, a48, 152, 186, 196

Christian Democratic Union (CDU), xvi, 1, 4, 12, 19f, 23f, 25, 30ff, 35–42, 43ff, 54, 59ff, 69, 104, 107, 112, 116, 121, 151, 157f, 160, 183f, 186, 193

Christian Social Union (CSU), 1, 4, 7, 30, 35, 43, 60, 69, 112, 116, 121, 157, 160, 183f, 186, 193

Commerzbank AG, 34, 155

companies (see corporations)

competition authorities, xviii, 34, 92, 201

competition policy, 33, 35, 36, 38, 42, 104, 117

Concerted Action, 15, 116

corporations, xviif, 2, 11, 34, 42, 44, 53, 64, 79, 80, 85, 91, 93, 110, 144, 146, 147f, 149, 150, 151, 153, 154, 160, 196, 201

largest German corporations, 92

size of companies in east Germany, 144

Council of Economic Experts (*Sachverständigenrat der deutschen Wirtschaft, SVR*), 6, 12, 13, 29, 106, 112, 114, 115, 121, 134, 184

currencies, 27, 28, 37, 41, 68, 74, 75, 79, 85, 86, 87, 88, 94, 95, 100, 104, 106, 107, 108–10, 111, 117, 128, 130, 133, 134, 140, 162, 171, 180

Bretton Woods, xvi, 4, 5, 10, 27, 41, 75, 78, 85, 88, 109, 130

currency futures markets, 65, 74

currency reform, 104, 107–9, 110, 117, 198

People

Index